W9-AEW-069

If all parents were to employ with their children the depth of honesty and openness that Dr. Dobbins advocates, what a society we would create! I can only hope that his message will be distributed as widely as possible so that a maximum number of parents and children can benefit from his guidance.

—Lynne Cola, MD, FACOG

As parents of three small children, we are grateful to Dr. Dobbins for the practical help his book is providing us and other parents in protecting our children while raising them to be sexually healthy adults.

—Alan and Tamara Houston
New York Knicks

Teaching Your CHILDREN *the* TRUTH

RICHARD DOBBINS, PHD

Most Strang Communications/Charisma House/Siloam/Realms products are available at special quantity discounts for bulk purchase for sales promotions, premiums, fund-raising, and educational needs. For details, write Strang Communications/Charisma House/Siloam/Realms, 600 Rinehart Road, Lake Mary, Florida 32746, or telephone (407) 333-0600.

Teaching Your Children the Truth About Sex by Richard Dobbins
Published by Siloam
A Strang Company
600 Rinehart Road
Lake Mary, Florida 32746
www.siloam.com

This book or parts thereof may not be reproduced in any form, stored in a retrieval system, or transmitted in any form by any means—electronic, mechanical, photocopy, recording, or otherwise—without prior written permission of the publisher, except as provided by United States of America copyright law.

Unless otherwise noted, all Scripture quotations are from the New King James Version of the Bible. Copyright © 1979, 1980, 1982 by Thomas Nelson, Inc., publishers. Used by permission.

Scripture quotations marked KJV are from the King James Version of the Bible.

Cover design by Bill Johnson/Judith McKittrick
Interior design by Terry Clifton

Copyright © 2006 by Richard Dobbins
All rights reserved

Library of Congress Cataloging-in-Publication Data:

Dobbins, Richard D.
Teaching your children the truth about sex / Richard Dobbins.-- 1st ed.
p. cm.
ISBN 1-59185-877-1
1. Sex instruction. 2. Family life education. 3. Child rearing. I. Title.

HQ57.D58 2006
649'.65--dc22

2005031353

First Edition

06 07 08 09 10 — 987654321
Printed in the United States of America

This book is dedicated to parents who understand the importance of being the primary sex educators for their children and have the courage to welcome the challenge.

Acknowledgments

Putting together a book like this requires the help of so many people, one hardly knows where to start in expressing his appreciation. Then, there is always the fear of forgetting someone whose help played a major role in the project.

Let me begin by thanking my wife, Priscilla, for her constant encouragement and willingness to share me with my readers. I also want to thank Mrs. Esther Fedd for bringing me together with Strang Communications.

My executive assistant, LaVale Beiler, was of great help in guiding and encouraging me in this project. I am also indebted to Barbara Dycus, my editor. Her creative touch and organizing skills have made the original manuscript much more readable and appealing. Thank you also to copyeditor Deborah Moss.

Finally, I want to thank Dr. Lynne Cola for verifying the accuracy of the medical information used in this book. Margaret Carr, Mary Anne King, and Debby Berkey have added their editorial assistance.

—Richard D. Dobbins, PhD

Contents

Part V Preparing Your Children for Marriage

Part VI After Your Children Say "I Do"

Appendices

Chapter 1

Sex...Sacred or Secular?

I remember a time in our society when children could enjoy living a rather sexually innocent life until they were approaching puberty. Then, even though you might not have known how to go about it, you realized it was time for you, as their parent, to have the *BIG* talk with them. You were awkward, and they were embarrassed, but you got through it.

You and I know this "head in the sand" approach to the sex education of our children is no longer practical in our society. They will be exposed to sex long before they reach puberty, probably before they start to school. So today the questions that confront you as a parent are not: "When should I tell my children about sex?" and "What should I say?" The urgent questions you face are: "Who will teach my children about sex?" and "What will they learn?"

Today, most children learn about sex from peers, pornographers, and public schools, but not necessarily in that order. As you know, none of these sources are going to address the spiritual and moral issues innately embedded in our sexuality. Nevertheless, these are the issues that strike at the core of a child's sexual identity and morality.

The sex education goals of today's public schools focus mostly on giving children information designed to help them protect themselves from sexually transmitted diseases and from complicating their lives with pregnancy. In many public schools children are encouraged to see their sexual preference, heterosexual or homosexual, as unrelated to their morality. They are taught to view homosexuality as *different* but normal, in spite of the fact that a majority of their parents will not share this point of view. Getting this kind of information in an amoral environment leaves children confused and uninformed about and unprotected from the moral and spiritual consequences of their sexual behavior. It also encourages them to define their sexual values very differently from those held by their parents.

The moral and spiritual issues inevitably involved in your children's sex education will determine whether their lives will be blessed or burdened by their sexuality. The fact that you are reading this book indicates that you understand this and feel the urgent need to be involved in the sex education of your children. However, most of us don't know how to go about it.

After all, you may have grown up with parents who were uncomfortable talking to each other about sex. You may remember how awkward it was for your parents to try to discuss this vital part of life with you. In the past, by the time many parents got around to talking with their children about sex, those children probably knew more about the subject than their parents knew. You don't want to make that same mistake with your children. So, when should you begin the sex education of your children?

Good sex education begins at birth. If it shocks you to discover that it really should begin this early, relax. Most parents would react to this information in the same way—but it's true. In the next chapter I will tell you why it should begin this early and how to go about it.

Healthy Sex Education Is More Than Talk

Helping your children grow up healthy and comfortable with their sexuality isn't determined so much by the information you give them in a series of conversations over the years as it is by your ability to create an environment that treats sexuality as a normal part of life. Evidence that you are succeeding in meeting this challenge is seen in the ease with which your children can ask you any questions they may have about sex, and also in the freedom they feel to check with you about any sexual information they may be picking up from their peers or sex education classes. When your children feel free to raise these kinds of issues with you, you know you are doing a good job.

As you can see, if you are comfortable with the subject yourself and begin the task early enough, becoming your child's primary sex educator is easier than you think. In fact, this can be one of the more enjoyable tasks of parenting—and, at times, hilariously funny!

Through the years many parents have sought my help in enabling them for this task. In this book I will be sharing with you what I have shared with them.

Get Comfortable With the Subject

If you are going to help your children grow up to be sexually healthy adults, then you need to be comfortable with your own sexuality. Unfortunately, many parents are so ill at ease with their own sexuality that they cannot talk openly with each other about this intimate dimension of their relationship. So, the very thought of talking to their children about sex raises the level of their anxiety so high that they just can't get the conversation started. Children pick up on these vibes and conclude that the subject of sex is too uncomfortable for their parents to discuss with them. Helping married couples get comfortable in talking with each other about sex is the subject of my next book: "Breaking the Silence of Your Bedroom."[1] If you find yourself in this category, here are some ways to deal with the anxiety.

First, be sure you are comfortable using the medical terms for the sexual parts of the body. If your parents did not acquaint you with these terms, then even saying them to yourself can be very embarrassing for you. So, begin by rehearsing them silently in your mind. Repeat to yourself, over and over again, words like *penis, testicles, scrotum, vagina, labia, clitoris, anus,* and so forth until you are comfortable with them. (You may find reviewing the clinical drawings in chapter ten helpful in this process.) These are the terms you will want to use when acquainting your child with his or her body.

If you are married, start using these terms when talking with each other about your own bodies. By becoming at ease in using these terms with each other, you will not reflect any awkwardness or embarrassment when introducing them to your children.

You will also want to become comfortable with the "street terms" for body parts and sexual functions. After all, if you want your children to share with you what they are hearing about sex from their friends, then you need to get ready to hear it in "street talk." When children talk to each other about sex, they usually don't discuss sex in clinical language. So, don't act shocked when they ask you what these terms mean. Just be prepared to tell them honestly in language you feel is all right for them to use when discussing sex with you.

Remember, if you act shocked when they talk like this to you, they will sense it. The silent message your shock sends is that you are uncomfortable with their questions about sex. Your children are likely to conclude it is better for them to find their own answers for their future questions, or simply to ask their peers.

This would be tragic because there is much more at stake here than just giving your child information about sex. Over the years, your neglecting to talk with your children about sex can affect the value they place on life—their own lives as well as the lives of others.

Life—Secular or Sacred?

Unlike those who take a secular view of life, people of faith see all life as sacred...particularly human life. We refuse to see human beings as ascending from the animal kingdom through a multimillennial, serendipitous, evolutionary chain of events that finally resulted in us establishing our place at the top of the animal kingdom's food chain. People of faith see human beings as a special creation of God, made in His image and set apart from the animal kingdom. We believe that the human family has been commissioned by God to care for other forms of life on this planet.[2]

Secularists hold a view of life that sees human beings slightly higher in the evolutionary chain than the most intelligent apes. We who take a sacred view of life see human beings created by God to be "a little lower than the angels."[3] These conflicting views are seen in sharp relief when you contrast the zeal of the animal rights movement in trying to provide legal protection for endangered species of animal life and the faith community's zeal in trying to protect unborn babies by resisting the legality of abortion on demand.

Currently, the secularists are winning this legal battle. Under present law, unborn sea turtles are given greater protection than unborn human beings. Even a casual observation of this absurd contrast in legal protection reveals how unnatural it is. To impute a greater value to other offspring than one ascribes to human offspring is outrageous.

Secularists can rationalize such a ridiculous comparison between animals and humans because they believe that death is the end of life. However, the person of faith believes that the end of natural life ushers us into eternity, where each of us will be held accountable by God for how we have chosen to live on earth.[4]

Currently, the secular view of life is prevailing in our society...not the sacred. Your children are being exposed to this secular view in the media and are being taught it in the public schools, and they are feeling unbelievable peer pressure to conform to it.

Of course, the way sex is viewed by the secularist is very different from the way people of faith see it. Your children need to be aware of this. Only you can be sure that they are. If your children are going to have clear understandings of the sacred view of life, it must come primarily from you. There is no more convenient opportunity for you to communicate this to them than when you are sexually educating them for life.

Sex Is Becoming More and More Secular

Today, fewer and fewer Americans see anything sacred about sex. Most nonreligious people in our country no longer strongly object to single people engaging in intercourse, so long as they protect each other from sexually transmitted diseases and the possibility of pregnancy. Such a view fails to foresee the crippling effects having many different sexual partners before marriage can have on a person's capacity to be monogamous in marriage. I'll go into this in greater depth later.

While a majority of Americans still agree that the conception of children belongs in marriage, a growing minority are challenging these views more and more. Such a reaction encourages more sexually promiscuous behavior, further erodes the sexual conscience of those involved, hastens the breakdown of marriage, and speeds the process of moral decay, already rampant in our society.

Children who are unfortunate enough to be born outside of marriage should be embraced compassionately and accepted by the community, but this does not mean that the irresponsible sexual behavior that conceived them should be approved.

There is an important difference between *acceptance* and *approval.* Jesus demonstrates this in His response to the woman caught in adultery. He extended His loving acceptance to her by saying, "Neither do I condemn you...." However, His strong disapproval of her sexual misbehavior is seen in His commanding her, "Go and sin no more" (John 8:11).

All of us are aware of how promiscuous and perverted sex is becoming in our world. Because sexual experiences can be so life defining, we do not want our children's futures to be poisoned by a morally decaying society. But neither do we want them to be crippled by sexual inhibitions and guilt. This makes it very important for you, as parents, to talk with each other about the sexual values you want to instill in your children.

For example, most of us want our children to save intercourse for marriage. So, how should we advise them to manage their sexual tensions during adolescence and early adulthood? Because of the early onset of puberty and the tendency to delay marriage longer than previous generations, the ten or fifteen years of adolescence are very sexually challenging for teens and young adults. So it is very important for you and your mate to discuss with each other and come into agreement on the spiritual and moral guidelines you want your children to respect during these formative years of their lives.

Secularists, in collusion with the media, seem determined to extract everything that is sacred and beautiful from sex. Even the definition of marriage and the family is being challenged. A growing minority of Americans are insisting that children fare just as well when raised by two "mothers" or two "fathers" as they would if raised in a traditional marriage by biological parents who love and care for them or by a loving adoptive mother and father.

Today, intercourse is being reduced to just another form of social contact, a little more intimate than kissing or, even worse, just an experience of sensual pleasure that is shamelessly indulged in and displayed as another form of *adult entertainment.* The tragic personal and social consequences of choices made in such a secular approach to sexuality are predictable.

By treating sex needs as part of our *animal nature* and ignoring the sacredness of human sexuality, people open themselves to the painful and far-reaching consequences of poor sexual judgments. Sooner or later, the lack of discretion and restraint in the expression of our sexual impulses results either in becoming a sexual aggressor who is callused to our deeper needs for intimacy and oneness with another, or becoming a sexual victim who is deeply wounded by the painful feelings of betrayal, rejection, and abandonment. Some people carry the scars of these wounds for the rest of their lives.

If we are to help our children avoid these tragic consequences, we must teach them to respect the sacredness of their bodies.[5]

Respecting the Sacred Nature of Sex

As your children grow, the personal moments you share with them will present you with priceless opportunities for helping them learn the sacred nature of their sexuality. Beginning when they are preschool age, you can gradually teach them to relate the pleasant genital feelings they have with their dreams of growing up and getting married as their father and mother did.

The ten to fifteen years between the time your children enter puberty and the time they get married will bring a rise of strong sexual urges. So, long before they reach these sexually turbulent years, caring parents must help their children prepare for them by understanding the wisdom of saving the excitement of sexual intercourse as a special celebration of love to be shared with their spouse on their wedding night.

In the meantime, what kind of advice will you give your children for dealing with their sexual tensions? Remember, if you do not guide them...others will. So, let's take a look at some of the spiritual and moral issues involved in healthy sex education.

Teach Children That Human Beings Are Unique

Your children need to learn from you that human beings are different from other creatures. An ideal time for introducing this idea to them is when you see them fascinated by seeing animals having sex.

For example, one day a little farm girl saw a rooster and a hen having sex. Because the activity seemed so violent to the child, she ran to her mother crying, "Oh, Mama, come quick. The big chicken is killing the little chicken!"

When the mother got to the backyard and observed what was happening, she calmly explained, "Honey, there is nothing to be afraid of. The big chicken and the little chicken are making love so they can have a little baby chick."

This brief explanation seemed to satisfy the little girl. She went back to playing, and her mother went back to work.

Several weeks later, her parents had some special guests for dinner. After the meal, the adults continued to sit at the table and talk. Times like this can leave children feeling so left out of the activity that their needs for attention inspire them to think of their own ways of sharing in the discussion.

When there was a break in the conversation, the little girl politely addressed the guests and proceeded to tell them what had happened between the big chicken and the little chicken. "I was really scared for the little chicken until Mama told me they were just making love so they could have a little chick." Then, all of a sudden the insight from this lesson of nature burst in the little girl's mind. To her parents' dismay, without hesitation she turned to her father and said, "Oh, Daddy, is that what you did to Mama so you could have me?"

Of course, the whole table broke into uproarious laughter. The parents blushed, but the guests were impressed with the sexually honest way they were raising their daughter.

Human Sexuality Is Different From Animal Sexuality

Children need to know that human beings are different from animals. Animals have limited choices. Their behavior is determined by their instincts, but human beings are free to choose their behavior. God has given us a will and a conscience that enable us to choose very good behavior or very bad behavior, and the ability to know the difference.[6] No other creature shares these unique qualities of life with us. Our capacity for good and evil makes us different from animals, which are bound to behave according to their nature.

God loves and values the animals, but He loves people more because He made us in His image.[7] So, when your children wonder why God made us different from the animals, tell them it is because He loves us more and values us more than He does the animals.[8]

Children need to learn the sexual distinction between themselves and the animals very early in life. They deserve to know that their bodies are a precious gift from God. He chose to give them bodies because He wants their lives to be expressions of His life. He chose to make them sexual because He wants them to grow up, get married, and have children who will also give expression to His presence. That's why He chose to make us male and female.

God did not *have* to give us a body. He *chose* to do it. He did not *have* to make us male and female. He *chose* to do it. After all, He is God. We have a body because God chose to give us one, and we are male or female because He chose to make us sexual.

Every child deserves to have some explanation as to why God made these choices. If children grow up knowing why God gave them bodies, why He made them male or female, and what His purpose is for their sexuality, it helps them find meaning and direction for managing these unique expressions of their personhood. Providing your child with this kind of background will help him or her to make sense of the sexual rules and guidelines you will be giving them.

Schools Cannot Give Moral Training

Your children will not get this kind of information from the sex education programs in public schools. Unfortunately, any reference to God as the creator of our bodies and our sexuality in public schools is against the law in many countries of the world, including our own. This forces the public school to take a secular approach to human life. Such an approach disregards marriage as the only safe environment for freely celebrating our sexuality.

Extracting God from public life has gone a long way toward the destruction of public conscience as a restraint for lawless and immoral behavior. Secularism has degraded human beings to the level of other animals sharing life on this planet. When we teach our children that they are animals, why should we be surprised when they act like it? In fact, as mentioned earlier, the offspring of certain endangered species are afforded greater legal protection in the United States than unborn human beings. Legally, abortion has become a way of trying to erase the consequences of poor sexual choices.

Secularism breeds these kinds of disparate moral judgments. After all, if there is no God, then, contrary to what the Scriptures teach, there is no ultimate accountability for our choices.[9] And if there is no ultimate accountability for the choices we make, then why should we assume ultimate responsibility for the way we live?

Historically, on the other hand, institutional religion has gone to the opposite extreme. Religion has implied that our sexuality is the enemy of our spirituality rather than an expression of it. It has assigned such a taboo to sexuality that parochial schools are not likely to provide your child with a healthy sex education either. What your child will learn about sex in a parochial school is more likely to be guilt provoking and repressive of their sexuality. Such an approach to sex education denies children the anticipation of a celebration of sexual freedom in marriage.

So, as you can see, if your children cannot count on you to answer their questions about sex, they are likely to go into adolescence and adulthood without a practical appreciation for the sacredness of life or for the role healthy sex is to play in it. This is why it is so important for you to "step up to the plate" and accept your responsibility as the primary sex educator of your children.

The Challenge You Face

No one else is going to answer the theological questions about your children's bodies and their sexuality for them and, at the same time, give them healthy and wholesome ways to view their sexuality. Your children cannot afford to have you fail them in this task!

At best, secular sources will do a good job of informing them about how to avoid pregnancy and sexually transmitted diseases. At worst, pornographers will sexually arouse them, erode their consciences, and rush them into promiscuous sexual activity that will severely cripple their ability to form a strong and healthy marriage bond with their future spouse.

When you help your children understand that their bodies and their sexuality are unique gifts God has given them for their enjoyment in marriage, they are more likely to develop responsible and healthy ways of dealing with their sexuality between now and then. They are more likely to understand the importance of keeping their pleasurable genital feelings and the anticipation of marriage connected in their fantasy life.

This connection gives them practical reasons for saving sexual intercourse for marriage. First, it helps them see that this is a way of being sexually true to their spouse years before they know who that person will be. Second, being sexually true to their spouse before they are married will make it easier for them to be sexually true to their spouse after they are married.

In a survey of American teens, three-fourths said that their first intercourse was unplanned, and they wished that they had been older when it happened. Studies show that frank and open discussions about sex between parents and teens tend to postpone the time and circumstances of the teens' first intercourse.[10] We can only hope that our teens' first intercourse will not occur until after they are married. But we can know that it is a fact that the longer we can delay it, the less complicated their lives will be.

Chapter 2

What Does the Bible Say About Sex?

You want your children to be well informed about sex, but you also want them to grow up fully aware of the spiritual, moral, personal, and social consequences of their sexual choices. Many people base their spiritual and moral beliefs about sex on what they believe the Bible teaches. So, it is very important that your children have a fair and honest biblical understanding of sex.

In this chapter I offer a very brief and limited theology of sex. Its purpose is to provide you with a helpful spiritual framework for giving your children moral guidelines that can spare them the painful consequences of poor sexual choices while encouraging them to look forward to celebrating sexuality in marriage.

The taboo way in which sex is dealt with in many churches and religious families would leave you believing that the Bible discourages sexual expression. Nothing could be further from the truth! However, this kind of deep-rooted ecclesiastical bias and discomfort with sexuality so enshrouds the subject that many married couples have difficulty talking about sex with each other.

What the Old Testament Says About Sexuality

The Bible presents a healthy and forthright view of human sexuality. The account of Creation found in the first two chapters of Genesis makes it clear that we are made in the image of God—body persons and sexual persons by divine design.

These passages state that after God formed Adam from the dust of the ground, He breathed a part of Himself into Adam. No other creature shares this uniqueness with human beings. Then, He gave Adam and Eve the mission of establishing dominion over the earth.[1]

God formed Eve from the body of Adam to be involved with him in the mission of establishing divine dominion over the earth. Notice that God chose not only to make Adam and Eve body persons, but He also chose to make them sexual persons: Adam male and Eve female. Then He commanded them to multiply the number of human bodies on the earth so that by living in people God's divine dominion could be extended over all the earth.

On each day of Creation, God pronounced His work *good*. But on the sixth day when He created Adam and Eve, He looked at them, naked and unashamed, and pronounced them "*very good*."[2] He not only said that the way He had made them was *very good*, but He also said it was *very good* that He had made them *naked and unashamed!*

In the Old Testament the Jews had very strict rules governing sexual behavior. Any sexual behavior that was inconsistent with a strong and healthy marriage bond was forbidden. The penalties for infractions were very severe. Adultery, incest, homosexuality, and bestiality were forbidden under the Jewish law and carried punishments ranging from social ostracism to death.[3]

Since God was creating the Jewish nation, men were not permitted to practice contraception, and it was generally forbidden for women as well. We find this graphically illustrated in the sin of Onan.[4]

Every Jewish man wanted a son to carry on his name. So, if a man died before his wife had a son, the dead man's brother had an obligation to impregnate his dead brother's wife until she had a son to carry on the name of his dead brother.

Onan took sexual advantage of his brother's wife, but he hated his brother so much that when he was about to ejaculate, he withdrew from her and spilled his semen on the ground. For this God killed him. However, Onan did not die for spilling his seed on the ground; he died because he hated his brother.

Notice that this story has nothing to do with self-pleasuring or masturbation. In the New Testament we are told that a person who hates his brother is a murderer.[5] It was because he hated his brother that Onan was judged so severely.

The Old Testament takes a very healthy view of sexual expression in marriage. Read the first eight chapters of the Song of Solomon. You will find them filled with delightful sexual fantasies shared between a man and his wife. When you read those chapters in *The Living Bible*, you discover that the sexual fantasies of men and women have not really changed that much over the centuries.

In the seventh and eighth chapters of the Song of Solomon, you will notice how visual the husband's fantasies are. He doesn't fantasize about the sound of his wife's voice. He fantasizes about her nudity, her breasts, her navel, and her genitals.

A man's fantasies are very visual. Many times a man expects his wife to fantasize as he does, but a woman's sexual fantasies are not that visual. What does the woman fantasize about? She fantasizes about the sound of her husband's voice, his arm under her, his embrace, his kisses. A woman's fantasies are most likely to be auditory and tactile, while a man's fantasies are visual and tactile. At the appropriate time, we should make our children aware of this.

What the New Testament Says About Sexuality

Luke reminds us that the life of Jesus was conceived in the womb of Mary in a miraculous moment when the power of the Most High *overshadowed* her.[6] We don't understand the mystery of Christ's conception and the virgin birth. But notice that God did not bypass the human process of conception and gestation in bringing His only begotten Son into the world.

In some mysterious way, an ovum from the body of Mary was impregnated by God so that the body of Jesus came from Mary's ovum, while His blood was from His heavenly Father.[7] By using the human reproductive process in the creation of His only begotten Son, God sanctified the sexual process of bringing children into the world.

Historically, within the institutional church some have taught that sexual intercourse is a sin unless the man and woman intend to have a child as a result of the intercourse. According to this teaching, any sexual activity without the intent to have a child is sin.

The Bible does not support such sexually repressive teaching. God sanctified the sexual relationship between a husband and his wife when He created Adam and Eve for each other. Paul urges every man to have his own wife and every woman to have her own husband in order to prevent sexual misbehavior. And, in order to avoid sexual temptation, he urges the husband and wife to carefully meet each other's sexual needs.[8]

Jesus was chaste and celibate. This means He did not act out any of His sexual impulses. However, if we are to believe He was "... in all points tempted as we are" (Hebrews 4:15), we must assume that His hormones presented Him with the same sexual urges that men experience today. If He didn't have normal testosterone levels in His blood, then He could not be tempted in all ways like we are.

Some people in the church have difficulty believing Jesus was this human. Viewing Him as the Son of God is easy for them, but seeing Him as being just as much the Son of man troubles them. However, Jesus was just as much the Son of Mary as He was the Son of God. So, when we bring our sexual temptations to Him, we are not talking about a subject that is strange to Him. He has been a human male on earth. He knows what we are feeling. He conquered His passion, and He can help us conquer ours. Our children need to know this about Jesus.

What Did Jesus Have to Say About Sex?

Jesus acknowledged that only an unusual man could live without sex.[9] After His debate about divorce with the Pharisees, His disciples came to Him wondering if it would be better for a man not to marry again, even if he divorced his wife because of her adultery.

Jesus said this would be very difficult. He acknowledged that some men are born eunuchs, some are made eunuchs of men, and some become eunuchs for the kingdom of heaven.[10]

What did He mean by this? Usually, eunuchs were male servants of the royalty.[11] Jesus said that some males are eunuchs from birth. That is, they are born with little or no sex drive. This is rare, but it does happen. Then, in His day, some men were castrated to serve as eunuchs and to give personal care to royal families without posing any sexual threat to them. For example, eunuchs often bathed the women and children of royal families.

Then He referred to some men who became eunuchs for the kingdom of heaven's sake. This means they were able to sublimate all of their sexual energy into serving the kingdom of God. However, Jesus acknowledged that this is a very difficult way for a man to live, and only those who are given the ability to live this way should attempt it.

In other words, knowing human nature, Jesus told His disciples that most normal healthy men need a wife. Paul adds that most normal healthy women also need a husband.[12]

Further evidence that Jesus blesses sexual lovemaking in marriage is seen in the fact that He used the setting of a wedding feast as the scene of His first miracle.[13] If He didn't approve of what was to follow the marriage, why would He choose to bless the wedding feast with His first miracle?

What Did Paul Have to Say About Sex?

Early Christian converts brought their pagan Greek and Roman sexual histories into the church. In these cultures, sexual orgasm was a pleasure not necessarily associated with marriage, but indulged in for the sheer enjoyment of it from whatever sources could provide it. So, Paul had to address the differences between pagan and Christian views of sex.

Pagans sought sexual pleasure as an end in itself. Often, it was a part of their religious ceremonies. Temple prostitutes were common in Paul's day. Even when a person became a Christian, there was a strong tendency for him to cling to some of these pagan practices. This is why Paul found it necessary to stress the need for Christians to discontinue these pagan practices.[14] He argues that the body was not created for selfish sexual behavior. The body was created for the Lord.

Sex Outside of Marriage Involves Serious Risks

Since prostitution was a major business of the day, Paul wanted to be sure a man understood that when he had sex with a prostitute his body and hers became one. Today, through the study of sexually transmitted disease we understand the scientific truth of this statement.

When two people engage in sexual activity, their body fluids mix and remain a part of each other's body chemistry for many years. This means that the body fluids of every person with whom you have sex continue to be a part of your body chemistry. When you have sex with someone, your body chemistry intermingles with that of your partner. You are affected physically by the chemistry of every person with whom you or your partner has had sex with during the past several years. Young people need to know this—and they need to know it before they have sex with anyone.

Sexually transmitted diseases have a way of casting a long shadow across the future of a person. Paul warns us about this when he reminds a man that if he has sex with a prostitute, her body and his become one.

A Greater Pleasure

Then Paul tells the Corinthians about a pleasure greater than sex can ever provide, which occurs when our spirits becomes one with God's Spirit.[15] When you are united with the Lord in a moment of spiritual ecstasy, you experience a joy and pleasure that exceeds even that of sexual orgasm.

This is difficult for a man to imagine. Most men tend to see sexual orgasm as one of the greatest, if not the greatest, pleasures in life. I believe this is one of the reasons the devil provokes men to resist spiritual ecstasy. He wants to keep men in bondage to sexual temptation. He knows that once a man experiences the greater pleasure of becoming one spirit with God, he will discover what David had discovered when he exclaimed, "In Your presence is fullness of joy; at Your right hand are pleasures forevermore" (Psalm 16:11).

Once the pleasure of God's presence breaks in upon a man's life, he is not as likely to be dominated by his search for bigger and better sexual orgasms. Finally he has a benchmark for measuring the relative importance of sexual pleasures that helps him discipline his sex drive. His desire to keep the greater pleasure of God's presence encourages him to put the lesser pleasure of sexual orgasm into proper perspective.

Many men would find it difficult to believe that when the Lord fills you with His presence, you experience greater joy than any woman can give you, but it is true. This is what Paul challenged the men of Corinth to discover.[16]

The Divine Purpose of Sexual Orgasm

However, other than the pleasure of His presence, God designed sexual orgasm to be the most intensely pleasurable experience human beings can know. This is why it tends to be so addictive. God deliberately designed it to build and reinforce a bond of pleasure between a husband and wife over the years of their marriage. A husband's greatest pleasure on earth is to be found in his wife's body, and her greatest pleasure should be found in his.[17]

The adhesive nature of this bond plays a vital role in making a man and woman one with each other. Its strength provides for the permanency in marriage. This bond is necessary for having healthy children, raising them in an emotionally secure environment, and launching them into lives of their own. This is why Paul warned couples not to neglect reinforcing this lifelong bond of pleasure for each other.[18]

When you experience sexual orgasm outside of the fantasy of marriage or the reality of marriage, it will build an attachment between you and the source you allow to provide it for you. The same kind of pleasure God meant to attach you to your spouse brings you under bondage to whatever stimulus you substitute to provide this pleasure for yourself.

For many men this becomes some form of pornography—colored pictures on paper or colored pixels on a computer. Remember this: the experience of sexual pleasure that God meant to form a bond between you and your spouse can bring you under bondage to whatever stimulus you use to bring you to orgasm.

God designed the pleasure of orgasm to be so addictive that marriage is the only safe environment in which it can be experienced. God intended it to reinforce the bond of passion that grows between a husband and wife over the years.

Sexual Sins Are Not the Most Evil Sins

In his discussion of sexuality, Paul is not saying that sexual sins are the most evil sins we commit. James tells us the most evil sins are committed by the tongue.[19] Sexual sins are certainly not any more difficult for God to forgive than the other sins we confess to Him.[20] The special nature of sexual sins is that they are life's most complicating sins.

Sexual sins have a long and predictable future. They never simplify life. They always complicate life, even when people believe they are successful in keeping them secret. I will have more to say about this in future chapters as we begin to look at a developmental approach to sex education.

Paul concludes the sixth chapter of 1 Corinthians by asking, "Do you not know that your body is the temple of the Holy Spirit who is in you, whom you have from God, and you are not your own? For you were bought at a price; therefore glorify God in your body" (1 Corinthians 6:19–20).

Paul is bringing us back to this one basic truth: the greatest pleasure the body was designed to experience is not a sexual experience; it is a spiritual experience. Some people who have never had that spiritual experience seek to fill the void left in their lives from its absence with sexual pleasure. Sadly, they discover that not only is sexual pleasure a poor substitute for the pleasure of God's presence—but also it can ruin their lives.

Why Did God Make Us Sexual Beings?

Our sexuality is a part of God's image in us, designed to serve His divine purposes in our lives. What are His purposes?

The unitive function of our sexuality

First, there is the unitive function of our sexuality. God said that it is not good for human beings to live alone.[21] So He made males with a penis and females with a vagina so that the joining of these organs could physically symbolize the interpenetrating intimacy that grows between a husband and wife throughout their marriage.

When a wife welcomes her husband's penis into her vagina, she is inviting him and all of his personal history into her life. When he enters her, he is inviting all of her personal history into his life. Healthy intercourse is not only about the interpenetration of male and female sexual organs, or even two bodies. It is about the interpenetration of two lives. Over years of marriage this all-encompassing experience creates the spiritual unity for which each spouse longs. This is what marriage is all about.

The interpenetrating nature of sexual intercourse physically symbolizes two people becoming one. The pleasure of sexual orgasm reinforces the strength of that unity. This is why it is important for both spouses to develop the art of lovemaking and to acquire the good orgasmic skills necessary to provide each other with the sexual pleasure each of them needs.[22]

The reproductive function of sexuality

The second divine purpose of sexuality is the reproductive function. Over time, healthy sex not only makes two people one, but in the child-bearing years of life it makes two people three... or more.

Over the years, many people have asked me, "Is it God's will that all married couples have children?" My answer has remained the same. If they are physically capable of having children, it is God's will for them.

However, every couple needs to understand the divine purpose of reproduction. Why do people of faith have children? Of course, becoming parents is a wonderful way of fulfilling our personhood and extending our family.

However, people of faith do not have children simply to perpetuate their family's name. We have children to share our faith with them. We pray that they will embrace our faith so that when our bodies grow old and die, the presence of God housed in us can live on in them. Children are a heritage of the Lord.[23]

Our children belong to God. It is our privilege to introduce Him to them and to help them discover the gifts and talents given them for the purpose of serving God and others during their lives. He has loaned them to us so that we can teach them how to serve Him. Ultimately, the purpose of having children is to continue giving physical expression to God's presence on earth through another generation.

For example, my mother died as a result of my birth. She was just nineteen years old when she died. My father died when I was in my early thirties, but the energy that I'm using to write this book can be traced back to the moment of my conception when my father made love to my mother. Isn't that amazing! We will never do anything more creative than conceiving and having a child.

As I understand the Scriptures, God leaves with each couple the freedom to choose when and how many children they should have. A husband and wife who have children from previous relationships may, or may not, choose to have children of their own. Couples who, for whatever reasons, are unable to conceive can count on God's grace to help them discover compensating fulfillment in other ways. However, when we understand that the divine purpose for the human body is to express the presence of God on Earth, the desire for children takes on a deeper meaning.

The recreational function of sexuality

The third divine purpose of sexuality is the recreational function it serves between a husband and wife. God meant for sex to be fun for married couples. He meant for it to be exciting and pleasurable for us.

As a couple with a normal, healthy sex life, sometimes you will find making love to each other to be almost as awesome as a deep spiritual experience. Lost in the passion of your love, you become one in such an intimate way you can hardly sense where one of you ends and the other begins. The two of you just seem to melt together in the rapturous moments that follow.

On the other hand, sometimes making love with your spouse is like going over the top of the world's tallest roller coaster. It's just frolicking good fun.

At other times, sex is just the routine satisfaction of a bodily need, about as romantic as orange juice, toast, and coffee for breakfast. A healthy love life runs the gamut of all of these experiences. Before your children enter marriage, they need to know this. Unrealistic sexual expectations can become the source of unnecessary sexual frustration in marriage.

In the following chapters I will present you with a developmental approach to sex education designed to help you know the sexual information you should share with your children at each stage in their growth and development. And I will suggest some appropriate ways for communicating this information to them.

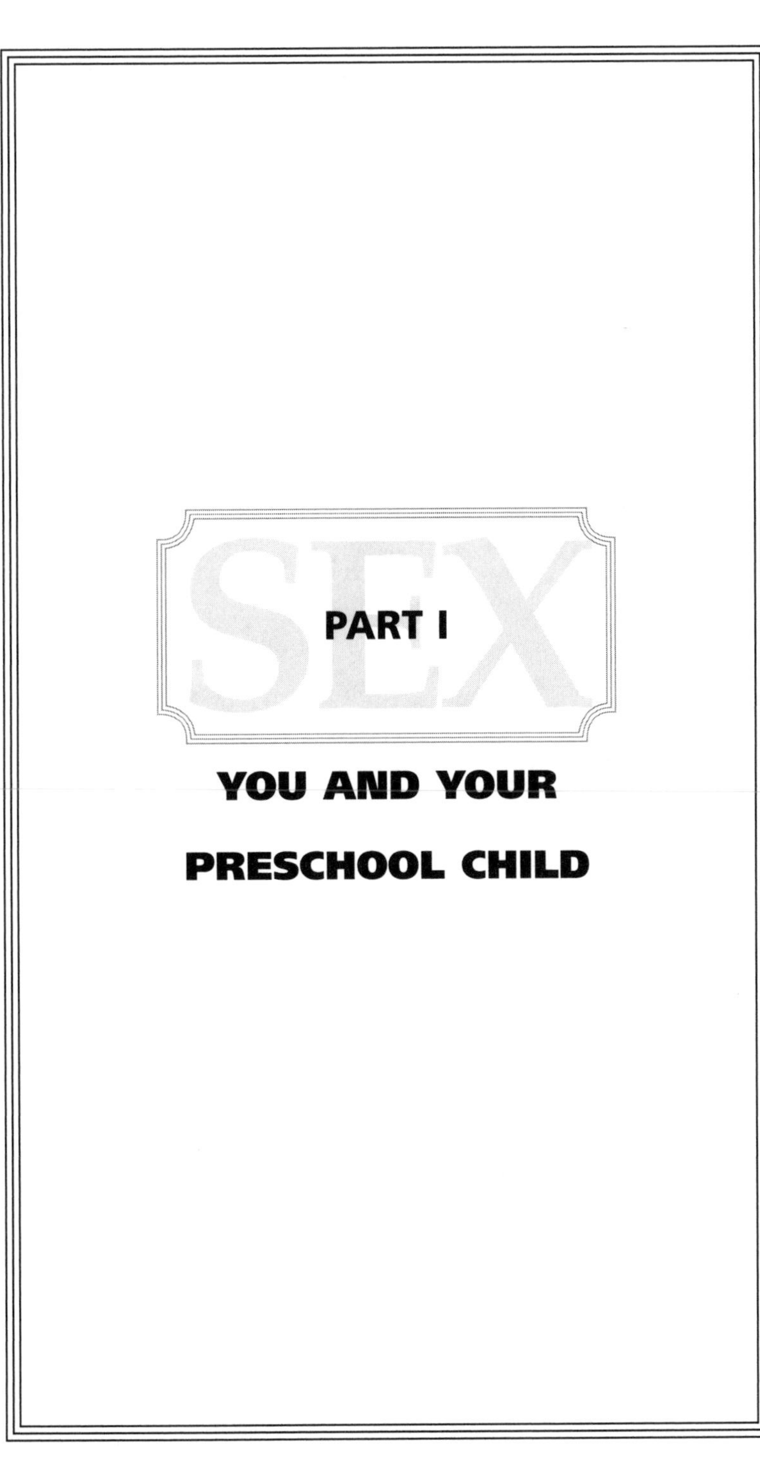

PART I

YOU AND YOUR PRESCHOOL CHILD

Chapter 3

The Preverbal Infant's "Total Experience"

Believe it or not, healthy sex education begins as soon as your child is born. Your baby enters this world already wired for sexual pleasure. A little boy's ability to erect and a little girl's ability to lubricate are awakened by nature before they are born. They first begin to experience genital pleasure the first time they are diapered or bathed.

The first person who diapers or bathes your baby will likely be the person who introduces them to sexual excitement. Usually this is an obstetric nurse. Fortunately, they know how to make bathing and diapering a comfortable experience for your baby. However, as soon as you feel better they turn this responsibility over to you. Of course, you see that Dad gets involved as soon as you and the baby are home from the hospital. This is why it is important for both of you to understand the role that diapering and bathing plays in the sex education of your child.

Diapering and Bathing Are Sensual

Naturally, as a parent you will tend to see diapering and bathing as part of the good hygienic care you want to provide for your baby. After all, keeping the baby clean, warm, and dry is an important part of nurturing.

Nevertheless, very few of us consider diapering and bathing our baby as two of our favorite parental responsibilities. Even though it is *our* baby, diapering for most of us is a stinky, messy job. Perhaps when you understand what an important role these activities play in the sex education of your child, the tasks will be somewhat more tolerable for you.

Naturally, your baby is not old enough to understand the hygienic importance of diapering and bathing, so that little one trusts you to take care of that part. But from the baby's point of view these activities are his or her introduction to sexual pleasure. You may have never thought of them as sexual experiences for the baby. However, when you look at the process from the baby's point of view this becomes obvious to you.

Notice what you do when you diaper or bathe your baby. First, you wash the genitals with warm water and a soft cloth. (If your little boy has been circumcised, be particularly gentle with his penis until he heals.) Then, you carefully dry the genitals with a soft towel.

Next, you usually oil the baby's genitals with some kind of baby oil before wiping them off again with a soft towel. To top everything off, you sprinkle that little bottom with talcum powder. You would have to be dead for this not to feel good to you!

Memories of these sexual feelings begin to be stored in your baby's brain long before he or she can talk. I have had parents say to me, "Well, I never thought of sex education starting during the first two years of life. After all, what can a child learn about sex before they can talk?" Far more than you think they can.

Genital Fondling Is Normal

Even though we are the ones who introduce our babies to genital pleasure through the diapering and bathing process, some parents are horrified when they discover their babies fondling themselves. Some have even asked me if this activity is evidence of our fallen sinful nature.

While restoring some reasonable perspective to the situation, I have tried to reassure them and lessen their anxiety by jokingly suggesting, "So the two of you feel your baby's fascination for genital fondling may indicate you have given birth to a demon-possessed baby? No, I don't think so, and neither will you when you understand what's going on from the baby's point of view.

"When the two of you give this kind of attention to each other, it feels good to you, doesn't it? So, why should you think it is strange that these things feel good to your baby?" Once this insight dawns on them, their anxiety subsides, and they begin to understand how their baby came to this discovery.

Your reaction to your baby's genital fondling is the first lesson in their sex education—and one of the most important. Babies learn whether genital pleasure is approved or forbidden during the years they are being diapered and bathed by observing their parents' reaction to this activity. Remember, your response to your baby's fascination with genital fondling is the first, and one of the most important, lessons in his or her sex education. What makes this so important?

Your Baby Lives in a World of "Total Experience"

In the years before your baby learns to talk, he or she lives in an unmediated world—a world of *total* pain or *total* pleasure. Once language development begins, your baby can start to learn how to lessen his pain or intensify his pleasure by using language.

Thank God for language. When used in healthy ways, it helps lessen our pain and increase our pleasure. However, until your baby learns to talk, he lives in a world of unmediated reality.

For example, a preverbal baby whose diaper is pinching him cannot say to himself, "Wow, this diaper is hurting me, but when Mom or Dad comes back into my room and finds me hurting, they will fix my diaper so it doesn't hurt me anymore." As far as the baby is concerned the pain is *total.* He has no way to mediate it, and he has no way of knowing how long it will last.

On the other hand, when your baby is drawing a warm stream of milk from mother's breast or a bottle, the baby is experiencing total pleasure. Genital fondling provides your baby with a similar pleasure.

Your baby is not only sensitive to physical pain and pleasure, but he is also very sensitive to emotional pain and pleasure. For further evidence of this, all you need to do is observe the expressions on your baby's face when you smile at him and then observe the difference when you frown. For preverbal babies, these preverbal emotional memories become the seedbed from which future feelings about themselves and their activities will spring. Your goal simply is to see that these memories are more pleasurable than painful.

Since you want your child to grow up to be socially and sexually healthy, you don't want to overreact when you discover him fondling his genitals. That is, you should neither overindulge this activity nor forbid it.

How Should You Respond?

Any pleasant, emotionally neutral response is healthy. Simply treat the activity as normal. For instance, gently remove the baby's hand from his or her genitals, pull a diaper up over them, and ignore the activity while you continue with the diapering or bathing process. This sends a clear and appropriate message to the baby: "What you're doing is no big deal!"

This is the lesson you want your baby to learn. *Normalize* the activity; don't *catastrophize* it. Every healthy baby finds this activity pleasurable and soothing.

By scolding, scowling at, or slapping the baby's hands you are sending a mixed message to your little baby's brain. The feelings from his or her genitals are good, but the feelings from the parent's reaction are bad.

This message gets locked into the baby's brain before he or she has a vocabulary—it feels good, but it is bad. As a result, good sexual feelings get mentally paired with parental disapproval. If it feels good sexually, it has to be bad. This is definitely not the message you want to send to your baby. A child growing up with these memories will have a tendency to feel guilty for having healthy, pleasurable sexual feelings.

When your preverbal infant is comfortable, but not preoccupied, with his or her genitals, pat yourself on the back. You have gotten off to a great start in becoming your child's primary sex educator.

In the next chapter we will be talking about how to help your child become acquainted with his or her body. We will also be giving you some practical ways for teaching your child the importance of healthy body privacy.

Chapter 4

When and How to Start Talking About Sex

Let's face it! Sooner or later, someone outside your family is going to talk to your children about sex. In spite of all you will do to control the social contacts in their young lives, there is no way you can *totally* protect them from the toxic sexual influences permeating our society today. So, if they are going to hear about sex anyway, why don't you determine to be the one who takes charge of their sex education?

Here are some things you can do to help your children grow up sexually healthy, even in our day. First, build a strong bond of affection between you and your children. Hugs, kisses, and compliments are vital ingredients in creating these ties.

Second, take advantage of the secure relationship you have with your children to carry on a healthy dialogue about sex with them from the time they are able to talk. By doing this you can be sure that whatever they hear from others won't surprise them.

By the time they venture out into the preschool or kindergarten world, you will have become their most trusted expert on the subject of sex. They will be prepared to compare what they have learned at home with what they hear from others.

For example, an older playmate who thought he was going to share some shocking sexual secrets with his four-year-old friend was taken aback when the little guy said, "Yeah, I know all about that stuff. Me and my mom and dad talk about it all the time." This sure let the air out of his older friend's balloon.

Keep the Subject Open

I guarantee you that if *you* don't close the subject of sex between you and your children, then it will always be open. They will see to that. By nature children are insatiably sexually curious.

As long as you are transparent and honest in responding to their questions, they will share their sexual curiosity with you. Such a frank and open relationship with your children makes it much more likely that they will bring sexual information they receive from other sources home to you for verification. This will give you the opportunity to correct any misinformation they may have received and keep the sexual dialogue open between you and them.

At times you may have to fight your own embarrassment when your children innocently ask you the meaning of "street terms" for sexual activities or body parts. However, if you have prepared yourself for these moments, as we suggested earlier, and treat their inquiries honestly and respectfully, your children will continue looking up to you as the most trusted source of sexual information in their lives.

When Should This Dialogue Begin?

Once your children begin to talk, it is time to further their sex education. During their second and third years be sure you add to their vocabulary the words that will help them talk to you about this vital part of life. As you know, one of the first challenges a child faces is labeling his or her world. For some children this begins before they are two.

Usually you go about helping your child by pointing at something, telling her what it is, and asking her to repeat what you said. For example, you point to yourself and say, "Mama" or "Dada," whichever is appropriate. You may show her an apple and teach her to say, "Apple." You point to a dog and teach her to say, "Doggie."

Somewhere in this process of labeling their world, you need to give your children the correct labels for their sexual organs. After all, you teach them what to call their eyes and ears, so why not also teach them what to call their genitals? By the time your children are three years old they should have this information and know how to refer to their elimination products.

"It" and "Down There"

Has it ever appeared strange to you that we give our children the proper names for all their body parts *except* their genitals? Some parents are so greatly embarrassed when faced with this challenge that they can only refer to their child's genitals as "it" or "down there." This is not a healthy practice.

When I was growing up, most parents were too self-conscious to speak plainly to their children about sex. Mine certainly were. Whenever they talked to me about my genitals, which was very seldom, they always referred to them as "it." I remember being cautioned not to play with "it," or not to touch myself "down there."

I never will forget a certain mentally challenged boy who would walk past our home at about the same time every day. One day, my aunt, who raised me, pointed to him and said, "Son, do you know why he's the way he is? He played with 'it' too much. And if you play with 'it' too much, you may turn out to be just like him." That was called *sex education* in my home.

Parents who give their children nicknames for their genitals are subtly telling the children that sex is something their family feels too uncomfortable to talk about. Of course, no parent intends to send this kind of message. Nevertheless, their discomfort sends a subtle message that encourages their children to address their sexual questions elsewhere.

On the other hand, by giving your children the proper names for their body parts when they are learning to talk, you are telling them that sex is a wide-open topic in your family. You are reassuring them that as they grow older they can continue to bring their questions to you and get any information about sex they feel they need by simply asking you. They clearly understand this. They know that you are there for them and are willing to talk about any sexual issues they want to discuss with you. As you can see, giving your children the proper names for their genitals gets you off to a good start in becoming their primary sex educators.

You teach your little boys that they have a penis, testicles, and a scrotum by simply pointing to these parts of their bodies and coming up with your own script. You may want to say something like, "This is your penis. This is your scrotum, and inside your scrotum are your two testicles. The fluid that comes out of the hole in your penis is called 'urine.' When you say it right, it sounds like 'you're in.' That is the adult word for it, but for now you can call it 'pee-pee' if you want to. The hole in your bottom is your anus, and the smelly stuff that comes out of it is called 'feces,' but you can call it 'poop' if you want to."

Similarly, by putting the information in your own words you teach little girls about their labia, their vagina, and their clitoris. Of course, you will have to go over this information again and again with your children, but their fascination with their genitals and those of their siblings will make quick learners out of them.

Simple conversations like these help your children overcome any shame or embarrassment they may have about their bodies. Once they have mastered this curious "lingo," you are in for some healthy, wholesome, family entertainment, because children like to share what they learn.

So, when Grandma comes over after you have given your little boy or girl this wonderful lesson in sex education...watch out! You and she are about to be treated to some unforgettably disarming hilarity.

On such an occasion, one grandmother had just gotten in the door of her daughter's home when her little granddaughter came running up to share with her the exciting things she had just learned from her mother.

"Oh! Grandma, Grandma!" she exclaimed, "You know what? I got a 'bagina.' You got a 'bagina.' And Mommy's got a 'bagina,' but Daddy don't got no 'bagina.' He got a penis."

Then the darling little girl walked innocently over to the wallpaper, pointed her finger at the design she found there, and proudly declared, "And that's a flower."

Obviously, the word *vagina* had no sexual connotation for her at the time. It was simply a label she had learned for a very personal part of her world. This wise mother, by talking to her daughter openly about her genitals, had made it obvious that she was ready to talk about any questions the little girl's sexual curiosity may put in her head. Mother was even giving her the proper words to use when she was ready to ask her questions. This is good, healthy sex education!

Body Privacy—the Next Big Lesson

After you have taught your children the proper names for their body parts, body privacy becomes the next big lesson in their preschool sex education. By the time children are about three, they should no longer be bathing with parents of the opposite sex.

At this age, children are old enough to begin assuming responsibility for bathing themselves. Of course, when they step out of the tub or shower you will still have to perform your own final inspection to be sure they have done a good job. If they have, brag on them. If you have to finish the job, patiently show them what they missed and how they can do better next time.

Of course, little girls can continue to bathe with their mothers and little boys can continue to bathe with their fathers. However, it's time to begin stressing the importance of body privacy around members of the opposite sex. This is also a good time to stop bathing children of the opposite sex together and to start teaching them how to bathe themselves.

If you are a single mom or dad, you may have to bathe your children, but only little boys should bathe with you as a single father. Only little girls should bathe with you as a single mother.

Bathing your child or bathing with your child gives you a wonderful opportunity to teach him or her about genital privacy. Your conversation may go something like this: "Honey, you know Mommy and Daddy have told you that your genitals are the personal private parts of your body. So, whether you are going to the bathroom, taking a bath, or caring for yourself in other ways, you always do this when you are by yourself, when you are alone. That's why we refer to our genitals as *our privates*. Remember, unless someone is helping you go to the bathroom or to take a bath, no one should ever touch your genitals. After all, these are your privates, and we call them *our privates* because we care for them when we are alone in private. Do you understand?"

Continue to explain to your child that most adults will respect his or her body privacy, but there are a few adults who want to touch the private parts of children. Then assure your child, "If any other person ever does that to you, you have a right to tell that person to stop it. Then, be sure to let Mother and Daddy know what happened."

You don't want to frighten your children unnecessarily, but you do want to warn them about child molesters. Later in the book I will share with you ten things you can do to protect your child from being sexually molested.

In stressing the importance of body privacy, I'm not implying that healthy families should guard against nudity as though it were the gold in Fort Knox. In the course of growing up in a healthy home, the occasional crack in the parents' bedroom door while they are dressing or undressing should provide all the opportunities a child will need to satisfy his or her curiosity about what a grown-up man or grown-up woman looks like without clothes. However, it is not healthy for parents to parade their nudity in front of children.

Here is a brief review of some ways you can teach your preschool children body privacy:

1. Give them little speeches like the one I just rehearsed for you.
2. Insist that your children respect your body privacy.
3. Instruct them to tell you if anyone tries to touch them in the private parts of their body unless they're helping them go to the bathroom or are bathing them.

When Bathing With Your Children

When parents are bathing with children of the same sex, they need to be aware of how sexually inadequate the child feels during this time. I guess I can best explain this by just simply sharing with you a cartoon I once saw. A little girl and her mother were pictured taking a bath together. As the little girl sat there facing her mother in the tub she said, "Mommy, how's come you're so fancy, and I'm so plain?"

Little children are fascinated with the adult nude body. In moments like this the thoughtful parent will take time to explain to the child, "Honey, when you grow up you'll be fancy, too. Your little breasts will develop, and you'll have hair on your bottom and on your genitals just like your mother. The reason Mother has these things now is because I have lived longer than you."

This kind of thoughtful consideration does a lot to prevent a child from feeling sexually inadequate during such times. In your own way, you just let the child know that the only difference between your body and hers is time. When she is as old as you, her body will be just as fancy as your body.

Does It Make That Much Difference?

Some people are haunted all their lives by feelings of sexual inadequacy. Girls are concerned with breast size. Boys are concerned with penis size.

When the male child bathes with Dad and compares the size of his penis with his father's, he is overwhelmed. His penis is smaller than his father's little finger. In comparison, his dad's penis looks huge. He is in awe of his father's penis and pubic hair. He sees the ancillary hair under his father's arms. He sees his father's body hair. Everything about his father seems so big. Everything about him seems so small.

It's important for the father to notice the son's preoccupation with the adult features of his body and to reassure his son by saying something like, "It's OK for you to look, son. When I was little and showered with my dad, I felt the same way you feel now. I felt like I was very small. But don't let Daddy's body make you think that your body is not just as good as mine, because the only difference between my body and your body is time. When you are a teenager, you'll have hair under your arms. You'll have pubic hair, and your penis will be just as big as mine." Such sensitive conversations can turn these moments into times when a father and his son form strong and healthy bonds with each other.

So the thoughtful parent will take the time while bathing with children of the same sex to explain to them that when they grow from girlhood to womanhood they will be just as fancy as Mom; when they grow from boyhood to manhood they will be just as big as Dad.

Genital Fondling

When your preschool child is obviously pleasuring himself or herself, it is time for another important lesson in sex education. How should you react?

A grandmother I talked to years ago knew just how to deal with such a delicate moment. She said, "One day when I went to babysit my grandchildren, my little four-year-old grandson had his hands in his pockets, obviously enjoying himself. So, I said to him, 'What's wrong, honey? Do your genitals itch?'

"The frankness of his reply was healthy, but it caught me a little off guard. He simply said, 'No, Grandma. It just feels good.'

"Then I said to him, 'Do you remember what your daddy and mommy told you about your genitals?'

"And he simply repeated to me what they had told him. 'They told me that my genitals were the personal private parts of my body, and that whether I was going to the bathroom, taking a bath, or caring for myself in other ways, I should always do this when I was by myself. That's why I call these parts of my body *my privates*.'"

"How did you respond to that?" I asked.

"Well," she said, "I just asked him, 'Are you alone now, dear?' Then he took his hands out of his pockets and said, 'No, Grandma.'"

What a healthy example of sex education in the home! Notice that the grandmother was addressing the inappropriate social context in which the behavior was occurring; she did not condemn the behavior.

She simply followed through on the instructions of the child's parents. They had told him, "Whether you're going to the bathroom, taking a bath, or caring for yourself in other ways, you always do this when you are alone. That's why we sometimes call these parts of our bodies *our privates*." He was not alone. So, the behavior was inappropriate, and Grandmother wisely reminded him of that.

Link Genital Pleasure With Getting Married

Take such an opportunity to link genital pleasure with the idea of marriage in that three- to five-year-old child's brain by saying something like this: "Isn't it neat that God has made us so that we can have good feelings in our genitals? That's His way of helping us look forward to growing up and getting married. Someday God will bring a woman into your life just like He brought your mom into your dad's life. So, when you have pleasant feelings in your genitals, think about marriage." If it was a little girl who was pleasuring herself, you would encourage her to look forward to the day when God would bring a man into her life that she would marry. The goal is to establish the link between genital pleasure and marriage so early in your children's minds that they cannot remember a time when they didn't make this connection.

Some people have asked me if I thought little three- or four-year-olds look forward to being married. Of course they do. One of their favorite games is playing house. They play being grown up. They play marriage. In today's broken world they even play divorce.

This is one of the ways by which children prepare for their adult roles. They practice them in childhood. That is what makes the early preschool years such an important time to link genital pleasure with the dream of being married.

Reassure your little boy that when he gets older, God will bring a woman into his life for him to marry. And help your daughter to look forward to the day when God will bring a husband to her. Encourage your children to think about marriage when they have pleasant feelings in their genitals. Remind them that this is God's way of helping them look forward to marriage when they can share these sexual feelings with the husband or wife He will send into their lives. Until then, they are not to share these sexual feelings with anyone else.

In this way your child will not remember a time when genital pleasure was not associated with the idea of marriage. The important issue is the fantasy that occupies the child's mind while he or she is pleasuring himself or herself—not the activity.

Jesus addresses this issue in Matthew 5:28 by saying, "I say to you that whoever looks at a woman to lust for her has already committed adultery with her in his heart." In this verse, He does not address the *activity* of self-pleasuring, but He does address the *sexual fantasy* accompanying it. The object is to train the child's feelings of genital pleasure to be linked with the dream of being married.

Notice how early you need to get the ideas of marriage linked together with pleasant genital feelings. This connection needs to be made in the mind of the child *before the child begins school.*

A young person does not begin to be monogamous as a senior in high school. He or she begins to be monogamous in preschool and kindergarten. A sexually healthy child links the feelings of genital pleasure with the dream of growing up and getting married. He or she looks forward to sharing pleasant genital feelings with that other person who will become his or her mate. It is a wise parent who gets these ideas linked in the mind of their preschool children.

As the primary sex educator of your preschool children, you want to:

1. Teach them the proper names for their genitals.
2. Reinforce the idea of body privacy.
3. Stress the social inappropriateness of fondling their genitals in front of other people.
4. Link together the idea of genital pleasure with marriage.

Games Children Play

Preschool children often rehearse for their adult roles in the childhood games they play. They have three favorite games. They play house. They play school. And, when Mother and Dad aren't home, they play doctor.

Playing doctor and nurse is a way children have of satisfying their normal sexual curiosity. The game is played by one child showing his or her private parts in exchange for another child showing his or hers. We'll talk more about this later in the book.

When these childhood games serve to satisfy the sexual curiosity of a child, they are a normal part of growing up. However, overindulgence in these games can create precocious sexual appetites that may be difficult for the child to manage. So, wise parents will not ignore these games.

You want to be aware that these games do go on and to supervise your children in such a way as to minimize the opportunities for them to be involved. If held to a minimum, these games usually satisfy a child's curiosity about how a person of the opposite sex looks. They become a sort of "rite of passage" into middle childhood. However, you will want to closely supervise your children to protect them from the temptation to overindulge in these activities.

Where Do Babies Come From?

Usually, sometime before they start to school, children become curious about where babies come from. Be prepared to tell them as much as they want to know—but no more.

If you are not prepared to be the primary sex educator for your children, you may panic when your child comes into the house and asks, "Mommy, where did I come from?" At such a time you may feel a need to go into the whole story about how little Sammy Sperm and little Ollie Ovum met in Mommy's body. But the child may not even be asking you about sex.

One four-year-old boy came rushing up to his mother asking, "Mommy, Mommy, where did I come from?"

So the mother started telling the whole story of how little Sammy Sperm and little Ollie Ovum met in the mother's body. She went on and on and on about how the little ovum grew and the little baby grew… and on and on and on. The little kid just stood there looking up into her face awestruck until she was finished. Finally, when she was done, the little boy shrugged his shoulders and said, "Oh, I just wondered because my friend just told me he came from Pittsburgh."

Simply telling the preschool child that he came from a seed planted in Mommy's tummy will get you started. Then the child will probably ask you how the seed got there. So, you tell the child there is a way through Daddy's penis that the seed is planted in Mommy's tummy. There's a door in Mommy's vagina that opens when it's time for the baby to come out, and that's how a baby is born.

This is an adequate explanation for the preschool child. It is honest, it is accurate, and it satisfies the child's curiosity. This will keep your child coming back to you when he wants more information.

You know you are doing a good job as the primary sex educator of your children when they begin to think of you like this: *You know, my parents taught me the proper names for my body parts. They know that once in a while I touch my genitals, and it feels good to me, and they haven't punished me for that. They haven't made me want to hide this part of my life from them, although they do insist that I keep it private. When I asked them where I came from, they gave me an honest answer. So when I have any more questions, why should I go to anyone else? I can always come to Mom or Dad.*

However, if the children get the impression that their questions embarrass you, and that somehow this is something you wish they had not asked you, then they retreat to sexual secrecy and turn to other people for their sexual education. We need to be careful how we manage the sexual curiosity of our children.

In Part II I will be addressing childhood sexual abuse. I will give you some practical guidelines for protecting your children from it and some steps to take if you feel your child has been abused. Then I will discuss the threats that today's media and pornography pose for your elementary school children and suggest ways you can shield your children from these current-day threats.

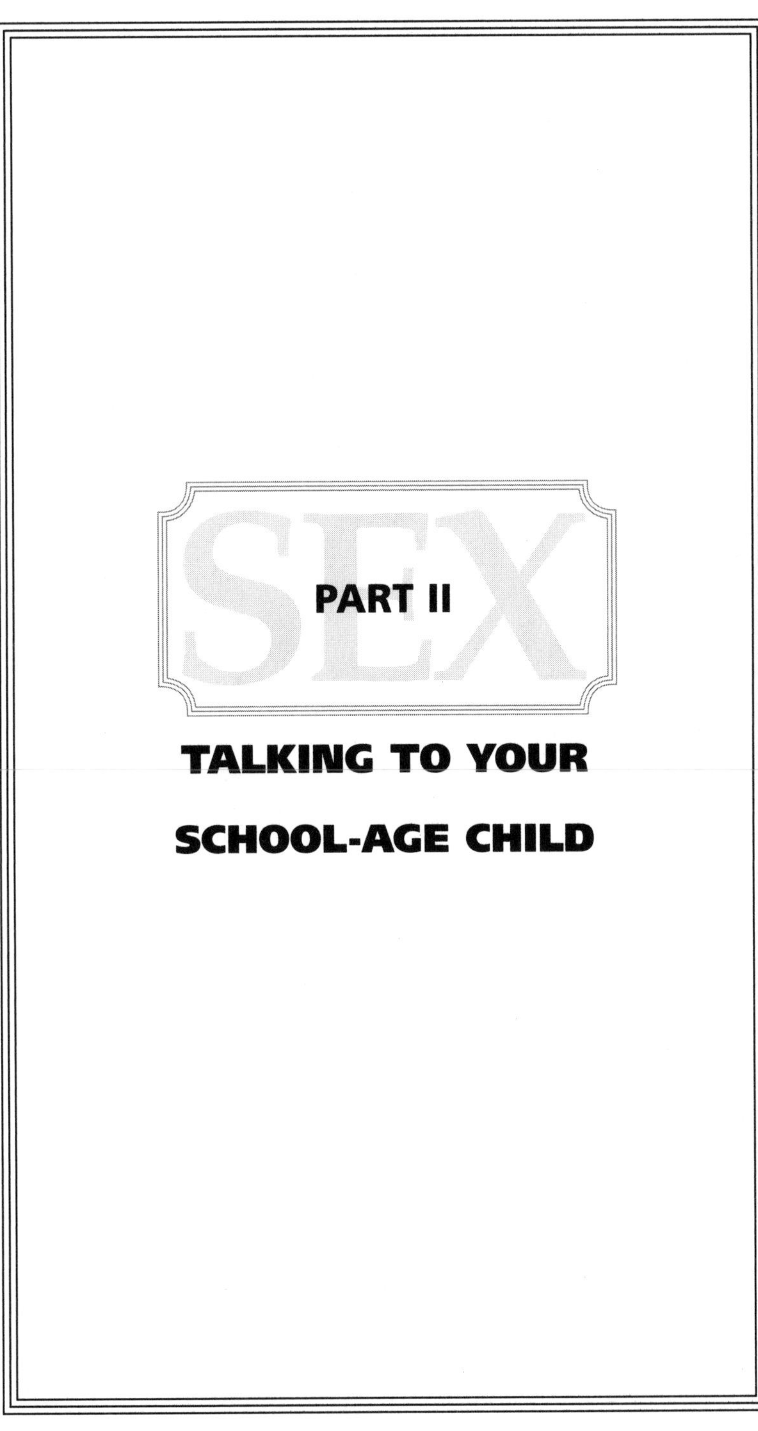

PART II

TALKING TO YOUR SCHOOL-AGE CHILD

Chapter 5

Protecting Your Children From Sexual Abuse

Watching your children move from the safety of your home to preschool, kindergarten, and the larger community makes you keenly aware of the menacing threats awaiting them in our "Megan's Law, Amber Alert" world. Today, any normal parent feels those fears, and national news stories about missing children reinforce them almost every week. And although child sexual abuse has been reported up to eighty thousand times a year, the number of unreported incidents is far greater, because the children are afraid to tell anyone what has happened.[1] So don't think yourself strange if, from time to time, you feel haunted by the subliminal awareness that you can no longer totally protect your children from the perverted minds of sexually sick predators who wait to seduce them.

This is why you, as a caring parent, want to stay informed about the harsh realities of childhood sexual abuse (CSA). As a well-informed parent you will be in a much better position to take the necessary steps to minimize these risks to your children. Or, if in spite of all you do, your child is still molested, then you will know immediately the steps you have to take to lessen the impact of this traumatic experience on your child's growth toward the healthy future you envision for him or her.

In this chapter I want to help you develop a strategy for protecting your children from CSA. In the following chapter I want to help you define a plan of action for dealing with sexual abuse, in the event your child is sexually abused.

In order to do this, we need to explore the following questions together:

- What is CSA?
- What are the risks of your child being abused?
- Who are the likely abusers?
- What can you do to protect your child from abusers?
- How can you tell if your child has been sexually abused?
- What should you do if your child has been abused?

What Is CSA?

Legally, childhood sexual abuse (CSA) consists of any sexual exploitation of or contact with a child by an adult or child who is five or more years older than the victim. If violence is used, then sexual abuse is involved even though the abuser may be less than five years older.[2]

Legal definitions like this can seem so cold and void of emotion when dealing with the realities of such a personal problem. So I want to paint a picture of this kind of crime against children that will be difficult for you to forget.

All parents have some idea about what is involved in the sexual abuse of a child and are so repulsed by it they prefer to push it to the back of their minds. Nevertheless, the best way to spare your child this trauma is to feed and maintain your own personal sense of outrage toward sick adults who lie in wait to prey sexually on children.

Be suspicious of any person who wants to develop a *special* relationship with your child, regardless of who that person may be. For example, when you take your child with you shopping, don't underestimate the predator's ability to lure your child away from you, regardless of how many times you have warned your child to stay away from strangers. Staying mentally alert like this can help you maintain the parental sense of urgency necessary to maximize your child's protection.

What goes on when the relationship turns sexual?

Here are just some of the activities the child abuser would like to engage in with your children: He wants to involve them in open-mouth kissing. He wants to touch their genitals. He wants to fondle or manipulate their genitals with his fingers, his lips, his tongue, or some other object.

Often, he enjoys performing oral intercourse on your children, and he forces them to perform oral intercourse on him. Regardless of how young your child may be, the abuser may try to force his penis into your little girl's vagina or even into your child's anus.

However, CSA may not always include physically touching your child. The abuser may *flash* his genitals to your child or show him or her sexually explicit pictures. He may ask your child to watch him while he masturbates, or he may seduce your child into performing sex acts with other children while he and other older children watch.

Since children are very curious about sex, the predator may show them videos of the kind of sexual activity he wants to involve them in. Of course, the violent predator will threaten children if they do not do what they are told to do.

Children may be encouraged to take their clothes off and be photographed naked in sexual activities or sexually seductive poses.[3] At times, even more bizarre activities may occur with children and adults. Video cameras may be recording what is happening during these sessions. These videotapes are likely to be marketed later as child pornography on the Internet.

Through the years of my practice I have sat with hundreds of adults who were sexually abused as children. Listening to the painful price they and their families have paid so that the sick sexual needs of some pervert could be satisfied leaves me with a fresh sense of outrage each time I hear a new victim review these nightmares from their past. This kind of morally reprehensible behavior against children carries with it such convincing evidence of evil that even the most devoted skeptic has difficulty continuing to deny its reality.

What Are the Risks of Your Child Being Abused?

Greater than you might expect! Since children are usually afraid to tell anyone that they have been sexually abused, experts agree that CSA is a highly underreported crime.[4] Some argue that an accurate estimate would find that one out of every three girls and one out of every four boys in our society are sexually abused before they reach eighteen years of age.[5]

Tragically, no child is safe from sexual abuse. Approximately one-third of those who are abused are below six years of age. A third are between six and twelve, and another third are between twelve and eighteen.[6]

Even when using the lower figures of the FBI, which indicate one female child in four and one male child in eight are sexually abused, approximately every five minutes around the clock, three hundred sixty-five days a year, some child in this country is being sexually abused.[7] Think about that! Living with this risk is difficult for any normal loving parent to grasp.

Don't let the fact that most children will grow up without being molested lull you into a false sense of security. Mentally force yourself to stay out of that trap! These figures are telling you that every hour of every day twelve children and twenty-four parents in the United States are being forced to deal with the shocking experience of childhood sexual abuse.

Let me use the same statistics to paint a startling different picture for you. Suppose your daughter was going to visit her grandmother, and you knew there was a 25 percent chance that the plane taking her there would crash before arriving. Would you let her take the flight? Of course not! And, even though the odds are only half as great for boys, you wouldn't let your son get on that plane either, would you?

Who Are the Likely Abusers?

There is no common personality pattern that defines sexual abusers of children. They come from all professions and all walks of life. Statistics show that 90 percent of sexual predators are male. Only 10 percent are female. Obviously, most abusers have serious personal problems. Typically they have very low self-esteem and have poor impulse control, but they are rarely mentally ill. The one thing they do share in common is a history of being sexually abused. Some studies have indicated that among sexual abusers of children in prison, as high as 95 percent of them were molested when they were children.[8]

So, get the picture of the child abuser as some *weird, dirty old man* out of your mind. The person most likely to molest your child is among your current friends, or may even be a member of your family. In fact, in only about 10 percent of CSA cases is the abuser unknown to the child. Approximately 60 percent of abusers are among the family's close friends and acquaintances. And in 30 percent of the cases, they are from the child's family.[9] In almost 90 percent of the cases the abuser is known by the victim—and often loved and trusted by the child.[10] This is what makes it so easy for the abuser to *groom* their victims for sexual favors.

Luring children into sexual abuse

During the courtship phase of the abuser's relationship with your child, he is likely to use a number of tricks to entice your child into a sexual relationship with him. Initially, he will be very affectionate with your child. The fear of losing this special attention sets your child up for keeping their sexual activities secret. Sometimes, bribery and money will follow.

When the abuser is a member of the family or a close family friend, he invests a lot of time with the child doing the things the child likes to do. This makes the child feel that he or she is special. The unsuspecting parents may feel guilty for not having the time they would like to have with their child, so they often feel relieved and grateful that another adult family member or close friend is willing to give the child so much attention.

Quickly sensing this, the abuser offers to relieve demands on the parents' schedule by agreeing to provide transportation for the child's social calendar. This allows him and the child to spend more and more time alone together. During these times is when appropriate touches are likely to be turned into inappropriate touches. Once the sexual activity begins, the abuser makes a secrecy pact with the child so that their *special* friendship can continue.

For example, years ago a children's pastor from a very large congregation was referred to me for evaluation as a suspected child abuser. He was very popular with the children—and their parents. He would take the children camping several times every summer. They all wanted to share his sleeping bag with him. This is when he would make his move on some of the children.

When I pressed him about the impropriety of sharing his sleeping bag with any of the children, he denied doing anything improper. He protested that some of the smaller children would get cold and would just want him to keep them warm.

When I asked him if he limited his activities to keeping the children warm, he failed to answer. His silence conveyed his own eloquent confession.

Like many other abusers, this children's pastor attempted to shift responsibility for the initiation of inappropriate activity to the children. He lamented that after children's church they all ran up to him and wanted to sit in his lap for a few minutes. "I wanted to give each child his turn, but this became very tiring for me. Finally, after so long a time, my arm would droop down into the child's groin area."

"You were not aware that this was an inappropriate place for your hand?" I asked. When he didn't answer, I inquired further, "Was that all you did?"

At this point he admitted fondling several children through their clothes during these brief times. Later, he admitted reaching through a little boy's shorts and fondling his genitals during a private time he had with the boy, but insisted this had happened only two or three times. Before the criminal investigation of this case was over, the abuser was found to have molested almost one hundred children and wound up in prison.

What Can You Do to Protect Your Child?

During the preverbal and preschool years of life, your children are particularly vulnerable to sexual abuse. They are so unsuspecting and innocent. They readily trust anyone who is kind and affectionate to them.

The best protection you can give them is your own personal supervision, even when they are playing outside with their friends. When you take them shopping or to other public places, don't let your children out of your sight! Never leave them in your car by themselves, not even for a few minutes. It is not safe!

To demonstrate the vulnerability of children, television networks have used hidden cameras and hired child advocate specialists to show how effective the ploys of child abusers are in luring small children away from their parents, even in public places like shopping malls and public parks. Parents were astonished to see that it only took a matter of seconds for their small child to walk away with a total stranger.

Here are some of the ruses that worked best:

- The abuser pretended to be ill and asked for the child's help in finding a place to sit down.
- The abuser pretended he had lost his little puppy and enlisted the child's help in finding the puppy.
- The abuser told the child he had a special gift for him in his car.

These twisted people know more ways to influence a child than any normal parent. Unfortunately, they are very skilled at what they do.

Stress the importance of your permission

Warn your children about strangers who may approach them when they are with you in shopping malls. If they stray from you and get lost, be sure they know how to go to the information desk at the mall or to a store clerk and have you paged. As they get older, warn them of the dangers of hitchhiking. Let them know that sometimes people who pick children up when they are hitchhiking intend to sexually molest them. Get them to promise you that they will never do this.

These are just more reasons why it is so important for your children to understand the importance of getting your permission before they go anywhere or accept any gift from anyone. Let them know that you want to protect them from any person who would harm them.

Before you trust your children with anyone other than yourself, be sure you know that person well—I mean really know them! See where he or she lives. Get to know the people that person chooses as friends. Could you trust your children to be around those friends? If the individual has children of his or her own, how well does that person protect the children? Until you know that person well enough to be sure of these things, don't trust that individual with your children.

Your children should have no doubt about whom they are permitted to be with and where they are allowed to go. Forbidden people and places should be just as clearly defined for them. Explain to them that the reason you are drawing such strict limits for them is because you love them very much and want to do everything you can to see that no one harms them. I regret that it is necessary to confront you with this grim reality, but our culture has become so sexually toxic for children that concerned parents like yourself have no other option.

Guidelines for Protecting Your Children

Here are ten guidelines to help you to protect your children from sexual abuse:

1. Make sure your children know that it is not safe to trust all adults. Tell them that most adults can be trusted, but there are some adults who want to hurt children.

   Remind them of this every time you are emphasizing the importance of body privacy. Help your children develop a healthy suspicion of older children or adults who want to become overly affectionate with them. Remember, child molesters are more likely to be successful in seducing uninformed and naïve children than children who display a healthy suspicion of those who show too much interest in them.

   Be sure your children are closely supervised at all times. There is no substitute for responsible parental supervision. However, in today's world this is not always possible. If you are going to leave your children with babysitters, be sure you get references before hiring them. If you are thinking of using teenagers as babysitters, know their parents well. Would you trust your children to be in their home without you? Remember, your children are usually sexually safer with female babysitters. Very few babysitters are child molesters, but among those few who are, males are more likely to be the culprits than females.[11]

   Don't allow babysitters to have their friends in your home when they are babysitting your children. You are paying them to take good care of your children. It's not party time!

If you are a single mom, be careful about trusting your children with your boyfriend. In most cases they would be safe, but men who want sexual access to children have been known to seek the company of single mothers.

2. Periodically quiz your child about what happens during these times when they are left in the care of other people.

3. Teach your children to stay away from people they don't know. Caution them against approaching a car driven by a stranger. Warn them to never get into that car, even if the man says, "Your mother has sent me to pick you up for her."

   Don't allow your children to accept gifts from strangers. Explain to them that child molesters often use gifts to lure children into a *special* relationship with them.

4. Don't allow your children to be alone on the street after dark. Teach them to look out for strange cars or people who show up in their play areas. Tell them to remember their descriptions and stay away from them. Ask them to bring these cars and people to your attention.

5. Since molesters are often relatives or trusted friends, it's extremely important for you to never leave your child alone with someone unless you are absolutely sure that person is totally responsible and trustworthy. You can't afford to make the mistake of assuming they are. You must know that person is safe for your children to be with! I am aware I'm making a BIG issue out of this, but I cannot stress it too much.

6. Be sure your children know they have an absolute right to refuse to be touched, especially in those areas of their body that are concealed by clothing, such as their genital and anal areas.

Frequently caution your small children to never let anybody touch them underneath their clothing, unless they are helping them go to the bathroom or take a bath. And, even when this happens, it should always be with your knowledge and permission. These steps are good precautions!

7. Be sure your child knows that no one should ask them to take part in any sexual activity. Make your children promise to tell you or someone in authority whenever they have been inappropriately touched or sexually abused.

8. Locate any areas in the children's environment where molestation is likely to occur and bring those areas to your children's attention, including: back stairways, elevators, alleys, abandoned buildings, wooded areas, and public restrooms. Warn your child to avoid these areas.

   Never send your child into a public restroom by himself or herself. These are places where predators wait for unsuspecting children.

9. Tell your children there is safety in numbers. Once they start to school, encourage them to walk to and from school with their friends.

10. If your children have to be home alone, caution them to keep the doors and windows locked at all times. They should admit no visitors.

    Teach them to answer the phone in such a way that the caller will not know they are alone. For example, teach them never to say, "My mother is not home right now." Tell them to say, "My mom or my dad can't come to the phone right now." That's true. Explain to them that they haven't lied by implying that you are home, but neither have they exposed themselves to violation by saying Mom and Dad aren't home. They are simply telling the caller that Mom or Dad can't come to the phone right now.

Other Helpful Suggestions

In addition to these ten guidelines, here are some other helpful suggestions for protecting your child from sexual abuse.

- Maintain good records of your children. These should include a current photograph of the child, an accurate description, and his or her fingerprints.
- Don't put your children's names on their clothing. It's better for them to lose some caps and coats than to furnish a predator information that he could use to make it sound to your child that he knows his or her family.
- Show your children how to dial 9-1-1, and teach them how to tell the operator about their problem.
- If your child gets lost in a mall or a store, be sure he or she has been trained to go to a security officer or cashier and ask for help.
- Be sure your children know your phone number and address, including the street and town. And be sure your children know your family's cell phone numbers.

Unfortunately, in spite of the fact that you carefully see to all of these guidelines and suggestions, your child may still be sexually molested. However, you can have the comfort of knowing you did everything you could to prevent it.

Chapter 6

Helping Your Child When Abuse Has Happened

Childhood sexual abuse is often referred to as a *silent problem*. It remains silent and unreported because the victims are so often threatened about what would happen if they told, and they are filled with shame about the behavior. When the abuse occurs at the hands of a family member, the child may feel guilty for not protesting in the beginning and believe that he or she is partially or fully responsible for the abuse. The child also may fear getting the relative into trouble.

Childhood sexual abuse can occur at any time from infancy through adolescence, but it occurs more often between the ages of six and ten.[1] This means your child is most at risk during the elementary school years.

How frequently the abuse occurs and how long it continues vary, but it is usually determined by the identity of the abuser. When the predator is outside the family, the period of abuse may be brief and consist of only a few episodes. However, when the abuser is a member of family or a close friend of the family, the abuse is likely to span two to four years.[2] All during this time the child may feel fearful of telling anyone and keep what is going on as his or her own deeply held, carefully guarded secret.

Sexual abuse is more easily detected in preschool children. Even though they may not verbally tell you, they reflect what is going on in obvious changes in their behavior. Here are some things to look for in younger children:

1. Toilet-trained children may regress to wetting and soiling themselves.

2. Children who have been able to separate from you with comfort may suddenly show signs of severe separation anxiety, particularly if you are unwittingly trying to leave them with the abuser.

3. Children who normally sleep soundly may start having nightmares and be very afraid to go to bed.

4. Young children who are not old enough to know the social impropriety of their behavior may copy adult sexual behavior. They may use sexual words that are foreign to the family. They begin to demonstrate a knowledge of and intense interest in sexual activity.

When bathing your preschool children, always be watchful for unexplained swelling, bruising, or bleeding in the mouth and unusual discharges in the genital and anal areas of your child's body. Any of these signs should raise immediate suspicion of childhood sexual abuse.

Any of the following sudden changes in your child's behavior could be an indication of sexual abuse, so be on the alert for them:

1. You may notice your child is acting strangely or differently.

2. Your child may display an unusual air of secrecy. He or she wants to keep things from you more than usual.

3. Your child may be depressed or sad. The vibrancy that normally characterizes his or her mood is not there.

4. Inappropriate gifts may appear on the scene. This is one way child molesters bind children to them.

5. Be sensitive to your child's use of any sexual street language. If the words being used are not common in your home and, all of a sudden, your child is using them, then this may be an indicator that they are learning this language from the person who is molesting them.

6. Notice any preoccupation your child may have with a person who is not known to the family. Your child may be talking about that person all the time. This should raise suspicions. You need to meet this person as soon as possible and know more about the kind of relationship he has established with your child.

The older the child is when the abuse begins, the less obvious the signs may be. Children who are being abused are often severely threatened by the abuser to keep everything secret, and they will find it difficult to tell you about it. When they first determine to disclose the abuse, they may do so in very vague terms. When you get the feeling they are trying to tell you something without really saying it, you should be suspicious of CSA.

Some children are too afraid to tell their parents, so they will tell their friends. Their friends report the information to their parents, who usually will tell you about it right away.

Why Is It So Difficult for Your Child to Tell You?

You may be offended that your child did not feel free to tell you what was going on. Don't be offended! You never know how the child was being threatened by the abuser. Your child may even be afraid that you would blame him or her for what was going on.

If the abuser is a relative or close friend of the family, your child may have been urged to keep this sexual activity a secret from you. Abusers have an almost endless list of tricks and threats they use to intimidate the child to keep silent about what is going on.

Here are just a few of the threats an abuser may use:

- Sometimes the abuser will try to make the victim feel responsible for the abuse.
- Your child may be told that no one will believe her if she tells what is going on.

- The child may be told that he will be punished if he tells.
- The abuser may appeal to the child's sympathy by saying that if the child tells, the abuser will go to jail.
- When the abuser is a father or stepfather, he may try to make the child feel responsible for breaking up the family.
- Among the cruelest is to threaten the child that if she tells she will no longer be special to the abuser. The abuser will not love her any more.

What Should You Do If Your Child Has Been Molested?

First of all, don't panic! Your child has been traumatized, but his or her life has not been ruined. You should check with your pediatrician for further and more detailed instructions, but here are seven steps you will want to take once you know your child has been molested.

1. If you learn of the attack within eighteen to twenty-four hours after it has happened, take your child immediately to a medical center for a physical exam, and have the center call your pediatrician.
2. Since the child's clothes may be needed for evidence in the event of criminal prosecution, don't bother to wash your child or change his or her clothes before going to the medical center. Just get the child there. Some parents, in their efforts to make sure their child is presentable and dressed respectably before taking the child to the medical center, damage or completely destroy important evidence needed to prosecute the perpetrator that can often be found on the child's body or in his or her clothes.
3. For the sake of your child's privacy, quietly inform the person at the medical center what has happened, and ask that person to care for your child. You don't want to panic. Just approach the person in charge and quietly tell what has happened to your child.

4. Call the police and notify them of your child's examination. Tell the police your child has been sexually abused. They'll have someone in the department that specializes in child molestation cases. When you're talking to that person, tell him or her that you are at the medical center and your child is being examined. Explain that you have saved the child's clothes, and you haven't washed the child or changed his or her clothes since the attack happened.

5. Ask the medical staff to cooperate with the police in gathering evidence for possible prosecution. Parents who don't know what to do allow molesters to get away from prosecution because of a lack of physical evidence proving that the crime actually took place. We need to get as many of these people identified and off the streets as quickly as possible. Until they are removed from society, they will molest many children many times. Predators that can only be sexually stimulated by a child's body are responsible for abusing an average of 117 children before they are finally caught.[3] So identifying them and getting them off the streets is in the best interest of all of our children.

6. Since several community agencies will be involved in helping your child through this ordeal, be sure to write down names and telephone numbers for future contacts. Request that the people from the police department be the same sex as your child. This will make processing the report less traumatic for your child. In most communities today this is already standard practice. *Try to limit the number of people for whom the child has to recite this ordeal.*

7. In talking with your child communicate the following five ideas very clearly:

   a. "It is all right for you to tell me about what happened." This is particularly important if the molester has been someone in the family whom the child may feel the need to protect. You want to relieve the child of any guilt for telling you.

b. "I believe you." Some parents have blamed their children for their own molestation. It is enough that the child has been invaded and his or her innocence has been stolen. The last thing a child needs is to feel that somehow he or she is responsible for the molestation.

c. "It's all right for you to be angry at the person who molested you." This is a healthy reaction.

d. "It was not your fault."

e. "I love you and care about you."

Issues Involved in the Recovery Process

As soon as you discover your child has been sexually abused, you will want to arrange for an evaluation by a competent child therapist. Your pediatrician can help you find one if you don't already have someone in mind.

Childhood sexual abuse is treatable, and in almost all cases you can be assured of your child's full recovery with the help of a competent child therapist. However, the problem is not self correcting. Time alone will not cure it. So, be sure your child gets the professional help needed to overcome this barrier.

The earlier sexual abuse occurs, the more difficult it is for your child to remember what has happened to him or her. Pedophiles know this, and they take advantage of it.

When the abuse takes place in the preverbal years of a child's life, the memories of the experience are more likely to be stored in the sensory area of the brain. Therefore it may be difficult for that child to recall what happened. However, a child therapist takes advantage of many nonverbal ways of helping very young children deal with such trauma.

Why do the preverbal and preschool years present such a challenge in treating emotional trauma? Perhaps you can begin to understand the answer to this question by reflecting on how little you recall of your own life before you went to preschool or kindergarten.

For example, your child's brain is recording feelings, sounds, tastes, and achromatic visual sensations before he or she is born. Only memory for smells awaits birth for activation. These sensations are also recorded in specific parts of a child's brain.

After birth, chromatic vision, along with all these other sensations, begins to be associated with people, places, and things common to each person's environment, When your child begins to talk, you teach him or her to label the world, which makes it much more understandable for your child.

It takes about five years for your child's brain to develop the mental abilities to think abstractly, to conceptualize and orchestrate recall of specific senses stored in various parts of the brain well enough to put together a verbal history of his or her life.

All of these mental qualities are highly correlated with the onset of memory. This is why most children can remember very little about their preschool years. This is what makes children so vulnerable to emotional trauma during the preverbal, preschool years of life. And this is why your children need your special protection during this time.

However, by the time they are entering preschool or kindergarten, their memories are developing rapidly, and they can beat you regularly at games that require immediate recall. By this time they can do most personal things for themselves, even though they may still need your supervision in the process. So, not only are you relieved of much of their physical care, but also they are ready to enjoy life with you. And they are much better equipped to tell you if anyone sexually violates them.

Don't assume that the conversation you had with your child earlier about the relationship between genital pleasure and marriage is enough. This is a value that needs to be reinforced again and again in the mind of your child. So does the idea of body privacy.

From kindergarten through sixth grade your children will build most of their family memories. Once they are teenagers, their memories will be mostly of their peers. Unfortunately, these early memory-building years from six to ten are also the time when your children are at great risk for sexual abuse.

Even though at times you feel like your children's personal chauffeur, take advantage of those opportunities to show your personal interest in their world and to strengthen your emotional bonds with them. This will provide you with the influence you will need to guide them during their junior and senior high school days. Besides, by seizing these opportunities for personal conversation with your children, you make it easier for them to be open and honest with you about what is happening in their lives.

If anyone has invaded their body boundaries, they will need your help. And you will need to be aware of some of the issues they are facing. So, let me share some with you.

The very nature of the sexual abuse of a child carries with it deep and painful consequences. Realize that your child's recovery will likely extend over several months. If the abuser was a member of the family, and the abuse began when your child was very young, secrets kept that long form memories that must be shared thoroughly enough to be healed. The process is even more difficult for boys, because they don't like to be seen as victims; they don't like to talk about their problems. As you can see, all of this takes time, so be patient with your child.

Understandably, the emotions of abused children are all over the place. They feel angry. They feel confused. They feel violated. They feel afraid. They feel ashamed. They feel guilty. They feel sad and depressed. They feel undeserving of love. They feel powerless. They certainly feel different from their friends. They feel alone. Being sensitive to their emotional maelstrom will endear you to them.

Having some idea of the severity of your child's experience can help you to provide wiser support for him or her in their recovery. As you can imagine, the closer the relationship was between your child and his or her abuser, and the older the predator was, the greater the harm is likely to be.

When a child is abused by someone of the same sex, the child may fear this means he or she will become homosexual as an adult. If your child indicates any anxieties about this, simply explain that our nerve endings give us pleasure or pain regardless of who or what stimulates them. So it doesn't make any difference whether the person who molested your child was a person of the same sex or the opposite sex. Anyway, this is not about something the child did. It is about something that was done to the child. Be sure your child understands this.

It will be helpful for you to see recovery from childhood sexual abuse as an ongoing process, during which the abused child moves from victim to survivor—and finally begins to thrive in life again. Of course, as the child grows older, he or she may find himself or herself processing again and again what happened to them as a child. However, a healthy recovery will not leave your child emotionally or sexually crippled.

With good family support and competent professional help, a child who has been sexually abused can recover and move forward to achieve a happy, fulfilling life surrounded by loving relationships.

In the best of all possible worlds, you should not have to worry about what may be happening to your child when he or she is out of your sight. But, unfortunately, we don't live in that kind of world.

Fifty years ago, once a child's initial curiosity about sex was satisfied, that child's sexual interest was more likely to diminish during the elementary school years. The child's energies were consumed with school and games.

However, that world of childhood innocence disappeared with the advent of the Internet. It is a wonderful tool for gathering information and doing business, but it is proving to be disastrous for countless adults—and children. In the next chapter we will be talking about the dangers of the Internet and ways to prepare your children to deal with these dangers.

Chapter 7

Your Child's World...Invaded From Space

The invaders from outer space have arrived. No, I'm not talking about weird looking creatures from another world.

I'm talking about the invasion of your home by people unknown and invisible to you, who could care less about what happens to your children. Statistics indicate that nine out of ten children aged between eight and sixteen have viewed pornography on the Internet. In most cases, the sex sites were accessed unintentionally.[1]

You need to be aware of the arrogant way these people are using their technical and economic power to bypass you, as a parent, so they can communicate directly with your children through light waves, sound waves, computer pixels, and electronic technology, luring your children into their world—a world largely dominated by violence and sex.[2]

The impact these space invaders are having on your children and those of other concerned parents can be seen readily in the way the recreational center is shifting for American children from the playpen and the playground of the real world into the electronic world of media and virtual reality.

Typically, a child begins to retreat from the social world of family and friends to television in the preverbal years, and from there to the world of electronic games in early childhood. In many instances the preschool child is already playing games on computers and well on his or her way to the Internet world of cyberspace and computers in the early elementary school years.

Fascinated by what they see on television, discover in electronic games, and experience later on computer sites, our children are withdrawing more and more into this socially isolated electronic world. They are spending less and less time on neighborhood playgrounds where social skills are learned and bonds with friends are nurtured over the years.

Parenting Is Much More Challenging Today

These are just some of the issues that make parenting today much more challenging and demanding than when children got their information about their world through books and audiotapes. The electronic world, with the advent of headphones, is more difficult for you to monitor.

However, your children need your oversight now more than ever. With their limited judgment they cannot be trusted to determine what information they should be accessing from the media, and the industries involved certainly do not care about what happens to your children.

If you want to keep your children emotionally and spiritually healthy, you must take the time necessary to monitor closely their electronic world, which includes the world of their music. Trusting the judgment of your school children to know what media products are good for them is like expecting them to pick out their vitamins from the family medicine cabinet where your medicine is stored.

Beware of Electronic Child Care

Some parents may view their children's preoccupation with the new sophisticated *toys* of our impersonal world as a form of innocent child care that gives them some relief from their hectic efforts to keep up with an overextended work and social schedule. However, as a concerned parent you need to see this media invasion of your child's mind for what it is—a spiritual war that is being waged for the world of your child's urges, fantasies, and ideas, a world from which your child will ultimately make the choices that define his or her values and from which your child will choose his or her future lifestyle.

This battle is not just about money... although the *toys* of cyberspace are a lot more expensive than the old-fashioned toys of the playground. The people who control these industries are not satisfied with making hundreds of millions of dollars by captivating our children with interactive toys with their irresistible sights and sounds. They are determined to infuse these products with their philosophies, their values, and their politics. Over time, if you leave your children alone with these *invaders,* they will deliberately betray your family values and transform your child's view of life to conform as closely as possible to their own. This strategy is obvious to any thinking adult.

These invaders are gradually grooming your child from infancy through adolescence to become progressively attached to their electronic products. They are carefully targeting the pleasure centers of your child's brain so the child is easily moved from fascination with TV to electronic games, and from there to computers and to the music of the MTV networks. The ingenious brains behind these media giants are using the latest in psychological marketing techniques to prime the appetites of today's children for the adult products they are planning for tomorrow, thus guaranteeing the economic success of their giant corporations. No child is sophisticated enough to understand this.

However, every parent and teacher knows that the life-defining decisions you make in the course of becoming an adult have their roots in the philosophies, values, and ideas instilled in your mind as a child. As a parent, you are very careful to provide the physical protection your children need to travel and play in safety. However, in some ways your children are in greater need of your emotional and spiritual protection from those attempting to make millions by successfully invading their hearts and minds. Traditional sources of wisdom have told us that for centuries.[3]

How Serious Is This Media Invasion Problem?

In 2003 the Kaiser Family Foundation and the Children's Digital Media Centers studied media use by children who were six months to six years of age. What they found from their telephone interviews with 1,065 parents of children in this age group is astonishing. Here are some of the results:

1. As many as 43 percent of children under the age of two watch television every day. Twenty-six percent have a TV in their bedrooms, even though the American Academy of Pediatrics "urges parents to avoid television for children under two years old."

2. Children under two are using some form of screen media for more than two hours every day.
3. Slightly over a third of all children six years old and under have a TV in their bedroom. Many of them (27 percent) have a VCR or video game player in their bedroom, and a few (7 percent) even have a computer.
4. Over a fourth of the four- to six-year-old children in this study use a computer about an hour a day.
5. Over a third of these children can turn on a computer by themselves.
6. Forty percent can load their own CD-ROM.
7. Even though no one may be watching, two-thirds of these children were growing up in homes where the TV was on half of the time or more.
8. In over a third of these homes the TV was on always or most of the time. As you can imagine, this much TV exposure for children has a negative impact on their reading skills.
9. Ninety percent of the parents in the study realized this danger and placed limits on the amount of time children could spend watching TV. Almost 70 percent had rules about what their children could watch.

The study indicates the importance of parental control over the amount of time young children can spend watching TV and the kind of programming they are allowed to view.[4]

So, don't let your children determine these limits. You set them!

Media Skills—a Two-edged Sword

The unspoken message of this landmark study is that children are bringing sophisticated media skills with them to their *first* day of school. On the positive side, these children are equipped to benefit from the creative uses of these skills in the educational process. On the other hand, these same skills can also expose them to the dangerous electronic world of violence, cyberporn, and chat rooms that wait to prey on them. I will talk more about these later.

Carefully monitor the content and limit the amount of time your child spends interacting with the light and sound waves of the electronic world and the pixels of cyberspace. Leading pediatricians recommend that a child's media time should be limited to two hours a day; this includes television, electronic games, and computers.[5]

Presently, how well are we doing in helping our children observe this mental and social health standard? Researchers tell us: "By the time teenagers graduate from high school, they will have spent 15,000 hours watching television compared to 12,000 hours in the classroom."[6] You can draw your own conclusions.

The Importance of a Dialogue With Your Children

Once your children are exposed to the media, it is very important for you to keep an open dialogue with them concerning what they are learning about their world. You may have grown up in a home where your ideas and opinions were not solicited by your parents. Perhaps you just had to listen to them go on and on about what they did or did not want you doing. If so, remember how easy it was for you to tune them out. Because they had the power to control you at the time, you had to listen—but you didn't have to *hear.* As a teenager I looked at those one-way conversations as my parents *preaching* to me. So, I *reverently* listened to the *sermon* Mom and Dad felt they had to *preach.* But when it was over, I left *church* and went on with my life as though I hadn't heard anything they said. And... often, I hadn't.

That kind of parenting was not effective in giving me the guidance I needed when I was growing up—and it is even less effective today. Your children do need to hear from you, but you need to hear from them as well. This is much more likely to happen when you talk *with* your children rather than *at* them.

When your children come home from school, try not to be so busy that you don't have the time to get curious about the events of their day. Question them about how their day has gone, not as a detective would grill a suspect, but as a friend who wants to share their day.

Learn the Value of Open-ended Questions

Learn to ask your children questions that can't be answered with a simple *yes* or *no.* Listen carefully to what they have to say. You need to stay in touch with what is going on in the everyday world of your child. Very few things you could be doing at the time are as important as learning about the views of life that are slowly forming in the mind of your children. In the process you also will pick up on what they are learning about sex. However, if you don't engage them in this kind of daily dialogue, the formation of their personhood will proceed largely in secrecy.

For example, suppose you are rushing to prepare the evening meal so you can keep an important evening appointment. You don't really have the time to sit down and talk with your child, but you would feel too guilty for not saying anything at all. So you ask: "Did you have a good day at school?" Your child simply has to say, "Yes." This ends the conversation, and you both go on with what you were doing without the child having to open up a very big window into his or her day. You don't feel guilty for not talking to your child, but your child is left feeling that you were not really that interested anyway.

You'll learn more about what is really happening by asking, "While we're eating dinner, why don't you tell me about your day?" For example, I know a couple who requires each of their boys to tell them five important things about his day during dinner. When they first began this practice, their boys thought it was "too much." However, as their parents took the time to listen, the boys began a friendly competition to see who would be the first to tell their five events of the day.

Take the time to review your children's learning experiences. Ask questions like:

- "Who is your teacher?"
- "What do you like most about him or her?"
- "What are you studying now?"
- "Tell me about some of the interesting things you are learning."
- "How do you and your teacher get along?"
- "Who are your friends at school?"

- "Who is your favorite?"
- "Why do you like them better than your other friends?"
- "Where do they live?"

I'm sure you'll be able to come up with a far better list than this, but at least these suggestions will get you started.

Notice, none of these questions call for a simple *yes* or *no* answer. That is why therapists call these kinds of questions *open ended.* This is how we make it easy for those who seek our help to tell *their* story.

By opening up the information lines into your children's world with conversations like this, you will learn what you need to know about the ideas that are being introduced to your child's mind from sources outside the family. This gives you a great opportunity to affirm the things they are learning that you approve of and challenge those ideas that are contrary to the values of your family.

Teach Your Children How to Think

Be wise in the way you challenge your children's ideas. Don't try to dissuade your children from their ideas by just demeaning what they say. When you take a different view of some of the things they are learning, patiently explain to them what those differences are and why you think people who look at these areas of life as your family does will live a more fulfilling and satisfying life. Encourage them to discuss matters with you that you may not agree upon. Remember, the goal of your discussions is not to think *for* your children but to teach them how to think wisely about the important issues of life for themselves.

Encourage them to do well in school, but help them to understand the difference between the academic learning of the classroom and the life education they get in your family. Make it clear to them that schools primarily teach us what we need to know to make a living. They do not teach us how to live. Families are supposed to teach children how to live. Schools are for teaching the things we need to know in order to make a living and become good citizens. Families are for teaching us how to live.

Chapter 8

Pornography...How Big a Threat for Children?

One of the greatest moral threats your children face at school is the informal learning that takes place among them and their peers. Your children's peers will introduce your children to the practices and values of their own families. They will keep your children up to date on the latest video games. The children will share with each other advanced computer skills they have learned—skills that can be used for Web browsing and text messaging. Such skills enable children to take advantage of the wonderful opportunity the Internet presents for research and learning. However, these skills can also introduce your children to the world of cyberporn.

How big a threat is pornography to your child? First, let's just look at the size of the industry. Sex is the number one searched-for topic on the Internet. Currently there are more than 1.3 million porn sites on the Internet. More than 32 million viewers searched out these sites in 2003. To give you some idea about how rapidly this epidemic of smut is growing, in 1998 there were 14 million pages of hard-core pornography available on the Internet, but by 2003 the number had grown to 260 million pages, or about twenty times the number available in 1998. The astronomical growth occurring in the industry is not likely to slow down in the near future.[1]

Fed by Unbelievable Profits

The pornographic industry made $12 billion in the United States in 2003. Just how much money is this? It is more money than the 2003 revenues of all major league baseball, football, and basketball franchises in the country. It is twice as much as was earned by all the major television networks, ABC, NBC, and CBS in the same year. This is no small economic monster that is attacking our children. Where this much money is involved, you can be sure that whatever political protection is needed has been bought and is already in place. First Amendment rights under the Constitution were never meant to put our children at sexual risk.

How Many of Our Children Are Involved?

The *average* age of a boy's first exposure to cyberporn is eleven; for girls it is thirteen. This means that many boys and girls who are not that old have already been exposed to this lurid world of sex. Nine out of ten eight- to sixteen-year-olds have found their way to these pages, mostly while doing their homework. Estimates indicate that 80 percent of fifteen- to seventeen-year-old young men in our country have had many exposures to hardcore pornography on the Internet. In fact, twelve- to seventeen-year-old males comprise the largest group of consumers of Internet pornography.[2]

Children are spending 65 percent more of their time on the Internet viewing pornography than they are on game sites. Every day in the United States, more than two billion pornographic e-mails are sent. One can only speculate how many of these are aimed at teens. Telephone companies estimate that minors use the information they gain from porn sites to make 70 percent of the five hundred thousand daily calls to dial-a-porn.[3]

How Do Children Discover Pornography?

Most children first discover cyberporn by accident. They push a wrong key on the keyboard and are confronted with powerfully stimulating sexual images. As disgusting as they are, these erotic images leave lasting imprints in the minds and brains of our children. This information is much more likely to be shared with their peers than with their parents. So, peer pressure begins to add its impetus.

Pornographers also devise deceptive ways of snaring unsuspecting children in their traps. According to a recent article in the *Orange County Register*, pornographers are using "bait-and-switch" tactics to link porn sites to the Web sites of children's favorite cartoon characters. Children innocently attempt to get on their favorite Web site, only to discover that these sites are linked porn sites designed to appeal to the youngest viewers.[4]

Children who stumble onto pornography this way may find themselves accidentally "mouse-trapped." What is this? *Mouse-trapping* is a device that programmers of cyberporn use to open other porn sites when the viewer tries to close the one they are viewing. The only way out of this dilemma is to *crash* the computer by holding down the power button until the computer shuts down. This is why the process is called *crashing.*

Pornography in the World of Youth Music

The world of youth music introduces your preteen and junior high children to a more insidious form of pornography—one that is not only acceptable to their peers but also embraced by them. Because the music is usually so loud and rapidly paced, few parents can even understand the words. This is intentional. This crowd wants their own world—and music they love and you can't stand is one way they create it. Unless you make it your business to know what the lyrics are, you may be easily persuaded by the anxious pleading of your children to let them purchase a certain album just so they can feel *in* with their peers.

However, much of this music that begins to ensnare your preteen and junior high children is so trashy you would be too embarrassed to repeat the words even if you could understand them. As I am writing this chapter, the number one song on MTV according to *Billboard,* the industry's standard for determining popularity, is a song called "Candy Shop."[5] Just a few explicit lines from this song would shock you into discovering the world of sexual ideas your children are being exposed to during these impressionable years.[6]

This chorus is tame compared to the explicit sexual references of the verses. And the dances that accompany this kind of music on MTV are very sensual and sexually suggestive.

Of course, by the time this book reaches you, another hit will be at the top of the list. Unless there is a sharp turn in the direction of the country's sexual morality, the lyrics of future hits are likely to be even more lewd.

No doubt these invaders of our youth's media world spent millions of dollars promoting this song. However, it would not have been number one unless most young teens used their parents' money to buy millions of copies of it. Be sure you know what your teens are spending your money on.

I know peer pressure plays a powerful role in determining what music is popular. This is why I believe your preteens and teens need to have the benefit of your views as they determine the kind of music they will allow to be sung into their spirits.

You can refuse to give them money for this kind of music—and you should. You can refuse to allow them to have it in your home—and you should. However, the better approach is to discuss the music and its intentions with them so they can develop a better understanding of the impact this kind of music can have on their attitudes and behavior over time.

It won't take long for them to see that the people who produce this kind of music are using pornographic lyrics like these to encourage sexually irresponsible behavior. These artists are trying to turn your children into the kind of person they are singing about—not the kind of person your children want to be at all. By patiently discussing the music world's motives in producing this kind of tuneful trash, you enable your teens to make better decisions on their own about the fantasy material they allow to shape their character. It also avoids the resentment you stimulate by making these decisions for them.

Once your children are preteen, I would discuss the lyrics of the most popular teen songs with them at least once a year. You might call it something like, "Our family's annual review of *Billboard's* top ten teen tunes."

Be sure to draw your children into the discussion. Respect their views, even if you disagree with them. This will establish their obligation to respect your views and to learn from them. And believe it or not...you will probably learn some interesting things from them as they freely express how they feel about sex and what is going on in their young world.

You need to check the list of the top ten at least once a year. Print out a copy of the lyrics for the top three, making a copy for you and one for each of your children. Plan an evening when you can have a discussion with them about these songs. Let them know that their views are very important to you, because you want to know what the world they live in is really like.

Once the discussion begins, let them do most of the talking. Remember to use open-ended questions that make it easy for them to express themselves. All of you will have to work on overcoming your embarrassment in discussing the obscene nature of some of the lyrics, but one of the most effective ways you can impact the sexual world they live in is by engaging them in this kind of dialogue about it. Don't let embarrassment deny you this opportunity.

Somewhere in the discussion they may use the argument that these are just songs and insist that they would never do what the songs suggest. This presents you with a wonderful opportunity to ask them why music plays such a prominent role in the church services at their place of worship. Explain to them that it is precisely for the purpose of embedding the truth of the lyrics in our spirit that we sing spiritual songs. The music penetrates our spirits and helps us live out the truths of the lyrics.[7]

Don't lose your patience in these discussions. Keep your cool! A rational discussion of the spiritual differences between the morals and values of your family and those expressed in popular music can be an invaluable part of your child's moral education.

Believe me, the ideas about sex that they will be exposed to from these sources are very different from those you have taught them. You can count on that!

How Does Pornography Affect Children?

As noted earlier, a certain amount of childhood sexual play to satisfy a child's curiosity about the opposite sex is normal. However, exposure to pornography can adversely affect your children in several ways. The degree to which they will be affected will depend on a number of factors. How early in life were they exposed? How often did they view pornography? How bizarre was the sexual behavior involved?

The multidimensional impact on the brain and mind of the child are predictable.

Spiritual effects of pornography

In the sacred view of sex presented in Scripture, sex is seen as God's gift to a man and woman, a gift they are to share only with each other in marriage.[8] In any other arena, having sex is seen as sinning against the body. The Scriptures refer to these sins as *fornication*.[9]

As we mentioned earlier, the intense pleasure of sexual orgasm is seen by people of faith to be intended to intensify the pleasure bond between a husband and wife. When that pleasure is experienced with another person outside of marriage, either before or after one is married, it is no longer an exclusive experience between husband and wife. The unique purpose of sexual orgasm is compromised, and it is difficult, if not impossible, to escape the life-complicating consequences of this sexual misbehavior. This is why the Scriptures refer to sexual sins as sins against the body.

Pornography presents a totally secular view of sexual behavior. From the pornographer's point of view there is nothing sacred about sex. It is portrayed totally as a form of pleasure that can be bought and sold like any other form of entertainment. Consequently it perverts the divine purpose of sex into a form of self-indulgent pleasure, totally unrelated to marriage.

In her testimony before the U.S. Senate Committee on Commerce, Science, and Transportation, Dr. Mary Anne Layden, the codirector of the Sexual Trauma and Psychopathology Program Center for Cognitive Therapy at the University of Pennsylvania, had this to say:

> An example of Pornography Distortion would include beliefs such as "Sex is not about intimacy, procreation, or marriage. Sex is about predatory self-gratification, casual recreation, body parts, violence, feces, strangers, children, animals and using women as entertainment." All of these messages are regularly sent by pornography.[10]

The younger a child is when exposed to pornography, the more confusing the activity is to the child's mind. Since it is presented as some form of fun and games, the child is likely to want to imitate what he has seen and heard. Discovering their child in this kind of perverted play is often how parents realize that their child is involved in pornography.

Pornography dehumanizes women and desensitizes men. Women are presented as the property of men, obligated to do whatever the man desires sexually at that moment—and just as obligated to *enjoy it.* After all, the man reasons, he is paying for it.

In the course of degrading and humiliating the women who are being sexually used while he is watching, the man involved in pornography is desensitizing himself. He does not see the women he views in pornography as human beings. He is excited by watching other men do to them what he would like to do. He sees them as bodies whose shape and body parts he rates in his own mind. And, in the process, he is destroying his capacity for developing intimate, caring, and compassionate feelings for women. This severely damages his ability to be the kind of man any healthy woman wants as a husband and the father of her children.

Pornography not only spiritually damages the consumers of its filth, but it also imposes unbelievable damage on the performers and producers of pornography. These people become so callused to anything intimate or tender about sex that three out of four of those brave enough to attempt marriage divorce in three years or less.[11]

Physiological effects of pornography

Pornographers deliberately target the reward pathways of the brain. Using the same neurochemistry that drives us to satisfy our need for food and water, pornographers create an exaggerated need for sex. The chemistry of the brain is noticeably affected by the intense sexual excitement pornography produces.

When a child is frequently exposed to pornography, he develops an abnormal appetite for sexual fantasy. This triggers a need for more pornography. Repeated exposure to such stimulating sexual fantasy triggers an unusually high appetite for sexual arousal. Once the child is aroused, then he is driven to continue masturbating while viewing pornography until orgasm relaxes him.

Often this produces a sexually precocious child whose physical appetites for sexual excitement are far in advance of his emotional and social maturity. The observing parent will notice this behavior and feel the need to spend time talking with the child about sex and supervising his behavior more carefully. I will return to this subject later when we discuss how to protect your children from pornography.

If you understand how these pornographic images are neurochemically burned into the brain, then you develop a deep respect for the addictive potential of pornography. Pornography possesses all the qualities of the three major drug families involved in compulsive or addictive behavior. It stimulates your fantasy like the hallucinogens. It arouses you like the stimulants. And once you have achieved orgasm, it relaxes you like the opioids. This is what makes pornography so dangerously addictive—and the peddlers know it.

Just as with any other addictive drug, your brain accommodates to a certain level of pornography that formerly brought you to orgasm. However, to get beyond the level of accommodation and reach the higher level of excitement required to bring you to orgasm in the future, more of the kind of pornography you find sexually stimulating will be required. Once caught in this cycle you find yourself sexually addicted.

Researchers indicate that 40 percent of sexual addicts will lose their marriage, and 27 to 40 percent will lose their jobs because they use company computers to feed their addiction.[12] You need to put your teenagers in touch with these statistics.

Emotional and social effects

The earlier the exposure to pornography, and the more frequently it occurs, the greater the risk that the child will want to imitate this behavior with other children. Once this practice begins, the adrenaline rush of doing something that is forbidden but extremely pleasurable reinforces the need for more pornography and experimentation with other children. The tragic consequences of such a destructive cycle are that sexual pleasure outside of marriage becomes normalized in the minds of our children.

Think about what this means. A young man's desire for immediate sexual gratification dominates his behavior. He learns that sexual pleasure is available without the need for him to make any personal commitment or assume any responsibility beyond the moment. So, instead of allowing his anticipation of sexual pleasure in marriage to intensify his desire to be true to his wife before he finds her, he develops promiscuous patterns of sexual behavior that make it difficult for him to be sexually true to his wife once he does find her.

Over time, as noted earlier, this pornographically created sexual desire will require higher and higher levels of excitement in order to bring the child or teen to orgasm. Unless this cycle is broken early by parental intervention and moral instruction, pornography strengthens its control over the young person as he grows older, and he becomes more and more dependent on this destructive habit.

Pornography also distorts the teen's view of women. Usually they are pictured totally under the man's control. Without expressing love or commitment, the man has absolute power over the women in commanding them to provide him whatever he wants at the moment. They are reduced to becoming an accessory to the man's every sexual need. Even worse, the women are portrayed as loving every minute of it.

Unfortunately, the male is unaware that as he dehumanizes the woman in this way, he is also desensitizing himself. The romantic side of his nature, his sensitivity to women, his tenderness, his capacity for intimacy...these lie neglected and undeveloped within him. They are the very attributes that a normal healthy woman will desire in a husband. So, long before he reaches marriageable age, these capacities may be so severely crippled that the male withdraws from young women and becomes more and more dependent on the pornographic world for his sexual excitement.

Until now, we have not even mentioned the responsibility that supporters of the pornographic industry must assume for what it does to the performers, both men and women. Very few little girls grow up wanting to be porn stars. Men who patronize this industry would certainly not want to discover their mother, sister, or daughter in the trade. In the process of satisfying the perverted sexual appetites of a morally decaying culture, these people are destroying their own ability to form marriages and families that last.

What Can You Do to Protect Your Children?

Here are several suggestions to help keep your children safe from pornography within your home:

1. The American Academy of Pediatrics recommends no television in a child's bedroom.[13]

2. Children's media exposure should be limited to two hours a day...including TV, music, and computers.[14]

3. Set the family computer up in an open area of the house. Be sure you know your children's screen names and passwords.

4. Talk to your children about pornography ("trashy sexual stuff") on the Internet. Let them know you understand they cannot always control what comes on the screen, but tell them to let you know when pornography comes up on *their screen.*

5. Be sure you have a current version of parental controls on your computer. Your local computer store will be glad to give you the names of the latest and best. None of the programs are foolproof, but they will discourage indiscriminate Web browsing and protect your child from pop-ups.

6. Until a child is ten years of age, don't permit him or her to surf the Web alone.

7. Be sure you block chat rooms and instant messages. There is a 100 percent chance that your child will be contacted by a predator if he or she enters a chat room.[15]

8. Tell your children about *mouse-trapping* as soon as they begin to use a computer. Tell them to call you if they find themselves *mouse-trapped.* Then, teach your children how to crash their computer. You do this by simply turning the power off.

9. Forbid your children to share personal information on the Web. Pedophiles can access this information. Warn them about meeting anybody they have met online unless you are present.

10. Have a talk with your child about pornography that stresses the material we have covered in this chapter and earlier.

Monitoring Your Child's Internet Activity

Be sure your computer skills are adequate for monitoring your children's activities on the Web. According to a Media Awareness Network survey done in 2001, only 36 percent of youth say that they sometimes (24 percent) or always (12 percent) erase the history of their recent Web site visits.[16]

Here is a procedure for doing a weekly search of your child's computer and responsibly monitoring their activities on the Internet:

1. Simultaneously press the Control and H keys. This will give you a quick glance of the history of your child's recent Internet activities.

2. Place the mouse on the down arrow on the right-hand side of the address line. Then left-click it. This allows you to see the recent sites your child has visited.

3. The same approach can be applied to the down arrow by the right-hand side of the search window on your child's favorite search engines: Google, Yahoo, and others. This will provide you with a list of the subjects your child has searched for recently.

4. Put the mouse on the start button and left-click it. Left-click on Search. Then enter the word "cache" without the quotes. This should bring up a list of folders. Left-click your mouse on each of them to open the folder(s). They also contain folders that tell you where your child has been.

5. Enter each of the following prompts in the Search window and press Enter: *.htm *.html (be sure you leave a space between the prompts just as above).

6. By following the same procedure, enter into the Search window *.gif *.jpg *.jpeg *.bmp, and you will discover the images your child has viewed.

7. To see the video files your child has downloaded, use the same procedure by entering into the Search space *.avi *.mpeg *.mpg *.asf (be sure you leave a space between the prompts). Find the pictures your child has downloaded: cache, .jpeg, .jpg, .gif, and .bmp.

8. To discover which Web sites have placed *cookies* (these are files that a Web site can post on your browser to trace your Internet activities), simply type *cookies.txt* in the Search window and press Enter.

If your child's computer is clean, breathe a sigh of relief and thank God for keeping your child safe from peddlers of pornographic smut. If your child has been visiting pornographic Web sites, they will be obvious by their names. Of course, any pictures or videos he may have downloaded will speak for themselves.

Once you have found footprints of pornography on your child's computer, print a copy of the complete record. As you can imagine, the situation will be dealt with differently depending on the age of the child and the extent to which he has involved himself with pornography.

Of course, corrective steps will need to be taken, but remember, our goal is to raise sexually healthy children in this sexually sick world. Although realizing that your child has already been introduced to the pornographic world is cause for serious concern, it is no reason for panic. The goal of our suggestions is to turn this disappointing discovery into a practical learning experience for you and your child.

Some of the Web sites cited in the Notes for this chapter can give additional help. In protecting your children from pornographers, there is no substitute for parental vigilance. Monitor diligently, and carry on a running dialogue with your children about what they are learning on the Web.

The dangers of cyberporn are very real. However, the Web's information highway can also be an invaluable learning tool for your children. I hope you have found the information in this chapter helpful in protecting your children from pornography.

In the next chapter I will be talking to you about the importance of staying ahead of Mother Nature in preparing your daughters for sexually healthy womanhood and your sons for sexually healthy manhood.

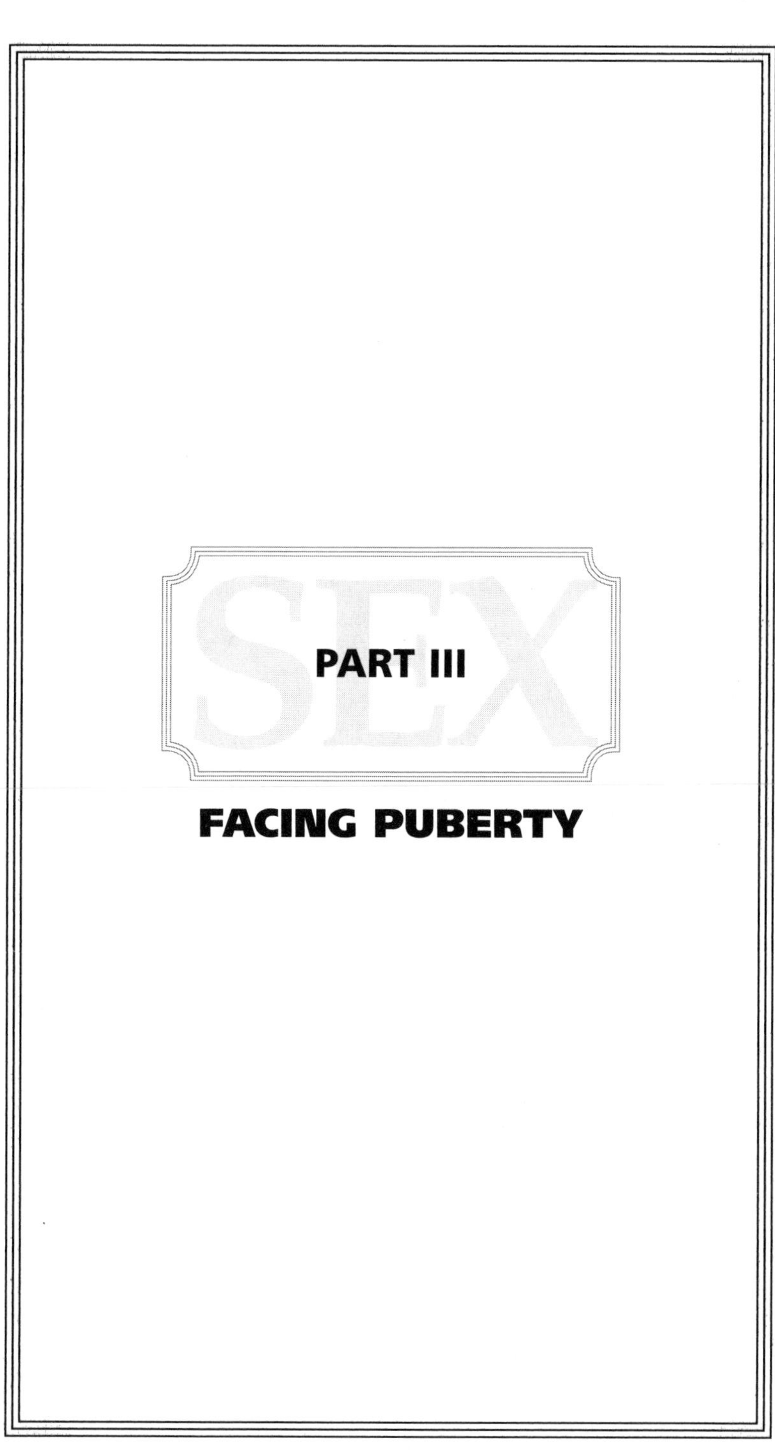

PART III

FACING PUBERTY

Chapter 9

When the Body Begins to Change

Most of today's parents lack the information they need to talk knowledgeably with their children about sex. Many of them were not offered sex education classes in their public schools. Consequently, what they learned about sex they learned from their peers, which often left them with inaccurate or inadequate information.[1]

With the information contained in this book, you can help your children have the training and information they need to develop a healthy, positive understanding of their own sexuality. This will be especially important as their bodies begin to change and they enter that difficult season of puberty.

During puberty and adolescence your children's bodies go through dramatic changes that transform them from children to adults. They have never experienced anything like the hormonal explosion responsible for triggering this process. Your daughter's moods are likely to be unstable and intense. It is difficult to tell when she wants to be coddled and when she wants to be left alone. The speed with which your son is growing arms and legs makes him somewhat clumsy and awkward. When he talks he never knows whether he's going to sound like a tenor or a bass. This should make you understand why adolescents are not known for their emotional stability.

Puberty Is Awkward—and People Are Unfair!

Once the pituitary gland (a little pea-sized gland in the brain) kicks off this process we call *puberty*, you and your child are off to the races. Your relationship will never be quite the same again.

For example, from your children's tenth birthday to their twentieth birthday their bodies will grow into very different sizes and shapes from the ones you and they have grown accustomed to during the first ten years of their lives. During the earlier years of their lives, they grew at a much more gradual and manageable pace. During puberty they can grow from two to six inches in one year.

So you can understand why it is not unusual for your children to feel like strangers to themselves during this decade of growth. The rapid and complex ways their bodies change can be very anxiety provoking for them and perplexing to us at times. This is one of those times in life when it is normal to be abnormal. Trying to predict the moods of children going through puberty can be very frustrating.

Just when you conclude they want to be treated more like an adult, they want to be treated like children. Yet when you want to treat them like children, they let you know in no uncertain terms that they are not children anymore.

Adding to the emotional challenges of this period of development is the fact that the pubescent growth does not occur uniformly. Some youngsters' bodies' shapes change and their growth spurt begins very early in puberty, while for others it is delayed until the middle teens.

Those for whom growth and change come early are often the envy of their peers, but beginning to look like an adult so early in life often puts them at the mercy of unrealistic expectations from the adult community. A fifteen-year-old girl with a fully developed body is not a woman. A fifteen-year-old boy over six feet tall, with facial and body hair is not a man. They both have the same fifteen-year history with the same fifteen-year judgment of their peers who have not yet begun their pubescent growth spurt. An advanced physical development also brings sexual attention from their peers that they are not emotionally prepared to manage.

On the other hand, when a young person's growth spurt is delayed, that young person can develop feelings of inferiority that can be crippling as an adult. Wise parents can help their youngsters understand that the body is important, but not as important as the person who lives in it. We want to take good care of our bodies because we live in them.

If the person living in the body keeps growing, sooner or later the body will catch up. However, when the person living in the body begins to feel so physically inferior to more rapidly developing peers that he or she neglects other aspects of personal growth and development, that adolescent will continue to be a child emotionally after the growth of his or her body has caught up with peers. Urge your children to keep their focus on personal growth and development, knowing that the future will take care of their physical growth and development. Helping them to put these changes in perspective should make the years ahead more comfortable for them and more tolerable for you.

Goals for This Section

In this section of the book, I will give you the information you need to enable you to help your children. It requires you to have information about the physical, sexual, and reproductive processes accompanying puberty and adolescence. If you are already familiar with this information, why not scan it again? This will serve as a useful review before discussing the information with your children.

Many of today's parents simply were not given an opportunity to learn about the changes of puberty when they were growing up. Few of us had parents who knew how to talk to us about them. When many of us went to school, sex education classes were not yet included in the curriculum.

Even in our sexually sophisticated society there is still a sexual information gap between parents and their youngsters, which leaves many girls not knowing what is happening to them when they experience their first menstruation and many boys mystified and anxious when they experience their first nocturnal emission. As parents, when we look back over our own lives, we are aware of the changes that took place in our own bodies, but often we are not comfortable enough to talk about these changes with our children.

Sometimes parents will give their children a book to read that explains the sexual changes that accompany puberty and adolescence. This is certainly commendable; it provides the necessary information youngsters need, but it doesn't take the place of the parental spiritual guidance and emotional support so important in giving children a healthy understanding of what becoming a young adult is all about.

This chapter will provide you with the clinical information you need to put yourself and your youngsters at ease as you chart the way to comfortably enter manhood and womanhood.

I will help you to anticipate many of the questions children raise about the physical changes they are experiencing as they leave childhood and began to enter adolescence. In responding to their questions, you will want to provide them the information they need at the time without overwhelming them with more than is necessary.

Your ability and willingness to address their questions will increase their respect for you as knowledgeable and loving parents. Helping them to stay ahead of Mother Nature will make puberty less anxiety provoking for them—they will know what is coming next. It will also nourish the emotional bond between you and them, making them more open to your influence and advice.

I will also model some ways you can share with your children the values you defined for yourself as you made your way through the painful experience of your own adolescence and early adulthood. This will also give you an opportunity to define the role a healthy faith plays in defining protective sexual boundaries in a person's life.

Puberty Is Awesome!

The physical and emotional transformation a child goes through in the process of becoming an adult is an awesome experience. Yet, before this process is completed your teenagers will be confronted with the responsibility for the miracle of human reproduction.

For this reason, I suggest that you separate these two events in your approach to the sex education of your children. Deal with puberty first. Then, two years later talk to them about conception and childbirth. Your first talk with your child about puberty should take place before his or her tenth birthday. When your child reaches the age of twelve, discuss conception and childbirth.

This approach makes a lot of sense when looked at from your children's points of view. Nine- or ten-year-old girls find themselves preoccupied with curiosity and some anxiety about the hormonal changes occurring in their bodies. However, during these later years of childhood the last thing that concerns them is the thought of having a baby. And, although twelve-year-old boys are concerned about being old enough to shave, unpredictable erections, and other physical changes that are turning them into men, they seldom give a serious thought to becoming fathers.

Putting *Ideas* Into Our Children's Heads

Of course, I still meet a few parents who mistakenly believe that giving children any information about sex and reproduction makes it more likely that they will experiment with what they learn. They fear this kind of openness between parents and children will "put *ideas* into their children's heads."

However, you and I know those ideas are already there. The question is, "What role are you, as a parent, prepared to take in shaping these ideas and being as sure as you can that they are healthy and based on accurate information?"

Our children are surrounded by all kinds of information about sex. What they learn from their sex education classes at school is most likely accurate but usually void of any spiritual or moral context.

Other information about sex comes to them from peers, pornographic books, magazines, television, movies, DVDs, cyberporn Web sites, and many other sources. A great majority of these resources are secular, many of them are inaccurate, and a lot of them are just downright evil.

Tragically, when parents fail to assume the primary responsibility for the sexual education of their children, they are abdicating this vital role to such sources. These people are not likely to be concerned about the spiritual, emotional, and social impact the sex information they provide will have on your children.

As we mentioned earlier, it is not a matter of whether or not your children will learn about sex. They will! The only unanswered questions are, "What will they learn?" and "Who will teach them?"

The fact that you are reading this book indicates you have already answered these questions for yourself and your children. You are going to assume the primary responsibility for putting the right kind of sexual ideas into their heads and hearts. Congratulations!

Staying Ahead of Mother Nature

Your preteen youngster is curious about the physical changes presently occurring in his or her body. However, forming close and intimate relationships with members of the opposite sex is not high on your child's list of priorities at the moment. So, right now our focus will be on just helping your child deal with *puberty.*

Puberty is the word we use to describe the beginning of the physical changes that introduce a girl into womanhood and a boy into manhood. Technically, the dictionary defines *puberty* as, "the condition of being or the period of becoming first capable of reproducing sexually marked by maturing of the genital organs, development of secondary sex characteristics, and by the first occurrence of menstruation in the female."[2]

Today, American children are entering puberty earlier than ever. As yet, there is no reliable research to indicate why this is happening. The average age of *menarche* for girls is around ten, but *menstruation* can begin as early as eight or nine.

However, if your daughter begins to go through puberty before she is nine or later than her thirteenth birthday, you might be wise to mention this to her pediatrician. She may need some medical attention. Your pediatrician will have excellent resources for helping you and your daughter deal with this special situation.

Boys begin puberty somewhere between twelve and fourteen years of age.[3] For both boys and girls, the whole process will take several years. As might be expected, girls are more comfortable talking to their mothers about puberty, but sons feel more comfortable talking with their fathers about it. As parents you need to prepare yourself for this important task.

Doing Your Homework

Surveys indicate that since the 1940s, American parents have largely abdicated the responsibility of talking with their children about puberty and adolescence to the public schools, their children's peers, and the media.[4]

So, if your parents were among this group, you may find the thought of discussing these issues with your children somewhat intimidating.

Nevertheless, the overwhelming majority of parents I meet today want to provide the information and emotional support their children need during this critical time of life. However, they frankly admit they do not feel well enough informed to approach this challenge with confidence.

In the next chapter I will discuss these important issues and give you the tools you need to help your adolescent children walk confidently through the season of puberty and become healthy, well-adjusted young adults.

Chapter 10

Getting the Facts About Puberty

Puberty is triggered by the *pituitary* (pe-tü-a-ter-ē) *gland*, a little pea-sized gland in the brain. It sends a hormonal or chemical message to the ovaries in a girl's body that it is time to begin the production of estrogen. The same gland sends a hormonal message to the boy's testicles to start producing testosterone. Once this process begins, your little girl or boy will never be the same again. They are on their way to womanhood and manhood.

Now that we know how the whole process begins, let's take a quick review of the reproductive systems of the female and male and see how they are affected by these changes. This will give you more confidence and help you to feel more comfortable talking with your children about the changes they can expect to experience in puberty. Since girls enter puberty approximately two years before boys, we will review their sexual anatomy first.

Anytime you discuss anatomy you deal with details. Therefore you may find the next few pages to be somewhat tedious. However, becoming thoroughly familiar with the anatomy and properly pronouncing the names of the organs is very important in achieving the necessary confidence to put your preteen at ease when discussing the subject with her.

So take a few days to review these next few pages again and again. Try to memorize the drawings of the female and male reproductive systems before you speak with your child so that you have a clear picture of them in your mind as you talk.

I will identify each of the organs for you, define how they change during puberty, and discuss the role they play in reproduction. I will also give you the correct way to pronounce their names.

After you are confident and comfortable with this information, I will give you some suggestions for the kind of prepubertal talk that your son or daughter will find helpful. Of course, you will want to adapt your talk to fit your own personality and way of communicating with your children. However, the suggestions and guidelines at the end of the chapter will provide you with some help in making this excursion comfortable and exciting for you and your children.

FEMALE SEXUAL ANATOMY

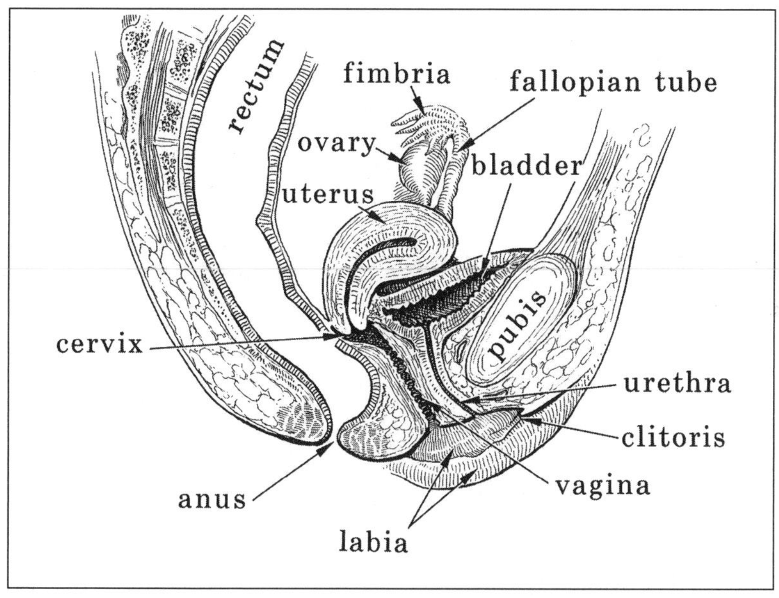

Diagram 1

1. The external female sex organs include the *mons veneris* (mänz ven-er-es), which literally means the "mountain of Venus" in Latin. This is the mound of fatty tissues just under the skin over the *pubis* or pelvic bone. Pubic hair grows over the *mons veneris* during puberty. This makes the *mons* the

most obvious member of the *vulva* (vul-va), or external female organs.

2. The *labia majora* (lā-bē-a ma-jor-a), or major lips, are two fatty lips that extend from the *mons veneris* and form the outer borders of the *vulva*, or the external parts of the female sex organs. They are covered with hair and usually hide the other parts of the *vulva.*

3. The *labia minora* (lā-bē-a mi-nor-a), or minor lips, lie just beneath the *labia majora.* They are two thin folds of skin richly endowed with blood vessels and nerve endings. They join at the top and form a single fold of skin covering the *clitoris.*

4. The *clitoris* (kli-te-ras) lies at the top of the *labia majora,* just below the *mons veneris.* It is a short cylindrical organ that consists of two spongy bodies that can quickly fill with blood, stiffen, and increase in size when sexually excited. This is why in some ways the *clitoris* is analogous to the male penis. The word comes from a Greek word that means "that which is closed in." This refers to the fact that the *clitoris* is partially covered by the *clitoral hood*, which may contribute to the formation of *smegma* (sm-eg-ma), a pastelike genital secretion that can cause irritation and contribute to pain during intercourse.

5. The *vaginal* (va-je-nul) *opening* lies below the *urethra* (yu-rē-thra). Unlike the male, the *urethra* of the female is independent from the sex organs and functions only to release urine from the bladder. It is very small and is located about halfway between the *clitoris* and the *vaginal opening.*

6. Although the *vaginal opening* is very large when compared to the *urethra,* it may be partially closed by a membrane called the *hymen* (hī-men). The *hymen* serves no known physiological purpose, although in the past, when the *hymen*

was intact, a woman was considered a virgin. However, some *hymens* are elastic enough to allow for the insertion of a *penis* without tearing. Other *hymens* are so thin and fragile that they may be torn by many activities other than intercourse. This makes the *hymen* test of virginity for females very unfair in countries where this is still the practice.

7. As a woman matures, her breasts are formed from two cushions of fat and tissue surrounding her *mammary* (ma-me-rē) glands. After she gives birth to a child, these glands begin secreting milk into special ducts leading to the nipples of her breasts. Although a woman's breasts are not sex organs in the strictest sense of the word, because of the erotic role they play in sexual arousal they can be considered as part of the woman's externalized sexual parts. Because the nipples of a woman's breasts contain so many nerve endings, they are very sensitive to touch and usually become erect during sexual intercourse. Even though breast size is determined by heredity, it continues to be the source of concern for many women of all ages.

8. The *ovaries* (ōv-a-rēes) are two walnut-sized organs located in the lower abdomen on either side of the female *uterus* (yü-te-res). They produce *ova,* or eggs, and hormones such as estrogen, androgen, and progesterone. Estrogen and progesterone play important roles in a woman's *menstrual cycle,* which we will talk more about later.

9. The *ova* (eggs) are formed within the *fimbria* (fim-brē-a), or *follicles*, of each *ovary*. One *ovum* (egg) is usually produced each menstrual cycle, every twenty-eight to thirty-five days.

10. As the *ovum* is released, it begins its journey down the *fallopian* (fa-lō-pē-en) tubes or *oviducts,* where *fertilization* normally takes places. These tubes provide a passageway for the *sperm* to reach the egg. Fertilization usually takes

place in the upper part of the tube. The fertilized egg is then moved toward the uterus by the combined action of the wall of the tube and the movements of countless hair-like growths inside the tubes called *cilia* (ci-lē-a).

11. The *uterus* (yü-te-res), which is the Latin word for *womb*, is a muscular, pear-shaped organ about three inches long, located in the center of the lower abdomen between and slightly above the *ovaries*. The *fallopian tubes* enter the *uterus* near the top on either side. The *cervix* (cer-vix), which is the neck of the *uterus*, protrudes into the deep portion of the *vagina*. The *cervical opening* is plugged by impenetrable mucus, except for a certain period during *menstruation*. Every month, the part of the lining of the uterus called the *endometrium* thickens to prepare the uterus for implantation of a fertilized ovum. If fertilization does not take place, the endometrium deteriorates and is discharged through the *cervix* during menstruation.

It takes an unfertilized *ovum* approximately three days to exit the body. It travels through the *fallopian tubes*, the *uterus*, or womb, which is connected to the *vagina* by a small opening called the *cervix*, and finally leaves the body through the *vagina*, which is the canal that leads from the *uterus*.

12. *Vagina* is the Latin word for *sheath*. The *vagina* is a muscular tube about three and one-half inches long that extends from the *cervix* to its external opening. It serves three main functions: it provides a receptacle for the man's *penis*, a passageway for the *menstrual* flow to leave the body from the *uterus*, and a passageway for the baby to exit the body from the *uterus* at birth.

Like the mouth, the *vagina* hosts different kinds of organisms that live in a natural, healthy, ecological balance that should not be upset by chemical interference. For this reason, *vaginal* sprays and douches should be avoided unless they are prescribed by a doctor. The *vagina* provides secretions for its own cleanings and protects itself from infections.

The *vaginal* walls contain very few nerve endings. However, they do secrete a lubricant when the woman becomes sexually excited. Without this lubricant, intercourse could be painful for both the woman and the man.

The other organs depicted in the diagram are:

1. The *bladder* (bla-der), which holds the urine created by the kidneys.
2. The *rectum* (rek-tum), which is the terminal part of the intestine from the *sigmoid flexure* to the *anus.*
3. The *anus* (ā-nes) is the opening through which solid wastes called *feces* (fē-sēez) exit the body.

As I suggested earlier, thoroughly familiarize yourself with this diagram. Sooner or later, your daughter may have questions about it.

However, at first most of her questions are likely to express her concerns about whether or not she is normal. Later, we will talk about the kinds of questions these concerns will provoke in your daughter. We will try to help you anticipate most of her concerns and be prepared to give her reassuring answers.

However, before we get into this conversation, let's review your son's reproductive system and get you ready to respond to his questions as well. The following diagram will provide a good visual tool in helping both your son and your daughter better understand the male's reproductive system. Let's review it together.

MALE SEXUAL ANATOMY

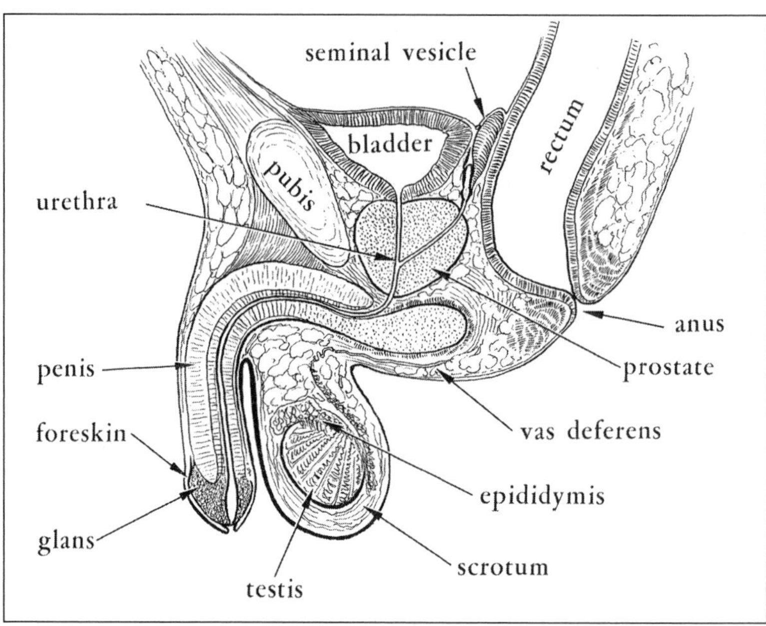

Diagram 2

1. The *penis* (pē-nas), which is the Latin word for *tail,* serves as the male's reproductive organ, but it is also the organ through which he is relieved of *urine.* The *penis* is cylindrical in shape and contains three long, spongy tubes of erectile tissue. The one underneath houses the *urethra,* which is the duct through which both *urine* and *semen* (sea-men) are passed. As you know, *semen,* or seed, is the name given the male's *ejaculate* (i-ja-kya-lāt). As these large arteries fill the spongy tissue of the *penis* with blood, it increases in size and erects. The loose skin of the *penis* makes this possible.

2. The *foreskin* is a fold of skin that covers the *glans* of the *penis.* In an uncircumcised male, the part of the skin that extends beyond the end of the *penis* is called the *foreskin* or *prepuce* (prē-pyüs).

3. The *glans* (glanz) is a conical glandular body that forms the extreme end of the *penis.* During erection the *glans*

protrudes from the *foreskin.* The Latin word *glans* means "acorn." The smooth surface of the *glans* is filled with many nerve endings that make it extremely sensitive to touch, especially around the rim or *corona* (ka-rō-na). The *glans* is attached to the *foreskin* on the underside by the *frenulum* (fren-ye-lem). This is the most sensitive part of the *penis.* A pastelike substance called *smegma* is secreted by the *glans* under the foreskin near the *frenulum.* This may accumulate and irritate the *penis.* Boys must be taught that good personal hygiene requires washing the *glans* and removing the *smegma.* In order to do this, the *foreskin* has to be pulled back. Circumcised males do not have this problem.

When flaccid, or soft, the adult male *penis* ranges from three to five inches long. When erect, the length will vary from five to seven inches. However, you cannot infer what size a flaccid *penis* will be when it is erect.

A male may be very concerned about the size of his *penis,* even though he has no reason to be. If his *penis* is only two inches long when erect, he can experience satisfying and fulfilling lovemaking with his wife.

4. The Latin word *scrotum* (skrō-tem) means "bag or pouch." The *scrotum* hangs at the base of the penis between the male's thighs and contains his *testicles* (tes-ti-kals). There are two compartments in the *scrotum,* each containing one *testicle.* Muscles in the *spermatic cord* contract in cooler temperatures and relax in warmer temperatures. By adjusting the distance of the *testicles* from body heat, it acts like a thermostat to be sure that *testicular* temperature is kept from two degrees to four degrees lower than body temperature for the production of *sperm.* Without this provision a man would be sterile. This is one of the body's many wonders.

5. The *testicles* are reproductive glands, oval in shape and about one and a half inches long. The left one hangs slightly lower than the right. The *testicles* perform two functions: they

produce *sperm* and secrete hormones directly into the bloodstream. Once the male reaches puberty, his testicles produce approximately 300 million *sperm* every day. They are absorbed back into the body when they are not ejaculated. *Sperm* are only 1/600 of an inch long, which makes them among the smallest cells in the human body. Each of them is shaped like a skinny tadpole and has three parts: a head, a body, and a tail. The head is only 1/10 of the sperm's length. There are twenty-three chromosomes, which represent a unique combination of the genetic heritage from the male's family. One of the male's chromosomes will determine the sex of the child.

6. The *epididymus* (e-pe-di-de-mas) is a system of small ducts emerging from the back of the *testis* that hold sperm during maturation. These ducts form a tangled mass before uniting into a single coiled duct that is continuous with the *vas deferens.* The entire process of sperm production may take as long as three months. When they are mature, the sperm move up the *vas deferens* toward the urethra.

7. The *vas deferens* (vas-de-fe-ranz) is a thick-walled tube about two feet long that begins at and is continuous with the tail of the *epididymis*. It eventually joins the duct of the *seminal vesicle* to form the *ejaculatory duct* in the human male.

8. The *seminal vesicles* (sem-in-al ves-icles) are glandular pouches that lie on either side of the male reproductive tract and secrete a sugar- and protein-containing fluid into the ejaculatory duct.

9. The *prostate* (präs-tāt) is a firm, partly muscular, partly glandular body that is situated about the base of the male *urethra* and secretes an alkaline fluid that is a major constituent of semen, the male ejaculatory fluid. Also contributing to the ejaculate are secretions from the Cowper's glands. The alkaline content from these secretions neutralize any acid in the urethra that would interfere with conception.

10. The *pubis* (pyü-bes) is sometimes called the *pubic bone.* During puberty it becomes covered by hair. The bladder, rectum, and anus serve practically the same purpose in the male body as in the body of the female.

You will want to familiarize yourself thoroughly with these diagrams so that you will be prepared to answer any questions your children may have about them.

Finally, let's take a look at the woman's menstrual cycle so you can explain it clearly to your daughter. Your son may not show much interest in understanding it at the time, but go through the explanation with him anyway. This will provide a good foundation for revisiting it with him later when he begins to go with girls.

THE MENSTRUAL CYCLE

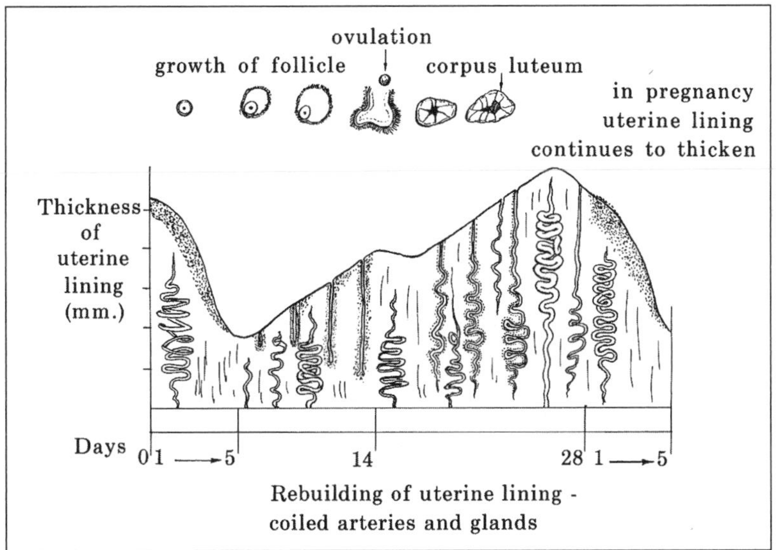

Diagram 3

Ovulation takes place approximately fourteen days before the first day of the next *menstrual* period as indicated in Diagram No. 3. This is the fourteenth day of a twenty-eight-day cycle or the twenty-first day of a thirty-five-day cycle.

The time period between *ovulation* and the next *menstrual* period varies very little. However, the time period between the end of menstruation and the next ovulation may vary considerably. This is critical in determining the time of the month when a woman is most likely to be fertile. We will talk more about the significance of this in the next chapter.

When a baby girl is born she has approximately four hundred thousand *ova* in her little *ovaries*. By the time she begins to menstruate, all but thirty thousand to forty thousand of them have been absorbed by her body.

A girl's first *menstrual* period usually occurs between her tenth and thirteenth year. This is referred to as her *menarche* (me-när-kē), or the beginning of her *menstruation*. It is triggered by the pituitary gland sending a chemical message to the *ovaries*, stimulating them to release an amount of *estrogen* large enough to result in the ripening of *ova*, or eggs. These are the girl's reproductive cells.

Once a girl reaches puberty and produces her first ovum, either of her ovaries may produce one or more eggs during each menstrual cycle. The production of an ovum is referred to as *ovulation* (äv-ye-lā-shan) and begins to occur approximately once a month after her *menarche*.

This process will continue for thirty to forty years, during which a woman will produce approximately three hundred to four hundred mature eggs. So, during her fertile years she will have about three hundred to four hundred opportunities for pregnancy to occur naturally.

This monthly event, along with all of its accompanying physical changes, makes up the woman's *reproductive cycle*. Since each woman is unique, her *menstrual cycle* will differ slightly from that of other women.

Often during adolescence a young woman's *menstrual cycles* are irregular. However, once she matures, her cycle will range from twenty-eight to thirty-five days. Even then some irregularity is possible and quite normal.

The *menstrual cycle* involves three phases. During the first phase the *uterus* is prepared for ovulation. The lining of the *uterus* is very thin following menstruation. So, every month the special tissue of the endometrium begins to thicken under the influence of *estrogen*. This prepares the uterus to support implantation, should fertilization of the next ovum occur. At the same time, the growth of *follicles* containing immature *ova* is also already being stimulated by estrogen.

Then, after about two weeks, the second phase of the cycle begins. By this time, the lining of the *uterus* has thickened and is almost ready for the *implantation* of a fertilized *ovum.*

Once an *ovum* is released from an *ovary,* it enters the nearest *fallopian tube* and begins its journey toward the *uterus.* A few days later, the *ovum* is mature and ready for fertilization. If it is fertilized, it develops into a cell cluster and continues its journey toward the *uterus.*

This process is depicted in the following diagram. Notice that the *ovum* enters the *fallopian tube,* and, once it is fertilized, it continues its journey toward *implantation* in the *uterus.*

OVULATION, FERTILIZATION, AND IMPLANTATION

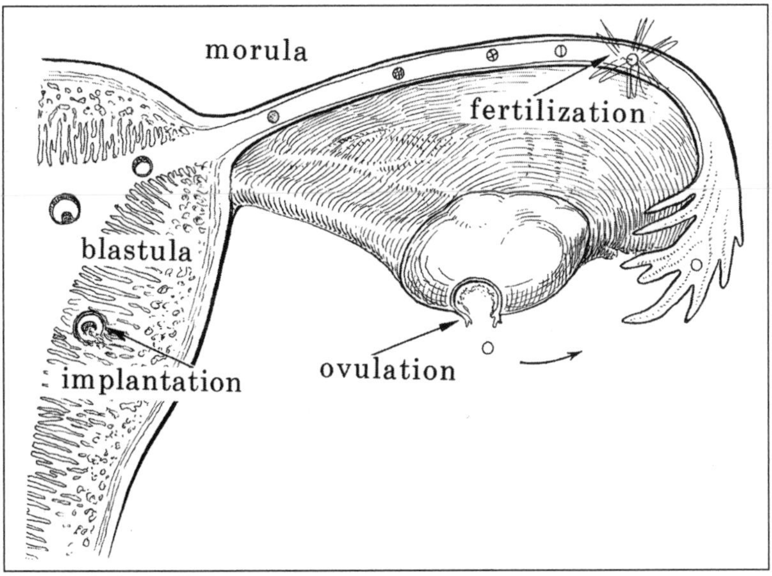

Diagram 4

Every month, the special tissue of the endometrium thickens to prepare the uterus for implantation of the fertilized egg. However, if no sperm cells are encountered during the first twenty-four hours after *ovulation*, the *ovum* simply dies and disintegrates. Additional *estrogen* and *progesterone* are not produced. The lining of the *uterus* begins to break down.

The third phase of the menstrual cycle now begins. Since the nutrients prepared for nurturing new life are no longer needed, the resulting waste material is discharged from the woman's body through the *cervix* in *menstrual* bleeding, which continues from three to seven days, preparing the uterus for another possible pregnancy following the next ovulation.

The blood that is lost during *menstruation* is caught with a tampon or sanitary napkin. Be sure you have samples of these when you talk to your daughter. Show her how to use them. Then let her know she can choose which she prefers.

Since we usually associate bleeding with illness, explain to your daughter that the bleeding occurring during *menstruation* is not a sign of sickness but a sign of health.

Let her know that the chemical changes that occur during a woman's *menstrual* period may result in varying degrees of discomfort, often referred to as *premenstrual* or *menstrual* tension. Usually this consists of headaches, lower back pain, and abdominal cramps. Discuss with her some of the ways she can relieve this premenstrual tension if it occurs.

Discussing the Changes of Puberty With Your Daughter

Sometime *before* your daughter's tenth birthday, as her mother, you need to have a private talk with her. Before your son's twelfth birthday, as his father, you need to have the same kind of talk with him. Although the primary focus of your conversation will be on the changes in their reproductive systems, you will also want to discuss other important physiological changes that they will experience during puberty. The goal is not just to educate them sexually, but to normalize this awkward period of life for them.

As a mother, you might say something like this to your daughter: "Honey, I've noticed that your body is beginning to change. Before long you will become a young woman. How do you feel about that?" Give her a chance to respond.

If she has any misgivings, talk with her about them. Then go on to say, "What is happening to you is that you are going through puberty. Puberty is the time when the pituitary gland in the brain stimulates the creation of hormones in your ovaries. This happens for girls when they are about ten years of age. We all go through this as girls. I went through puberty when I was a girl.

"During this time our arms, hands, legs, and feet grow faster than the rest of our body. This makes us feel kind of clumsy. Sometimes you feel like you are the only one who is going through this, but you are not.

"I remember how weird I felt when I was your age. There is just no way to grow from being a girl to being a woman, or from being a boy to being a man, without feeling clumsy at times.

"Unfortunately, puberty begins for girls about two years before it begins for boys. As girls, this makes us feel like we are the only ones who are changing. The boys are staying the same. This is why it may be socially awkward for us during the fourth and fifth grades. We are growing at a faster rate than most boys. However, their bodies begin to change about two years later. Then, in the sixth grade they will begin to catch up, and everyone can feel weird together for a little while.

"Not everyone's body changes at the same time or at the same pace. However, everyone will be through puberty by the time of high school. In the meantime, whenever you're anxious about the way your body may be changing, you know you can always share that with me.

"I know your health teacher will soon be talking to you about all of this. However, you and I have always been able to talk about personal things with each other, and I don't want our relationship to change that way, do you?" Give her a chance to respond, and then continue.

"Life is such a special gift from God. I have never been able to think about the process of menstruation, pregnancy, and childbirth without feeling overwhelmed by the wonder of it all. It seems incredible that at some time in our lives, most of us women will experience the miracle of life growing in our bodies. I want to be the first person to share with you how this happens.

"As you go through puberty, the changes you will begin to notice are the widening of your pelvis, the rounding of your hips, and the beginning of your breast development. You will also begin to develop hair under your arms and between your legs. The hair between your legs is sometimes called *pubic hair* and usually indicates the beginning of menstruation."

At this point, show her the diagram of the female reproductive system found earlier in this chapter. Review with her the names for her sex organs. Then indicate where the ovaries are by pointing to them on the diagram and continue, "On either side of your tummy there is an ovary. These are the organs that produce the eggs from which babies can come. Approximately every twenty-eight to thirty-five days, one of your ovaries will produce an ovum, or egg."

Pause to allow her to ask any questions she may have.

Then continue your conversation. "Ova (that is the word for more than one egg) are the largest cells in our body. Each ovum is about as big as a period at the end of a sentence. It will take two or three days for that ovum to travel through the fallopian tubes, the uterus, and to make its way out of your vagina." (While you are talking, use some kind of pointer to trace the journey of the ovum on the diagram.)

"That's an awful lot of information. Do you have any questions?"

If she does, then respond to them. If she doesn't, then give her the pointer and ask her to trace the ovum's journey from an ovary and to identify the parts of her body through which the ovum will pass on its way out of her body.

Then continue the conversation: "About two weeks after the egg is out of your body, the part of the uterus (point to the uterus) that is no longer needed because the egg was not a fertilized by a sperm will pass from your body in a flow of blood that is sometimes referred to as the *menstrual flow.* This bleeding will last from three to five days and is called *menstruation.* Even though you bleed during menstruation, you are not sick. This is just the normal healthy way God designed your body to get rid of the potential food supply for an egg that is not going to become a baby."

Give your daughter a chance to ask questions she may have. Ask her to explain to you in her own words what you have just told her. This gives you the opportunity to clarify any points she did not clearly understand. Take time to commend her for the way she is learning about her body and her sexuality.

Then continue, "I want you to know that when this process begins in your body, you and I are going to celebrate. This means you are becoming a woman. You are not a little girl anymore. Isn't that neat?"

When you have given her time to respond to this new information about her body, then turn to the diagram of the male reproductive system shown earlier in this chapter. Point to the scrotum and begin explaining. "This sac or pouch underneath the boy's penis is called a *scrotum*. The scrotum has two compartments in it. In each of the compartments there is a *testicle*." (Then, point to the testicles.)

"The scrotum serves as a temperature-regulating organ by moving the *testes* closer to the male body to warm them or by hanging farther from the body to cool them. The boy's testicles produce sperm, just as the girl's ovaries produce ova. Sperm production can only occur properly if the temperature is two to four degrees below normal body temperature. Isn't that amazing!

"Within each of the testicles are a series of coiled, semeniferous tubules where sperm are formed. The sperm move to the epididymis just outside the body of the testis where they mature." (Trace the formation of sperm as you talk to your child.)

"Once mature, the sperm are ready to move up the vas deferens toward the urethra. Along the way, fluids are added from the seminal vesicles, prostate, and Cowper's glands to form the semen, which then leaves the male body through the urethra during an ejaculation. The entire process of sperm production may take as long as three months.

"When a boy reaches puberty, which is what we call the time when he can become a father, he will have millions of sperm cells stored in each of his testicles. When he is sexually stimulated, he reaches a peak in his excitement when two hundred thousand to five hundred thousand sperm cells spurt out of his penis in a fluid called *semen*. This spurting of semen is called *ejaculation*."

Give your daughter a chance to absorb this information and to interact with you. Then clarify her understanding of the information and continue your conversation. "When a sperm from a man's body penetrates an ovum from a woman's body, she becomes *pregn*ant. This is the word we use to describe a woman who is expecting a baby. This means that a *fetus* (what we call a baby before birth) is beginning to grow in the woman's uterus. In about nine months the fetus gets big and strong enough to live outside the mother's body and is ready to be born." Take time to review this information with your daughter.

Then continue: "The female sex glands consist of two ovaries located within the lower abdomen. The ova are formed within the follicles of each ovary. Normally, only one ovum is produced each menstrual cycle. The ovum is released at ovulation and begins its migration down the fallopian tube where fertilization normally takes place.

"Millions of sperm are ejaculated into the vagina. The sperm then pass through the cervix, up through the uterus, and into the fallopian tubes or oviducts. Fertilization takes place when an egg is passing down one of the oviducts at the same time as the sperm is going up.

"The egg secretes a chemical that attracts the sperm. One sperm breaks through the membrane around the egg, and the sperm cell nucleus enters the cytoplasm of the egg cell. This causes the membrane around the egg to change, and it stops other sperm from entering the egg. The sperm nucleus fuses with the egg nucleus, which forms the *zygote*."

Then reassure her, "This won't be the last time you and I will have this kind of personal talk. I want you to feel free to ask me anything you want to know about the sexual side of life. God has made this to be such a beautiful part of our lives once we are married. I don't want anyone making it appear ugly to you. I want you to look forward to enjoying this wonderful way of making love after you are married to someone you love as much as I love your father."

Acne

Acne is a common concern for both boys and girls during puberty and adolescence. Explain to your youngsters that these pimples are caused by hormonal changes that accompany puberty. They will learn what works best for their peers and for them to help clear their face. However, if the condition worsens, reassure them that their pediatrician will prescribe a medication that will take care of the problem.

Discussing the Changes of Puberty With Your Son

As a father you can use much the same approach with your son as I have suggested for a mother to talk with her daughter. Simply modify the information appropriately. Your son will have his own concerns about how his body is changing.

One thing that will bother him is the way his voice is changing. Explain to him that during puberty his *larynx* or voice box will get larger, and his Adam's apple will get bigger. As a result, his vocal chords gradually grow longer. This is what makes the pitch of his voice unpredictable for a while. One moment it can be high, and low in another moment. Eventually, it will even out. This is nothing to worry about.

He will also be concerned about his penis and testicles. Explain to him that it is normal for his penis to become erect when he is sexually excited. Sometimes his penis will become erect even when he is not sexually excited. Let him know that this is normal. Be sure he understands that the average penis is three to four inches long when it is soft and five to seven inches long when it is erect. Reassure him that when his penis is fully developed it will fall within this range.

When he examines his testicles he will discover them to be round. They produce several million sperm a day. At night, he may have a sexually exciting dream and wake up to discover that he has ejaculated. These are sometimes called "wet dreams." This is perfectly normal and nothing to be anxious about.

Body hair will also be a concern for him. Explain to him that some boys have more body hair than others. This is determined by his genes. Nothing he can do will change the amount of body hair he has, and it has nothing to do with his masculinity. It is normal for him to discover hair growing under his arms, around his penis and testicles, on his chest, legs, and other parts of his body.

If the boy's father is inaccessible or reluctant to talk to his son, then it is better for the boy to hear this information from his mother than not to hear it at all. Such a conversation keeps the door open for later talk with children of both sexes about their adolescent sexual concerns.

In the next section we will talk more about conception, pregnancy, and childbirth. We will also be reinforcing the advantages of abstaining from intercourse until after marriage and making some suggestions for practically controlling your relationships with the opposite sex until then.

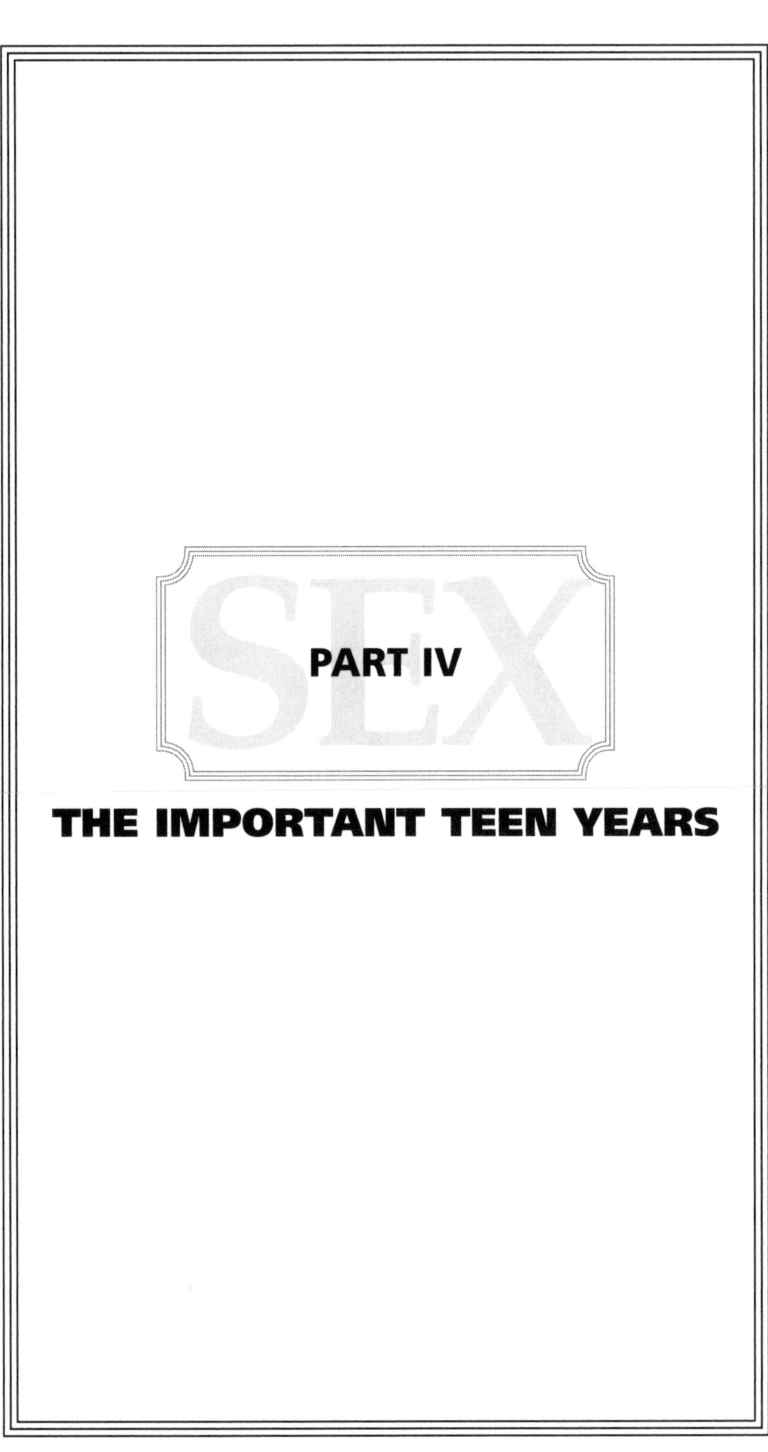

PART IV

THE IMPORTANT TEEN YEARS

Chapter 11

Avoiding Traps With the Opposite Sex

The teen years are the most sexually hazardous years in your child's life. Addiction to pornography, potentially fatal trips to chat rooms, sexually transmitted diseases, and pregnancy are among the most dangerous traps and tragedies bidding for them. Your role as a parent is critical in alerting your teens to these dangers. Peer pressure is subtle, pervasive, and powerful. For the sake of your kids, you cannot afford to be naïve. You need to know exactly what your teen is up to sexually. Your child's life depends on it.[1] No one else can take your place.

In 1997 the National Longitudinal Study of Adolescent Health looked at ninety thousand children in grades seven through twelve from one hundred forty-five schools across our nation. The purpose of the study was to determine what role family, friends, school, and the community play in helping teens make choices—healthy or self-destructive—during their junior and senior high school years. This is one of the most thorough studies ever done on teenagers and high-risk behaviors. Hundreds of questions were asked, and thousands of answers were recorded.

The results of this study were startling, yet simple. Feeling close to their parents and having access to one other adult figure at their schools were the two most important factors in helping teens stay out of trouble and make healthy choices for themselves. *Connectedness* was defined by the authors as, "a high degree of closeness, caring, and satisfaction with parental relationships, whether resident or nonresident, mother or father, feeling understood, loved, wanted, and paid attention to by family members."[2]

Your influence is particularly important in the decisions your children make about sex. In 2001, the National Campaign to Prevent Teen Pregnancy asked teens, "When it comes to your sexual decision-making, which is most influential: the media, friends, teachers and sex educators, brothers and sisters, religious organizations, or parents?" Parents were revealed as the number one influence in the sexual decisions made by their teens.[3] Are you shocked? See for yourself! Here's how the results stacked up:

- Parents—38 percent
- Friends—31 percent
- Religious organizations—9 percent
- Siblings—7 percent
- Teachers—6 percent
- The media—3 percent

Helping your teens safely navigate through the perilous waters of adolescent sexuality can be anxiety provoking. However, your *connectedness* with them is the most important influence in assuring them safe passage.

The Teens and Twenties Are Decades of Change

You can reduce the anxiety level of your teens significantly by letting them know well in advance about the changes they can expect to happen in the next ten years. When they are eleven or twelve, begin to talk about how exciting and important their teen years will be. At the same time, alert them to the awkwardness they will feel at times because of how quickly life will be changing for them.

Their bodies will be changing rapidly—not just outwardly, but inwardly as well. These changes could be dealt with more comfortably if they were happening uniformly to their friends at the same time. However, this is not the way it will be.

Hands, feet, ears, arms, legs, and noses have their own independent schedules for rapid growth and development during our teen years. These schedules are largely in control of the pituitary gland, a little pea-sized gland in the brain—and everybody's pituitary gland is on a different schedule.

Let them know that sometime during the next five years they will experience a growth spurt. Theirs may come sooner or later than their friends, but by the time they are seniors in high school they all will have gone through the same changes, and the physical playing field will be level again.

This little pea-sized gland will also trigger all kinds of internal hormonal and biochemical changes. From time to time their emotional world may be turned upside down. They may feel as if they are on an emotional roller coaster taking them from extreme highs to extreme lows. However, that also happens to everyone else their age.

During a young man's growth spurt he may add three to six inches to his height in one year. Girls do not usually grow as fast. However, their height and other body parts change rapidly enough to make them feel just as awkward.

Coordinating the movement of a body growing and changing this quickly can be challenging. Perhaps that is part of the appeal of youth music with a strong emphasis on rhythm. It serves at least one healthy function; it helps young people keep all these extra inches of arms and legs coordinated. It helps them *keep it all together.*

Timing Is Important

There is nothing any young person can do to alter the timing of his or her growth spurt. As I mentioned earlier, if children get their growth early, they may appear to be more adult than their years. Consequently, the adult community may unfairly expect them to be much more emotionally mature than is normal for someone their age. If their growth lags too far behind their peers, they may feel physically inferior for a while, but assure them that they will catch up.

Share the self-conscious feelings you suffered during your teens when the appearance of acne and voice changes seemed to be major catastrophes. It will be comforting to your children to know that you experienced the same kind of clumsiness and confusion they may be feeling and experiencing themselves.

Let them know that moodiness and anxiety are a normal part of the teenager's world. Dealing with rapid physical changes and emotional cycles are part of what makes this decade of life so awkward.

During the teen years young people are confronted by the strongest sexual urges of their lives. This is another factor that makes these years so risky. However, if they have a clear sense of vocational direction by the time they enter senior high school, their newfound sexual energy can propel them toward these goals and away from the temptations of drugs and sex that are all around them. So, encouraging the early definition of their vocational goals is one way you can help your teens manage their sexuality responsibly.

Young People Need Well-Defined Goals

Wise parents will motivate their children to define their vocational goals early in life. You are doing your teens a favor when you remind them that in the future they will spend more of their time working than in any other activity except sleeping. This is why it is so important for them to choose a career they will enjoy.

Once those choices are made, young people can devote much of their time and sexual energy to pursuing the education and training necessary to attain these goals. Point out to them that being able to earn a living doing something you really enjoy is a pleasure few people ever realize in life.

Unfortunately, without the *encouragement* of parents or some other concerned adults, most young people do not see the wisdom of focusing their time and energy in pursuit of long-term vocational goals. Consequently, as adults many find themselves settling for jobs they really do not enjoy but must have because they need the money to support the lifestyle they want. How sad!

When teens have well-defined goals by the time they enter senior high school, it adds to their excitement about the future. They know where they are headed in life and are anxious to get there. This helps them manage their passions more constructively and makes it much less likely that they will get sidetracked by drugs or sex—two big threats to their future.

Ask Teens About Their Future

Whenever I meet a young person, I make a point during the first few minutes of our conversation to ask: "What are you going to do when you get out of school?"

Usually, their response is, "I don't know."

Once in a while a young man or young woman will tell me that he or she is going to college. So, my next question is, "What will be your major?" Their most frequent response is, "I'm not sure."

You don't have to be a navigator to realize that if you don't know your destination, you can't define the best way to get there. If a person doesn't know where he or she is going, it's unlikely that they will ever arrive. After all, when one aims at nothing in life, they are highly likely to hit it!

So, give serious attention to the vocational guidance of your children, particularly during the elementary and junior high school years. It really doesn't take that much time. Simply notice the things that your children do well, and encourage them to use these gifts in defining their future. Talk about the vocational doors these talents can open for them, and get them thinking about which would be the most attractive to them.

Three Kinds of People in the World

Let them know that in general there are three kinds of people in the world: people who make things happen, people who watch things happen, and people who never quite figure out what is happening.

Appeal to them not to be simply a spectator in life. Encourage them to get out of the grandstands and onto the playing field. Let them know that you believe they will be among those who make things happen. Remind them that people who only *wish things would happen* create their own disappointments. You have to make things happen.

Express your confidence in their abilities. Challenge them to dream big, work hard, and make their dreams come true. This is a very important part of good preventive sex education.

Few young people recognize the teens and twenties to be the defining decades of their lives. As your children enter their teens, make sure you make them aware of the difference the next twenty years will make in their lives.

Why Are These Years So Important?

Repeatedly remind your children that the choices they make during their teens and twenties will define them as adults. Between our twelfth and thirtieth birthdays, most of us discover our faith, define our values, determine our vocation, and decide whom we will marry. The next forty to fifty years of our lives largely will be spent living out the consequences of these choices. To a great extent, our destiny is defined during our teens and twenties.

Some parents feel that reminding children of the seriousness of the role these decision-making decades play in casting the mold of their futures is too burdensome for young people. "After all," they reason, "these should be the fun-loving years of a young person's life. They will only be young once." However, very few of the people who make a significant difference in their worlds are those who spent most of their teens and twenties having fun.

Unfortunately, during these decades sexual attraction so dominates youths' priorities that many young people fail to see the traps and tragedies that can delay or destroy their potential destiny. This is why teens desperately need parents who can and will talk to them about sex.

So, engage your teenagers in meaningful, factual conversations about adolescent sexual morality, but don't *preach* to them. Preaching will only drive them further from you. What you want is the kind of open, confidential relationship that makes them feel free to bring you any questions they have about sex.

What Are the Traps to Warn Them About?

Nothing has greater power to destroy your children's dreams or to turn them into nightmares than misinformed, irresponsible, or unwise sexual choices. Be sure they understand this!

In a moment, overheated passions can nullify their intelligence and rush them into impulsive behavior that threatens their dreams, crippling them for years—if not for life. See that you dialogue informally with them about the kinds of sexual traps and tragedies that can be destructive for them.

The greatest tragedies stalking our teens are the sexually transmitted diseases raging in epidemic proportions among America's young. Every year, four million *new* teenagers in our society contract a sexually transmitted disease.[4] This is one of many practical reasons for abstaining from sex with another person until marriage. We'll talk more specifically about this epidemic in chapter thirteen, but first let's zero in on three of the most dangerous traps confronting today's youth. I will give you some suggestions for helping your teens avoid them.

Trap #1: Chat Rooms

The numbers of Internet chat rooms pose crippling and potentially deadly risks for your preteen and teenage girls. Most of our children are exposed to these risks. According to the U.S. Department of Justice, 77 million children are online in the United States. As many as 90 percent of children between the ages of five and seventeen use computers, and nearly 60 percent of them use the Internet.

In 2002, the Girl Scout Research Institute found that 30 percent of teenage girls in their study reported being sexually harassed in a chat room, but only 7 percent shared that information with their parents.[5] Over 80 percent of the teens in one study had private e-mail accounts. Only 68 percent of their parents knew about these accounts.[6] Almost half of the teens in another study (47 percent) had links to pornographic Web sites.[7] Don't be naïve about your children's Internet activity! Frequently monitor where they are going and what they are doing by using the information shared earlier.

Girls often are seeking to find their needs for understanding relationships met in the very risky rendezvous of a cyberworld chat room. Unless closely supervised, chat room sessions are highly likely to expose your teens to ideas about sex that are very different from your family values.

Warn your children about the presence of sexual predators on the Internet. These perverts frequently disguise themselves as teenagers when interacting with teens in chat rooms. The U.S. Department of Justice reports there are four million child molesters in the United States.[8] Internet chat rooms are convenient waters for them to troll in attempting to hook their next victims.

Although more girls than boys are involved in chat rooms, these activities pose high risks for both sexes. Young girls and boys are easily deceived into believing that the sexual predators who have invaded their innocence actually have a sincere personal concern for them.

Be sure you tell them that sexual predators deliberately design their conversations with teens in ways to *groom* them for later personal contacts and sexual activities. Your naïve teenager is no match for the lustful heart and seductive mind of a sexual predator. Warn them that engaging in conversations with such a person can threaten their futures—and in some cases, even their lives.

Share the following information with your children.

Your Daughter Needs to Know the Risks

To discover what was really going on in the cyberworld of adolescents, Doctor Patricia Greenfield, director of UCLA's Children's Digital Media Center, entered a Web site devoted to teenagers. She was shocked by what she found. Here is how she describes it:

> The sexuality expressed in a teen chat room was public, linked to strangers, and had nothing to do with relationships. It was very explicit and focused on physical acts, and often associated with the degradation of women. I started to receive private instant messages, including a crude sexual advance, just by hanging out at the chat room, even though I had not participated in any of the ongoing conversations. The unsolicited nature of these messages could be daunting for adolescents, particularly younger ones.[9]

Most of the time, what teenage girls talk about in chat rooms are the same kinds of things they talk about in their locker rooms at their schools. Usually, it's pretty innocent stuff, but they still protect the privacy of their Internet conversations with elaborate acronyms that afford them a code of secrecy to keep adults from knowing what they are talking about. For example, POS means, "My parent is looking over my shoulder, so I can't talk right now."

As you can see, it is very difficult for you to accurately monitor the chat room activity of your children, but you can educate them regarding the dangers that lurk there and teach them ways to protect themselves. So, here are some guidelines for chat room safety you can share with them:

Chat Room Safety	
1.	Remember, dangerous adults can be in chat rooms posing as teenagers. Don't use your real name. Don't give them your real address or any other personal contact information.
2.	Don't provide them with your e-mail address, particularly if it includes part of your name.
3.	Don't define your routine for them. For example, don't let them know what school you go to or the route you take to get there.
4	Never personally meet anyone you have only met in a chat room.[10]

Be sure your teens realize how dangerous it is to meet someone in person that they have only known in a chat room. It could cost them their life.

Trap #2: Cyberporn

Cyberporn is a bigger risk for teenage boys. They do enter chat rooms, but they prefer to visit explicit porn sites. There they are exposed to rapidly sequenced seemingly endless streams of highly erotic shapes, sizes, and activities. There, from the files of hundreds of thousands of explicit pictures, videos, movies, and camcorder shows, they can choose the ones they find most sexually exciting and that are most likely to provide them with intense and powerful orgasms.

These avenues of sexual excitement do not require them to develop the art and skills of interpersonal relationships, intimacy, and emotional vulnerability needed later for healthy sex in marriage. And the women on the Internet never say no to them, regardless of what they want them to do.

You cannot afford to be uninformed about the extent of this problem. A 1998 study indicated that nearly half of our children from nine to fourteen years of age reported visiting Web sites with *adult* content.[11]

There are more porn sites and chat rooms on the Internet than there are McDonald's restaurants in the world.[12] This kind of accessibility, along with peer pressure to participate and the Internet's provision for anonymity, helps to explain why 80 percent of fifteen- to seventeen-year-old young men have had multiple exposures to hardcore pornography.[13]

These temptations occur at a time in life when many young males are already masturbating from once a day to once a week. When a young man pairs the pleasure of sexual orgasm with pornographic images, over time he can seriously impair his ability to form a healthy sexual relationship with his wife later in life.

As a parent, help your son realize that the pornographer's goal is to make him sexually dependent on his products. This is why the pornographer makes sure your son is exposed to very exciting and intensely explicit sexual activities that will bring him to orgasm every time he visits this particular site on the Internet. This kind of immediate sexual gratification is available twenty-four hours a day, seven days a week. Can you imagine the temptation this poses for teenage young men whose testosterone levels are at an all-time high?

Be sure to warn your son that pornographic sex can become habit forming and addicting very quickly. When he wonders how this can happen, explain to him that pornography possesses the addictive pleasures found in all three major drug families.

Pornography will stimulate his fantasy like hallucinogens such as marijuana, LSD, mescaline, and peyote. It will excite him like stimulants such as cocaine, crack, and speed. It will relax him like narcotics such as heroin, opium, and morphine. Be sure your son understands that once he becomes dependent upon or addicted to pornography, marriage will not break this habit.

Pornography produces orgasm...not intimacy!

After all, when a male turns on a porn site, he is not looking for sexual intimacy. He is looking for sexual orgasm. Such immediate and selfish gratification bypasses the need for any spiritual or emotional interaction with a spouse during lovemaking, and it eliminates the sacred purpose of orgasm, which is the formation of a strong pleasure bond with the body of one's spouse.

When a man with a pornographic habit enters marriage, he is sexually crippled. He lacks the spiritual and emotional skills involved in becoming vulnerable and intimate with a woman. His involvement with pornography denied him the opportunity to develop these necessary skills during his teen years when he should have been learning how to build healthy friendships with girls. So, as a married man, he is unable to form the kind of relationship with his wife that encourages her to be sexually open and orgasmic with him.

God designed sexual orgasm for marriage.

During your son's adolescent years, continue to remind him of the thing you have been telling him all his life: God designed sexual orgasm to bind him to his wife. Let him know that if he chooses some other source of sexual excitement, he will come under bondage to it. Sooner or later, he will not be able to reach orgasm without it. At that point, what God meant to form a pleasure bond between him and his future wife will be a source of sexual bondage to him.

However, when his sexual fantasy is about lovemaking in marriage, the orgasm that results has been stimulated by his anticipation of experiencing this pleasure with his wife in marriage. Often remind your teens that sexual orgasm is God's gift to married couples—and their gift to each other.

By being the source of such pleasure for each other, a couple forms a powerful physical, emotional, and spiritual bond between them. It is part of the glue that holds them together. The strength of this bond is vital to forming the secure spiritual, emotional, and physical environment necessary for raising healthy children.

A healthy wife feels replaced by pornography.

Teens need to clearly understand that when they divorce sexual orgasm from the idea of marriage and begin to use pornography to create it, over time it will replace the body of their spouse as the source of their sexual pleasure. This helps to explain why a wife is so devastated when she discovers her husband's pornographic habit.

More than once, out of desperation, a wife has said to me, "If he were involved with another woman, I think I could deal with that, but I can't compete with this stuff." Pornography leaves a wife feeling totally inadequate in sexually satisfying her husband.

When a man indulges in pornography he is not being sexually true to his wife. In this age of virtual reality, pornography becomes a form of adultery often more difficult to break free from than an adulteress relationship with a real woman. I cannot overstress the importance of getting this basic spiritual principle embedded in your son's mind.

Debunk the sexual myths of pornography.

Your son needs your help in understanding the deception, lies, and perverted myths about sex that are conveyed by the pornographic industry. The physical characteristics portrayed in pornography are not normal. Men are carefully screened for penis size, and women for the size of their breasts and other erotic dimensions, before they are hired in the industry.

This is done deliberately to leave the viewer coveting the genitals of the actors and lusting after what he sees them do. Remind your son that the average man does not have a penis as large as that of a porn actor. The average woman does not have breasts or other sensual characteristics similar to a porn actress. The pornographic world is a fantasy land that is deliberately designed to lure men away from marriage.

Trick photography is used to amplify the erotic nature of the visual images. The soundtrack is recorded, distorted, and repeated to intensify the level of sexual excitement. The rhythmic beat of the music is arranged to simulate the movements of intercourse.

If porn actors were not getting paid huge salaries, they wouldn't be in the business. No normal child wants to grow up to be a porn actor. The people who staff this industry are troubled and pathetic. They sell themselves to make sexual cripples out of men and women who are foolish enough to indulge in their products.

Explain to your son that powerful neurochemicals deeply imprint in his brain the pornographic images he sees. Over time, these sensual memories will define his sexual appetites and seriously impair his ability to enjoy a healthy sex life with his wife. Be sure your teen knows that the pornographic industry is not dedicated to helping him become a sexually healthy man. The pornographers' goal is to get rich by making your son sexually dependent on their products.

Affirm Normal Healthy Sexual Urges

At the same time you are warning your teens about pornography and chat rooms, reassure them that their sexual urges are normal and healthy. Let them know that learning to manage a strong sex drive for several years is a challenge every young person has to face in becoming an adult. Express your confidence in their ability to do it.

Assure them that if they are thinking about making love to their future spouse when they are taking care of their own sexual needs, they have done nothing morally wrong. Teach them to view caring for their own sexual needs as a part of their personal grooming, like taking a shower, shampooing their hair, or using deodorant. Taking care of their own needs will relieve their sexual tensions and keep them from imposing their sex needs on others until they are married.

Keep on telling them what you have been telling them since they were small children. Repetition is an important method of teaching. Remind them that there is nothing morally wrong about having pleasant feelings in their genitals. After all, this is God's way of helping them anticipate what they have to look forward to in marriage.

By confining their sexual fantasies to marriage, your teens are learning to be true to the spouse they will eventually marry years before they know who that person will be. They are also building their anticipation of a healthy and exciting sex life in marriage. Assure them that if they save themselves for each other, sex in marriage will feel much better and will be far more emotionally satisfying than fantasizing about it before marriage.

Chapter 12

Discussing Masturbation and Fantasy

Today's teenagers face far greater risks and challenges in getting acquainted with the opposite sex than we did when we were teenagers. Why? First, as we discovered earlier, puberty is awakening a teenager's sexual desires from one to two years earlier than in previous generations. Teenagers' pituitary glands are cascading more sex hormones into their bloodstream than they will ever experience again in their lifetimes. As a result, they must deal with the emotional and physical changes accompanying secondary sexual characteristics while they are still children.

In addition, a generation ago young people were more likely to marry when they were in their early or middle twenties. Today's young adults are remaining single until their late twenties or early thirties. So, today's youth must manage their sex drives five to ten years longer than previous generations.

Teens are also being exposed to more sexually stimulating media programming than in previous generations. Unregulated streams of eroticism pour into our homes from an entertainment industry more concerned about its ratings and profits than it is about the moral character of our young.

Today's youth live in a highly erotic society. A brief look at the television programming tolerated today will convince any reasonable person of how much more permissive and sexually provocative our society is becoming. About two-thirds of today's programs contain references to sexual intercourse and other sexual behaviors.[1]

Defenders of the media would have us believe that the program content of their industry has no direct bearing on the sexual behavior of the people watching it. However, you and I both know that when we are young and impressionable, our social behavior is largely learned through imitation. We particularly want to imitate our society's celebrities. After all, modeling is one of the most powerful forms of teaching. Nevertheless, until recently the entertainment industry has successfully disclaimed any responsibility for the escalation of sexually permissive behavior among our youth.

Science Confirms TV's Sexual Influence

At last, the impact of TV on the sexual behavior of our young is being clearly defined by research. The Rand Corporation, in a study funded by the National Institute of Child Health and Human Development, interviewed a national sample of 1,792 adolescents ranging in age from twelve to seventeen.[2] The purpose of the interviews was to determine specifically what effects watching television with strong sexual overtones would have on the sexual behavior of these teenagers. A year later the same teenagers were given a similar interview.

An analysis of the results revealed that young people who watched large amounts of television containing sexual content were twice as likely to begin engaging in sexual intercourse in the following year than were their peers who watched little of this programming.

The study also indicated that youth who watched large amounts of television with sexual content are more likely to engage in sexual activities other than intercourse, such as mutual masturbation and oral sex.

Understanding Masturbation and Fantasy

Recent surveys in the United States indicate that about 55 percent of all thirteen-year-olds (both boys and girls) masturbate. By the time they reach age fifteen, the figure rises to more than 80 percent. About 95 percent of adult men and 65 percent of adult women practice masturbation.[3] Many young people are confused about this practice, and some are troubled by it. So you need to talk to your teens about masturbation.

Even though the word *masturbation* is not in the Bible, it is a common source of guilt for people, especially for young people. Although the practice is not mentioned in the Bible, the Scriptures clearly teach that fantasizing about having sex with someone to whom you are not married is sinful.[4] Since only a small percentage of young people report masturbating without fantasies, your teenager's sexual fantasies while masturbating *are* a cause of serious spiritual concern. Why?

God created sexual orgasm to be one of the most powerful pleasures a human being experiences. He designed your brain to form a neurochemical link between the pleasure of sexual orgasm and the fantasy you used to bring you to that level of sexual excitement. This is why the source of sexual excitement a person uses to bring himself to orgasm becomes such a critical spiritual issue. The source of sexual excitement becomes linked with the experience of sexual excitement. Explain this to your teens.

Keep Sexual Fantasies About Marriage Impersonal

Help your teenagers to understand that sexual fantasy is a normal part of puberty. Until your children are engaged to be married, their sexual fantasies should be about marriage in general. Suppose your son asks you, "I'm really in love with Suzie. Can I fantasize about *Suzie* when I masturbate?"

Obviously, the answer is, "No." After all, if your son is a typical fifteen- or sixteen-year-old boy, there are likely to be many Suzies before God brings into his life the woman he is to marry. Help him see that using a specific person as the focus of his sexual fantasy while he is masturbating is an abuse of that person.

However, he can fantasize about how much better his wife will be able to make him feel than he can make himself feel. At the same time, he can reinforce his determination to save himself for her.

Teach your sons to understand that when they want to experience sexual orgasm, their brains will automatically conjure up the fantasies they have learned can provide this experience for them. If these fantasies are about how good it will feel to have sex with their wife when they are married, then there is nothing morally wrong with it. If their orgasmic skills have been learned through the years by pairing orgasm with fantasies of making love to their future spouse, then they will bring into marriage orgasmic skills trained to respond to the body of their spouse.

Once your children are engaged, their fantasies can become personal. On their wedding night their spouse's body will become their body, and their body will become their spouse's body.[5] Then what both of them have been dreaming and fantasizing about for years can be celebrated freely without the risk of complicating each other's life by bringing into their marriage a history of sexually transmitted diseases or pornographic habits.

Once a man and a woman have married, they will both want to train their minds to make each other the source of all their future fantasizing. As a young person, your son could only think abstractly about his future spouse when he is fantasizing about marriage. Now he can place the image of his wife as the source of his fantasies. He can remember actual love-making events with his wife, or imagine those he would like to have. But once married, the husband's mind should be restricted to sexual thoughts about his wife, and the wife's mind should be restricted to sexual thoughts about her husband.

When other fantasies are used, a man will bring into his marriage a need for the stimulus he has learned to depend upon for helping him reach this level of sexual excitement. So, while he is making love to his spouse, his fantasies will not be with her. They will be fixed on whatever he has trained his mind to need for sexual excitement. Any intuitive wife will realize that although her husband is physically present when they are making love, he seems to be emotionally removed from what is going on.

Because of his history with masturbation, a man often brings more advanced orgasmic skills into marriage than his wife. When this is the case, the couple is mystified by the ease with which the husband reaches orgasm and the difficult challenge it is for the wife at times.

Neither Condone It... nor Condemn It

When talking to your teens about masturbation, neither condone it nor condemn it. As a part of your conversations with them, you may want to share with them how you dealt with this practice when you were a teen-ager. Such information will be helpful to them. Let them know that when you were their age you had your struggles with your sexual urges, too. Don't go into detail, but be honest—particularly about masturbation. Be honest enough to tell them if you felt guilty and, if so, how you dealt with that guilt. Assure them that the Lord helped you through those years just as He will help them. If their fantasies are of marriage while they are masturbating, and they don't feel guilty, don't impose guilt!

At the risk of being too repetitive, have the following conversation often with your teenager.

> Remember, when you are pleasuring yourself, it is very important that your thoughts are on marriage. If you use pornography to stimulate your sexual excitement, then you will carry the need for pornography into your marriage. Sooner or later, your wife will discover this. You will feel embarrassed and humiliated. She will feel angry and inadequate.
>
> So, when you are pleasuring yourself, think about your future marriage. Realize that when God brings His woman for you into your life, sex with her will make you feel better than you have ever been able to make yourself feel. When you are married to her, she will love you deeply and get to know your body well enough to give you the pleasure God has designed you to experience. Her body will fulfill your fantasies, and sexual orgasm will bond you to her.
>
> Your fantasies of her before you meet her will only add to the intensity of that bond. By restricting your sexual fantasies to her and keeping yourself for her you won't be thinking about what sex was like with this girl or that girl when you are making love to your wife. You won't be using the fantasy of another woman's body to satisfy the lust you have for pleasure. The fantasies that have sexually excited you and brought you to orgasm have always been of the wife God would eventually bring into your life. Being true to her before you know her will make it easier for you to be true to her after she is yours.

What if they still feel guilty?

If your teen feels guilty, or expresses shame about his feelings or desires, even though his fantasies are confined to marriage, then teach him how to manage his guilt. How do you go about doing this?

First of all, don't tell them they should not feel guilty. Respect the sensitivity of their consciences. Remind them that God has promised to remove our guilt. Teach them how to bring God's grace into this part of their lives until they are married.

God's grace is sufficient!

Encourage your teens to ask God for forgiveness every time they are morally prompted to do so. Let them know that God knows how difficult it is to deny all of their sexual urges until they are married. So, if they are willing to keep themselves for their future spouse and focus their sexual fantasies on marriage, God will give them grace and forgiveness for pleasuring themselves as often as is necessary until they are married.[6]

Unfortunately, some parents leave children thinking that God won't forgive them for masturbating unless they stop doing it. Now, just think about how theologically wrong this idea is!

Does this mean that parents cannot be forgiven unless they stop what makes them feel guilty? How many times has God forgiven you of saying things you shouldn't say? Does He withhold forgiveness from you because you don't stop doing it? No, of course not! He forgives you again and again and again and again and again. The last thing a teenager needs dogging them for years is a cloud of masturbatory guilt. Let me say it one more time: *The spiritual issue is the fantasy accompanying the activity, not the activity itself.*

With your help, your teens can learn to carefully focus their fantasies and desire for sexual pleasure on their future marriages. Inspire them to ask God to help them keep themselves pure for their future marriage partners. Encourage them to rely on God's mercy and grace to help them through these turbulent years of puberty. Pray with them that God will bring their marriage partners to them—in His own time and with the assurance that marriage will bring them more and greater sexual pleasure than anything they could have imagined.

Your teens need to know how to conduct themselves safely around members of the opposite sex. This is the topic in chapter fifteen. The next chapter will help you to know how to discuss the problem of sexually transmitted diseases with your children and to help them develop a commitment to sexual purity.

Chapter 13

Alcohol, Drugs, and Sexually Transmitted Diseases

Getting acquainted with the opposite sex should be an interesting and exciting time of life for your teens. However, the two tragedies that can turn their world upside down and your dreams for them into nightmares are *sexually transmitted diseases* and *pregnancy*. The common link between these two tragedies is obvious—sexual experience. As youth begin to use alcohol and have sex at a younger age, the risk of unplanned pregnancies, of exposure to sexually transmitted diseases, and of sexual violence increases.[1] In this chapter we will consider the issue of sexually transmitted diseases (STDs). The next chapter will discuss the issue of pregnancy.

You cannot protect your teens from these life-altering crises. However, you can arm your teens with the truth. There is no way anyone can have sex with other people and be completely safe from pregnancy and STDs. You should also warn them that both of these risks are heightened by unprotected sex.

Alcohol, Drugs, and Sex

Unfortunately, during the same time your teens are being confronted with sexual temptations, they are experiencing mounting pressure from their peers to experiment with alcohol and drugs. In 2005, the Kaiser Foundation and the National Center of Addiction and Substance Abuse at New York's Columbia University came out with the results of one of the first surveys to look at the relationships among drugs, alcohol, and reduced sexual inhibitions.[2] They interviewed twelve hundred young people from fifteen to twenty-four years of age. Here are some of the interesting things they found:

- Almost one in four said they had unprotected sex while using alcohol or drugs. If their sample is representative, this means more than 5,500,000 young people in this age range are willing to take these kinds of risks with the future.
- Twenty-nine percent of the sample said they "did more sexually than they had planned" because alcohol or drugs were involved.
- Seventy-nine percent of the high school students in the sample said they had experimented with alcohol at least once.
- Those who drank alcohol were seven times more likely to have intercourse than those who did not drink.
- Those who drank or experimented with other drugs were more likely to involve themselves with more sexual partners than those who did not drink.[3]

In reflecting on the study, Joseph Califano Jr., president of the National Center of Addiction and Substance Abuse and former Secretary of U.S. Health, Education, and Welfare, said, "Those are big differences and this is really dangerous activity. Kids do not understand this. When you mix drinking and drugs and sex, you then move into the world of the danger of getting AIDS, which is life threatening, or sexually transmitted diseases, teen pregnancy and rape."[4]

I cannot overstress how important it is for you to make your teens aware of the damaging influence alcohol and drugs have on their consciences and impulse controls in managing their sex drive. Today, young people in America are using alcohol at an earlier age than ever before. Children ages twelve to seventeen are more likely to abuse alcohol than any other age group in our society. According to *Adolescent Medicine*: "By the time they graduate from high school, two-thirds of today's youth have become regular drinkers and two-fifths are binge drinkers."[5]

How early do your children feel the pressure of their peers to begin drinking? Thirty percent of children from the fourth through the sixth grades say they have felt a lot of pressure from their peers to drink beer. Ninety percent of tenth graders and 75 percent of eighth graders say it is very easy for them to get alcohol. The average age when young people begin to drink is thirteen years and two months. However, use is seen more and more frequently among youngsters as young as nine years of age.[6]

Where Is the Good News in All of This?

Parents can, and do, make a difference. Teens who experience high levels of support from their parents are much less likely to get involved in alcohol, drugs, and sex. What do I mean by parental support? Care for your teens! Show them affection. Brag on them when they do well. Be fair with them. Caring fathers are just as important as caring mothers.

The absence of parental care leaves a void in a young person's heart that the young person is likely to try and fill by becoming intimate with one of his or her peers. Sooner or later this translates into sexual involvement.

Don't be put off by your teenagers' attempt to resist your affection. Even though you should be careful not to embarrass them in front of their peers, realize they need appropriate hugs and kisses now as much as ever before in their lives—perhaps even more. This is one of the ways you show you care about them.

Another way you show your teens you care about what happens to them is to stay informed about what is really taking place in their world. Don't stick your head in the sand. You may not like what you see when you stare their world in the face, but look anyway—even if it scares you.

Revealing that you are well informed about what goes on in their world means that you've done your homework. You have gone to legitimate sources and found the facts! Knowing you care this much tells your children that you really do want to protect them from the dreadfully dangerous world of today's teens.

Once you are aware of some of the risks they face every day, you will want to take a realistic look at some ways you can protect your teens from the risks—including the risk of sexually transmitted diseases.

Sexually Transmitted Diseases

There is an epidemic of sexually transmitted diseases currently raging among the youth of our country. How much worse is that risk today than it was when you and your parents were growing up?

During the 1960s there were only two prominent sexually transmitted diseases: syphilis and gonorrhea. Both of these could be cured by penicillin.

Today, forty years after the onset of the sexual revolution, according to the Centers for Disease Control and Prevention, our nation is faced with multiple epidemics of twenty-five sexually transmitted diseases. Some experts say this number rises to fifty when the various strains of virus groups are included.[7]

Because of the personal nature of these diseases, most parents and teenagers are unaware of this deadly tidal wave of sexually transmitted diseases threatening our youth. The following statistics graphically define the problem:

- Every year three million new teenagers are afflicted with a sexually transmitted disease or infection.
- The seventh leading cause of death among young people ages fifteen to twenty-four in the United States is human immunodeficiency virus (HIV).
- In the United States, the highest rates of chlamydia, a bacterial infection, occur among young adolescents fifteen to nineteen years old. When left untreated, chlamydia and gonorrhea become the most common cause of pelvic inflammatory disease (PID). More teenagers than older women are hospitalized for acute PID. This condition (PID) can be responsible for infertility, tubal pregnancies, and other health problems later in the lives of these young women.
- In a single act of unprotected sex with men who are infected with the disease, a teenage woman has a 1 percent chance of contracting HIV, a 30 percent chance of being

infected with genital herpes, and a 50 percent chance of getting gonorrhea.

- Teenagers and young adults have the highest incidence of syphilis in the United States.
- About 25 percent of Americans are infected with genital herpes. There is no known cure for this sexually transmitted disease. It can be contracted during oral, anal, or genital intercourse. Since herpes is transmitted by touching other parts of the body, condoms do not always protect a person against this disease.
- Approximately ten million people in the United States have genital warts. This is the most common STD in our country. One million new cases are diagnosed each year. This disease comes from the human papilloma virus (HPV). There is no effective treatment against the recurrence of genital warts.[8]

In her excellent book *Epidemic: How Teen Sex Is Killing Our Kids*, Doctor Meg Meeker comprehensively explores the risks of STDs with parents and youth. I highly recommend that you read this book and share it with your children.

Why Are Teens at the Center of This Epidemic?

During the sexual revolution of the 1960s, sexual intercourse between single people became a socially accepted practice. The common assumption was that since puberty is occurring earlier and marriage is being delayed, it is impractical to expect young people to reserve sexual intercourse for marriage. So the social stigma of premarital intercourse was removed, and our young people were given tacit approval to engage in sex before marriage. This was another giant step in the secularization of sex in our society.

Although many, if not most, Americans still believe that sex belongs in marriage, young people are no longer subjected to this form of social discipline. As a whole, our society ignores or denies that there is anything sacred about sex.

Such a drastic social change in sexual attitudes was followed by a sharp increase of sexual activity among young people on high school and college campuses. As you might expect, single pregnancies reached all-time highs. Subsequently, abortion was legalized. So, in order to reduce the number of single pregnancies and abortions, federal and state governments introduced sex education programs in public schools designed to teach young people how to have *safe sex*. Presumably, sex with condoms reducing the risk of pregnancy was *safe*.

Today, millions of young Americans are victims of this *safe sex* teaching learned in public schools. They were taught that properly using condoms and other contraceptive devices would not only reduce the risk of pregnancy, but would also protect them from sexually transmitted diseases. The last part of this statement is simply not true. Using condoms and other contraceptive devices have helped to *reduce* the number of single pregnancies and abortions among teenagers. However, young people are left with the illusion that what protects them from pregnancy will also protect them from sexually transmitted diseases. Along with youth's natural tendency to feel immune from tragedy, using condoms leaves them with this false sense of protection. Therefore they are far less restrained in the number of people they choose to have sex with than in previous generations in our history.

By age nineteen, 85 percent of our boys and 77 percent of our girls have had sexual intercourse.[9] By age seventeen over half of our teenagers have had sexual intercourse.[10] The earlier your teens have sexual intercourse, the more partners they are likely to have before they are married.[11] In one study, 31.1 percent of sexually experienced females and 45 percent of sexually experienced males reported six or more sexual partners by age twenty-one.[12]

As the number of sexual partners increases, there is an exponential increase in the risk of contracting a sexually transmitted disease. Few teens understand that. They think they are simply having sex with that one person.

Be sure your teens understand that when they choose to have sex with another person, they are not just having sex with that one person. They are having sex with every person that person has had sex with in his or her entire life.

What are the mathematical realities of having numbers of sex partners? When you have only had sex with one person, your risk is limited to that one person, provided you are the only person to have sex with him or her. However, if you have had sex with four people and those four people have had sex with four people, then you have shared body fluids with fifteen people and are exposed to the sexual histories of fifteen people.

Even if you limit the number of sex partners you have before marriage to 6, you are at risk for the sexual histories of 127 people. To give your teenagers some sense of how this risk exponentially multiplies, explain to them that if they have sex with 10 people before they are married, and these 10 people have also had sex with 10 people, then they have shared their body fluids with 1,023 people and have put themselves at the risk of all the sexual histories for each one of those 1,023 people.[13]

Be sure that your teens understand the implications of these numbers. Explain to them the dangers of contracting a sexually transmitted disease, and be sure they have the tools they need to assure a future free of disease.

In the next chapter you will be able to help them understand the greater risk of an unwanted pregnancy.

Chapter 14

Talking About Pregnancy

Pregnancy is a tragedy that can turn your youngsters' dreams into nightmares. When they had the body of a child, this was not a possibility. Even if you caught them in some kind of childhood sexual play, you didn't have to worry about it, and neither did they. As teens, they no longer have the bodies of children. Their bodies now house the miracle of life. They can make babies. However, being able to make babies and being mature enough to be responsible parents are two different things.

Teenagers Are *Not* Ready for Parenthood!

Be sure to stress to your teenagers the importance of waiting until they are grown, have completed their education, and are married for two or three years before they have a baby. This will allow them the preparation time necessary to develop the spiritual, emotional, and marital maturity to provide a baby with the kind of parents they want their babies to have.

When teenage children have babies, the responsibility of parenthood makes it difficult, if not impossible, for them to see their own dreams come true. In addition, their babies are deprived of the advantages of being raised by mature adult parents.

Do your best to help your teen understand that conceiving a child with another teen is something neither of them can ever erase from their history, regardless of how they choose to manage it. When a couple gets pregnant before marriage, it permanently links their histories together. It impacts the lives of the father, the mother, the baby, and both of their families.

Because the baby grows inside the body of the mother and she gives birth to the child, her life is more seriously affected than that of the father. However, having to assume the responsibilities of fatherhood before becoming a married adult is a heavy burden for young men as well.

Be Sure Your Teens Know How Pregnancy Occurs

Even though your teens are taught the basics about pregnancy in their health classes, many are still at the mercy of their own ignorance about pregnancy. For example, some teenagers believe a woman can only get pregnant if she achieves orgasm in intercourse. Some are unaware that the preseminal fluid secreted from the penis of a sexually excited male contains sperm at times. This means that genital petting can result in pregnancy. If they believe that pregnancy can't occur if a man withdraws before he ejaculates, their basic lack of information leaves them unprotected from pregnancy. Because the pre-ejaculatory fluid sometimes contains sperm, pregnancy can occur.

By the time your daughter is thirteen or your son is fourteen, they should have better information than this. They should know how a child is conceived, about the gestation of human life, and how childbirth occurs. Of course, you gave them the basic information about menstruation, nocturnal emissions, and pregnancy before they entered puberty. However, now it is time that they need to have a more detailed understanding of these awesome events of life.

Don't be surprised when you suggest having this kind of talk with them if they tell you they know all about it. Just assure them that a little review never hurts anyone. Then insist on giving them the details anyway.

Carefully select an opportunity when you know you will have enough time alone with your teenagers to share this information with them. Since there may be gender differences reflected in the appropriate responses to your child's questions, it is best when both parents can be involved in this dialogue. However, this is not always possible.

You may want to get the conversation started by saying something like, "I know life is changing a lot for you right now, and I thought it would be good for us to have some time to talk about it. On the one hand, you are no longer a child, but on the other hand, you are not an adult yet either.

"I remember how awkward I felt when I was in my teens. How do you feel about all these changes in your life?" Take time to let your child share his or her feelings with you. (Simply use plural pronouns when both parents are present.)

Then continue with something like, "Maybe it would help for you to think of yourself as a *tweenager* rather than a teenager. You are certainly no longer a child, and I am excited to see you grow toward adulthood. However, you are not there yet. You're sort of in between being a child and becoming an adult. So, since you are becoming an adult, I want to be sure you have the information you will need to manage your sexuality wisely.

"Until you are married, few things will complicate your life more than getting pregnant and having a baby. I'm sure you've seen this happen to some of your friends at school. Many times it happens because young people don't know as much as they think they know about how pregnancy occurs.

"When you have been married for two or three years, having a baby will be exciting. We are looking forward to sharing that time in your life with you. However, right now that is the last thing in the world we would want for you . . . and I know that's the last thing you want for yourself.

"Before you began your periods we had a talk like this, but we talked mostly about what was happening in your body. And we talked about boys and what happens in their bodies when they become young men.

"I'm sure since then you have gotten some information about birth control from school. They probably have talked to you also about sexually transmitted diseases. But you are too important for me to trust them to tell you everything you need to know until you are safely married."

Then continue with the following information. You may use these exact words if you choose, which will give a complete understanding of pregnancy. While you are discussing pregnancy with your children, be prepared to show them the diagrams in Appendix B that thoroughly describe each step of pregnancy from ovulation to the birth of the baby.

How Do You Get Pregnant?

"First, the only way to be sure of not getting pregnant is not to have sexual intercourse or any sexual contact with a guy or gal that involves the mixing of fluids from his or her body and your body. You do not have to have intercourse to get pregnant. Remember that! Here is how pregnancy occurs." (While you are explaining pregnancy, you may want to refer to the diagrams in the appendices from time to time.)

"When a young man becomes sexually excited, blood flows into the large arteries of the spongy tissue of his *penis*. This produces an erection. When you are older and your boyfriend hugs you, you will feel the firmness of his *penis* through his clothing.

"Sperm are stored in the *vas deferens* attached to his *testicles,* awaiting ejaculation. The *vas deferens* is a thin tube through which sperm travel and is part of the *spermatic cord*. It is the *vas deferens* that is severed when a man gets a *vasectomy*. This is a popular form of birth control.

"The genital ducts that transport a man's *sperm* include the *vasa deferentia* (plural) and the *epididymides,* which are collection tubes for *sperm*. Each of these tubes is approximately twenty feet long and lies on the surface of each *testicle*. A sperm cell takes several weeks to make its way through these tubes.

"Then, there is another tube leading from the bladder to the tip of the *penis* called a *urethra*. *Urine* is released from the *bladder* through this tube. *Seminal fluid*, which enters the *urethra* from special openings in the area of the *prostate gland*, is also released through this tube.

"Other parts of the male's *genitalia* involved in pregnancy include the *seminal vesicles*. These lie behind the *bladder* near the top of the *prostate gland* and secrete fluid that helps to activate the vigorous movement of sperm.

"The *prostate gland* is a firm, round body about the size of a chestnut. This gland, located below the *bladder,* constantly produces fluid, some of which is passed in *urine*. The rest makes up most of the *seminal fluid*. *Cowper's glands*, named for the man who discovered them, are two small, pea-sized glands that lie below the *prostate* and secrete a clear alkaline fluid into the *urethra* during sexual excitement. The purpose of this fluid is to protect sperm by neutralizing any acid urine may have left in the *urethra.* Sometimes this fluid contains *sperm.* When this fluid contains sperm, a woman can get pregnant through any genital petting that allows this fluid from the man's *penis* to come in contact with the lubrication of the woman's *vagina.* So she can become pregnant even though the man's *penis* never penetrates her *vagina.*

"You remember from our last talk that a male's *testicles* produce approximately 300 million *sperm* per day. The fluid his *penis* ejaculates when he has an orgasm is called *semen.*

"There are between 100 million and 200 million *sperm* in a healthy male's ejaculation. If any of these *sperm* are deposited in a woman's vagina, they will live at least forty-eight hours. This means several hundreds may still be surviving in the woman's *fallopian tubes* when her ovum arrives. Only one *sperm* is necessary to penetrate the *ovum.*

"The body of the *sperm* cell provides the energy to mobilize the *sperm.* The tail furnishes the mobility. The vigorous whiplash-like movement of the tail enables the *sperm* to move about one-eighth of an inch per minute.

"In contrast to the *sperm,* the *ovum* is the largest cell in the human body. An *ovum* is about the size of a period at the end of a sentence. Carried in its round body are twenty-three *chromosomes* representing a unique combination of the genetic heritage from the woman's family.

"Normally, pregnancy results from *coitus.* (*Coitus* is a Latin word that means "going together.") This may also be referred to as genital intercourse, copulation, "going all the way," or, in street language, "getting laid." The intense pleasure resulting from the rhythmic movement of a couple having genital intercourse produces an orgasm for the male and may produce one for the female.

"A man's orgasm involves an ejaculation of *semen,* a grayish white fluid, from his sex organs into those of the woman close to the entrance of her *uterus.* Although the total amount of *semen* ejaculated at any one time is less than a teaspoon, it contains from 200,000 to 500,000 sperm cells. These are forcefully ejected into the woman's body by the involuntary contractions involved in ejaculation. Of course, it is not necessary for the woman to climax for her to become pregnant.

"Once a man's *sperm* has penetrated a woman's *ovum,* the twenty-three *chromosomes* of the male's sperm join the twenty-three *chromosomes* of the female's *ovum* and fertilization takes place. The new cell, called a *zygote,* has twenty-three pairs of *chromosomes* that form a unique blend of the genetic characteristics from both parents.

"Segmentation follows, which is what happens when the fertilized *ovum* begins to produce other cells. Within a few hours after fertilization, the process of segmentation transforms the *zygote* into a mulberry-like cluster of cells called a *morula.*

"Three days later, when the *morula* arrives in the *uterus,* it resembles a hollow ball of cells called a *blastocyst.* Three or four days after the *blastocyst* arrives in the *uterus*, implantation begins. Implantation is the process by which the *blastocyst* implants itself in the wall of the *uterus.*

"The wall of the *uterus* is comprised of three different layers of tissue: the *perimetrium,* or outer wall; the middle muscular layer called the *myometrium;* and the inner layer known as the *endometrium.* In the event of pregnancy, the extraordinary muscular structure of the *myometrium* allows the *uterus* to expand to accommodate the growing *fetus,* or unborn baby. This same musculature provides the necessary pressure to expel the *fetus* at birth."

Ovulation and Pregnancy

"*Ovulation* takes place approximately fourteen days before the first day of the next *menstrual period.* This is the fourteenth day of a twenty-eight-day cycle or the twenty-first day of a thirty-five-day cycle.

"This time period between *ovulation* and the next *menstrual period* varies very little. However, the time period between the end of *menstruation* and the next *ovulation* may vary considerably.

"During the second phase of the *menstrual cycle*, the *uterus* prepares for the implantation of a fertilized *ovum.* Before ovulation the *follicle* encasing the *ovum* begins to produce *progesterone.*

"After ovulation, the follicle becomes a *corpus luteum,* or *yellow body,* and the production of *progesterone* increases greatly. The *corpus luteum* also produces *estrogen,* which contributes to building the lining of the *uterus* to its greatest thickness.

"This trip from the *ovary* through the *vagina* usually takes about three days. After another three or four days the fertilized *ovum* begins to implant itself in the nourished thickened lining of the *uterus*. This marks the beginning of pregnancy, which helps to sustain the yellow body production of *estrogen* and *progesterone*. This process prevents new *ovulation* from occurring and the lining of the *uterus* from deteriorating. The *menstrual cycle* is suspended at this time and pregnancy continues."

How Does a Woman Know When She Is Pregnant?

"If a woman has had sexual intercourse and misses her regular menstrual period, she may suspect pregnancy. This suspicion increases if she notices an enlargement of her breasts and a darkening of the nipples. Morning sickness and a more frequent need to urinate are further evidence that she may be pregnant.

"About three weeks after implantation, or six weeks after the last *menstrual period*, the hormone *chorionic gonadotropin* is detectable in the woman's urine. At this point it is possible to have a pregnancy test of the urine. Bear in mind that a positive result is almost always correct, but a negative result may not be reliable. That is, even though the pregnancy test may indicate the woman is not pregnant, she may be pregnant.

"More reliable blood tests for the detection of pregnancy within a few days after conception are available through your physician and local pharmacy. However, the surest signs of pregnancy are the heartbeat of the *fetus,* which can be heard at the beginning of the fifth month of *gestation*, and the movement of the *fetus,* which the mother can detect at about the same time.

"Now let's follow the progress of *fetal* development." (Use the diagrams in the appendices to follow fetal development.) "We have already covered what happens in the first month following fertilization. By the end of the second month, the *embryo* is almost an inch long and weighs about one-thirtieth of an ounce.

"After three months, the fetus is about three inches long, weighs about an ounce, and is beginning to look like a miniature infant. At the end of four months, the *fetus* is about eight and one-half inches long and weighs about six ounces.

"By the end of the fifth month the *fetus* has grown to twelve inches, weighs about a pound, and would live for a few minutes if it were born at this time. After six months, the *fetus* has grown to approximately fourteen inches and weighs about two pounds.

"At seven months in the pregnancy, the *fetus* is about sixteen inches long and weighs about four pounds. There is a 75 percent chance of survival if birth occurs at this time. By the end of the eighth month of pregnancy the *fetus* has grown to eighteen inches in length and weighs a little more than five pounds. If born at this time, the baby would have a 90 percent chance of survival. Birth at the end of a full-term pregnancy should find the baby about twenty inches long and weighing about seven pounds.

"For women having their first child, labor averages fourteen hours. After the first child this period is shortened to about eight hours.

"Once contractions are from three to five minutes apart and last forty-five seconds or longer, delivery is imminent. At some point in this process the *amniotic sac,* which surrounds and cushions the fetus, will rupture, releasing the *amniotic fluid* from the *vagina.*

"Delivery begins once the infant's head passes through the *cervix* and ends when the baby has completed its passage through the birth canal. This usually requires from twenty to eighty minutes. During this time, contractions occur about every two minutes and last from sixty to sixty-five seconds.

"Once the baby is born, the umbilical cord is cut. The mucus is sucked out of the baby's lungs. The baby begins to breathe on his or her own and is ready to take nourishment when he or she is hungry.

"After about five minutes' rest following birth, contractions will begin again so that the mother can discharge the placental sac, or afterbirth, from her body. This usually requires about twenty minutes."

Read this material several times before talking to your teens so that you can put all of this into your own words. Mentally rehearse the presentation so you can anticipate your teens' questions and prepare to answer them. Take time during the presentation to explain to your teens the terms they may not understand.

When Should You Begin Sharing This Information?

Once your daughter is thirteen or fourteen years old, plan a special night out with her to discuss her sexuality. To emphasize the importance of the occasion, plan it several weeks in advance. If possible, both parents should be present. The place should be carefully selected to provide the privacy you will need to talk about this intimate information.

During the evening, her mother should lead the conversation. Here are some highlights you will want to cover:

- The pleasant genital feelings she has from time to time are God's way of reminding her of marriage.
- When she entertains these feelings, she should keep her thoughts on marriage and how much more sexual pleasure she will experience with the man God will bring into her life than she can provide for herself.
- Assure her that the sexual attraction she is beginning to feel toward boys is normal and healthy. Desiring attention from young men is natural for someone her age. However, it may be awhile before young men her age began to notice any girls.
- Saving her virginity for her husband will not only protect her from pregnancy and sexually transmitted diseases, but it will also make it possible for her to give him this special gift that she has never given anyone else.
- Explain the more urgent sex drive that testosterone stimulates in young men than what young women experience. Because of this she may notice her boyfriend's penis gets erect at times when he is with her. This is normal.
- Review with her the levels of contact between young men and young women defined in the next chapter. Teach her the importance of keeping the focus of her relationship with guys on the social level rather than on the sexual level.

- Remind her that girls get pregnant. They have more at stake in the relationship with guys and should be insistent on being the one who controls the level of physical contact.
- Warn her that genital petting will put her at risk for sexually transmitted diseases and, at times, even pregnancy.
- Assure her that if a young man is personally interested in her, helping him to maintain control of his sexuality will only earn her his respect. If his interest in her is mostly sexual, then the sooner she finds this out the better it will be for her.
- Let her know that bragging on a young man and telling him how much she admires him will maintain his interest in her if his intentions are honorable.
- Be transparent about the challenge that the two of you faced with your own sexuality during your single days.
- Give her plenty of time to interrupt the discussion with her questions. Be honest and transparent in your answers.

At the end of the evening, the parents can let their teenager know how special it is when a man and a woman are able to present each other with their virginity on their wedding night. When you are finished with your conversation and her questions, give her a ring that you have purchased for the index finger of her left hand and ask her if she will wear it as a reminder to save her virginity for her husband.

When presented to her in tenderness and love, this symbol can be a powerful source of protection for your daughter. Every time she looks at the ring she will be reminded of the special gift she is saving for her husband. On her wedding day she can put the ring on a special chain and give it to her husband to wear around his neck as a symbol of the purity of their relationship.

When your son is fourteen or fifteen, he should have his own night out with you. This time the father should take the lead in the conversation. The same general areas of information should be shared with your son. His father also should remind him:

- How special it is for a woman to know that her husband has not had intercourse with any other woman. Her husband has saved himself for her.
- Of the need to avoid pornographic fantasies when he is pleasuring himself. Instead, urge him to imagine how much more fulfilling it will be when his wife sexually devotes herself to him.

At the end of the evening, present your son with a masculine chain and cross to wear as a reminder that he is saving himself sexually for the woman God will bring into his life as his wife. Then on his wedding day he can present this cross and chain to his wife as a symbol of the sexual purity he presents to her on their wedding day.

Chapter 15

Protecting Your Teens From Tragedy

As a parent you will want to do everything possible to protect your children from the tragic results of a lack of preparation or information about the important teen years. In this chapter we will discuss some of the boundaries your teenagers need to establish for their opposite sex relationships.

Begin by stressing to your teenagers the importance of not allowing alcohol or drugs to play a part in getting acquainted with members of the opposite sex. Be sure they understand the influence alcohol and drugs can have on their sexual behavior.

These drugs lower the resistance of a person's conscience and erode the controls a person would normally place on his or her sexual impulses. Be sure your teens understand that their futures could be sacrificed in a matter of minutes—if not seconds—once alcohol or drugs are allowed to impair their judgment.

Be sure they understand that God's love for them will never change—or your love for them. However, allowing sexual impulses to dominate their judgment in such moments can result in choices that carry tragic and lifelong consequences—consequences from which you, as their parent, cannot protect them. You would love them just as much and would try to help them make the best of the embarrassing situation resulting from making reckless choices, but not even God can protect them from the consequences of the decisions they make in such careless moments.

Teach your teens the importance of mutual respect in getting acquainted with friends of the opposite sex. Remind them that as soon as they could talk, you began to teach them to respect other people's privacy and not intrude upon them.

You would not allow them to slap or hit other people. You taught them to respect other children's toys. However, there are much larger issues to give attention to after the onset of puberty. Now that your children have the physical ability to be parents, they must learn the significance and importance of physical boundaries.

Each of Us Needs Our Own Space

In order to feel secure, each person needs about two or three feet of space. Teach your children to provide that space for others and to require others to do the same for them. This important lesson in social learning needs to be well in place as they begin to get acquainted with the opposite sex so they can exercise wise sexual discipline.

Every time you ride an elevator you compromise your personal space. The next time you get on an elevator notice how you behave. What do you do? Where do you look? Most likely, you look at the ceiling or the floor, avoiding direct eye contact with other people. Why? This is because each person on the elevator is aware that his or her personal space has been violated.

We permit this infringement on our boundaries for the convenience of avoiding the stairs. It is a temporary privilege we give to each other, but if we were not in an elevator each of us would feel uncomfortable with the others being so close.

This simple illustration will help your children understand why they feel uncomfortable when someone else gets too close to them. One of the ways we show our respect for others is to give each person the space they deserve for their own personal comfort.

Maintaining Physical Boundaries in Friendships

The need to teach teenagers the importance of physical boundaries is underscored by the fact that failure to maintain adequate boundaries has resulted in over half of them being involved in sexual intercourse by the time they are juniors in high school.[1] That's a startling statistic.

Even sadder is the fact that most teenagers do not make a conscious decision to have sex. They allow themselves to be influenced by the moment and adjust their personal boundaries accordingly. Help your teens understand their need to make a conscious decision *not* to have sex. If they have not made this commitment to themselves, then they are at the mercy of their friends and their impulses at the moment.

Unless you teach your teens something different, they are left to deal with a high school culture where peers often promote promiscuity and pornographers promote perversity. Some of their male peers will associate having sex with a girl with *becoming* a man. Some of their female peers think that having sex with guys will make them popular.

In fact, girls who are known to have sex freely are unpopular with other girls. And they are popular with the guys for the wrong reason. The guys who are driven to have sex so they will feel like men will *use* girls looking to find popularity by being sexually permissive.

Physical boundaries help protect us.

If you want your children to stay in control of their sexual impulses, teach them that there are distinct physical boundaries they need to establish for their sexual protection when relating to the opposite sex. The first is holding hands.

Explain to your teen that when getting acquainted with members of the opposite sex, holding hands is not just a casual contact. Actually, holding hands involves an intrusion of the boundaries between you and another person.

You allow this intrusion because you want to share affection with this person. It's a privilege you allow some boy or girl to enjoy with you. It's a sign of a special friendship.

The second level of affection teens share with each other is more sexually exciting. It involves activity above the shoulders. Sometimes we call this *necking* or *kissing*. Usually a couple engages in kissing on the lips first. However, if they continue to see each other, they will engage in open-mouthed kissing, sometimes referred to as *French kissing*. Your teens should know that allowing this activity exposes them to greater sexual risk than holding hands or kissing on the lips.

Sexual activity above the waist is even riskier than necking. Sometimes we call this *petting*. It usually includes hugging and caressing the girl's breasts. Call your teens' attention to the fact that each physical boundary they breach with another person leaves them less in control of the activity and more at the mercy of their circumstances.

The fourth boundary to be challenged is sexual activity below the waist. This may be referred to as *heavy petting*. Sometimes it includes mutual masturbation. Be sure your teen understands that allowing someone to violate this boundary places him or her at great sexual risk. During such activities their body fluids are mixed with the body fluids of the persons involved. Let them know that this activity carries with it a great risk for getting a sexually transmitted disease and puts them at some risk for pregnancy. They need to know this!

Finally, there is intercourse. Allowing this boundary to be broken is a violation of their future marriage. Help your teens understand that when this happens, they can no longer offer their future spouse any part of them that has not already been given to someone else. A violation of this boundary also exposes them to maximal risks of pregnancy and sexually transmitted diseases.

Let them know that when these boundaries are challenged you will not be there to protect them. It is important that they learn to protect themselves. Point out to them that each boundary that is penetrated makes them more sexually vulnerable.

Warn your teens that once sexual passions reach a certain level, they will lose control. These boundaries are there for their protection. Each one that is breached should intensify their awareness that they are losing control and strongly prompt them to retreat from their activities.

Encourage them to protect themselves sexually. Assure them of your confidence in their determination to do so.

Explain the Differences Between Love and Lust

Be sure your children unmistakably understand the differences between *love* and *lust*. Being able to clearly establish this distinction early in life can save them many heartbreaking situations. Here are the three distinguishing differences:

	LUST
1.	First, lust is the selfish use of another person for one's own sexual pleasure. Lustful guys do not want a relationship. They just want sexual pleasure. It is all about them. It never dawns on them that using your body for their own sexual pleasure is abusing you.
2.	Second, a lustful guy makes no meaningful commitment to the girl. He has learned to use the right words to make her feel he deeply loves her. He does this because he wants to sexually use her. Girls who are foolish enough to believe such a guy are going to be hurt. Once the novelty of a sexual relationship with her has worn off, the guy will be history. He will leave her wounded and brokenhearted. What he felt for her was just lust, not love.
3.	Third, a lustful person will assume no responsibility for a relationship. If he gets a girl pregnant or transmits some sexual disease to her, he will make her feel totally responsible for what has happened if he can. These guys are takers—not givers. They don't keep their word. They don't show up when they tell you they will. They are totally irresponsible!

	LOVE
1.	*Love* is the unselfish giving of one person to another person with no other motive than the welfare of that person. When a guy says to a gal, "If you really loved me, you would . . . ", he is telling her that he does not love her. If she's smart she will hear that loud and clear. If he *really* loved her, he would not ask her to compromise herself sexually just for his pleasure.

LOVE	
2.	When someone loves you, that person makes an unconditional commitment to you. They do not ask you to behave a certain way or do a certain thing in order for them to love you. And their attention is not divided between you and two or three others whom they love. They are committed to you!
3.	When someone loves you, that person is responsible to you and for you. He or she keeps his or her promises. When that person tells you something, you can rely on it.

Wise young people understand these distinct differences between lust and love. They see them for what they are. Consequently, they will be spared the pain inflicted by irresponsible lust and be rewarded by experiencing someone's unselfish love.

How Do You Know When Someone Loves You?

Today, most young people don't develop the spiritual and emotional capacity for unselfish love until they are in their twenties. Help your children to see the wisdom of using their teen years as a time when they discover their faith, define their values, and decide on their vocational future.

Social friendships with the opposite sex are an enjoyable part of adolescence. Healthy teenagers will want a number of them. By comparing the things they like and do not like about their different friends they are discovering the things they will want and the things they will not want in the person they later choose to marry. This is the healthiest purpose served by friendships with the opposite sex during the teen years.

Teenagers who are healthy and really love each other will not want to jeopardize each other's future by getting sexually involved when they are too young to marry. This is one way to know your teenage friend really loves you.

However, relationships that are driven more by passion than concern for each other's future can be dangerous and disastrous. They can result in pregnancy or sexually transmitted diseases. Wise young people will enjoy social activities with the opposite sex during their teens, but they will save the more passionate expressions of love for when they are older and in a position to consider marriage.

One father told me that when his daughters were in their twenties, they asked him, "Dad, how can we know when a man really means it when he says, 'I love you'?"

The father wisely responded, "When he makes a sizeable investment in something he puts on the third finger of your left hand. Where a man's treasure is there will his heart be.[2] So until then, protect yourself!"

My wife does not really feel loved because I tell her I love her. She feels loved because of what I do for her. If my deeds demonstrate my love, then she wants to hear me say that I love her because what I say is confirmed by what I do. Love is shown by our deeds and confirmed by our words.

Responsibly Supervise Your Teens!

There is no substitute for the responsible adult supervision of teenagers. This supervision should include your children's choice of friends and the schedule for permitting them to date members of the opposite sex.

Parents should agree on the social limits that they set for their children. Shortly after your children have entered puberty, you need to tell them about these agreed-upon guidelines. It will be helpful if the two of you can be together when you present this schedule to your children. Instead of announcing them as restrictions, you will be wiser to present them as expansions of your children's freedom.

For example, you can say to them, "Won't it be great when you're in the ninth grade and you can go out with groups of girls and boys together?" Notice, the emphasis is on greater freedom. This goes over much better than saying something like, "Just remember, you can't go out with groups of boys and girls until you're in the ninth grade."

Later, you can announce to them, "When you're in the tenth grade, you can begin boyfriend-girlfriend relationships as long as you are in groups." However, these activities should be carefully supervised. Tenth-grade boys and girls should never be left alone for long periods of time. Before you allow your teens to spend much time in the homes of other teens, be sure you know how closely they will be supervised. You will also need to know something about the television or movie fare your children will be exposed to in the homes of their friends.

Often, young people are first exposed to pornography by discovering where their father stashes his or by getting on his computer. If your teen's friend comes from a home where pornography is tolerated, you should know that.

Finally, you set the final boundaries, "When you're in the eleventh grade, you and your boyfriend or girlfriend can go out with another couple. Won't that be great?" Going out alone with a member of the opposite sex is a goal to be reserved for the twelfth grade.

The wise parent will not wait until the tenth grade to try to announce these extensions of freedom. You want to do this when your children are in the sixth or seventh grade. Remember, staying ahead of the developmental process is very important.

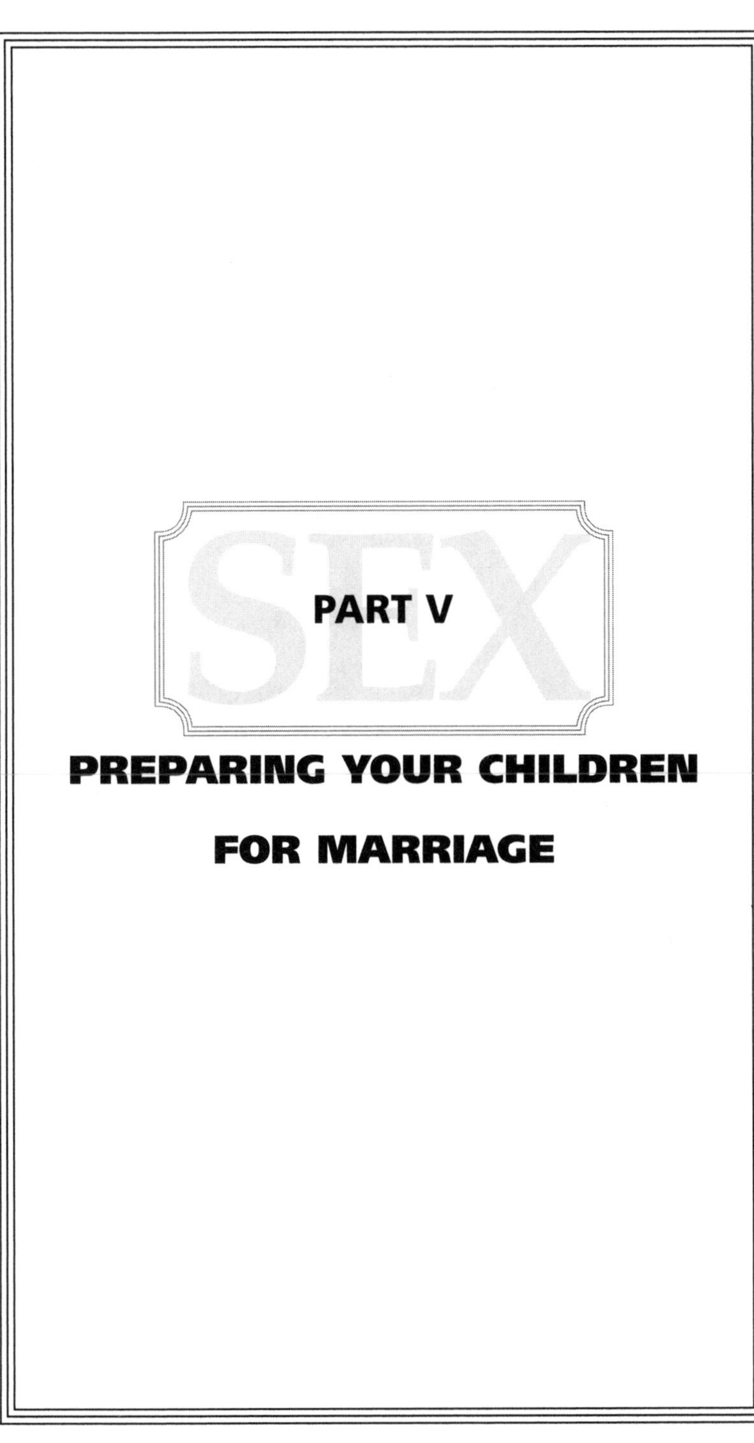

PART V

PREPARING YOUR CHILDREN FOR MARRIAGE

Chapter 16

Choosing a Life Partner

When your children enter junior high school, talk to them frequently about the important role their friends will play in shaping their future. Help them to see how extremely important it is to choose their close friends from among those who share their faith and values. Teach them to notice how friends tend to bring out the best or worst in you. Healthy friends bring out the best!

Later, when they begin to go with members of the opposite sex, stress the importance of limiting those friendships to young people who share their faith, values, and future direction in life.[1] Even though it will be years before they begin to think about marriage, this will protect them from developing a serious relationship with someone very different from them and their family.

When your children enter senior high school, help them to understand the seriousness of relationships they form with members of the opposite sex. Usually, they will *fall in love* for the first time when they are in senior high school. This is an exciting experience, but it seldom results in marriage—nor should it.

So talk to your teens about the importance of staying in control of the physical dimensions and boundaries of their relationships. This will spare them embarrassment when their *love* relationship breaks up. Encourage them to have a variety of dating relationships. This makes controlling the level of physical affection much easier.

Warn them about the *double-funnel theory of mate selection.*

They may think it is silly for you to talk about marriage to them when they are still in their teens. However, training in mate selection must begin early if it is to be effective. Once the heat of passion ignites a relationship, it is too late for reason to intervene. The wise young person uses his or her intelligence to screen relationships before he or she allows emotions to make another person sexually attractive.

The Double-Funnel Theory of Mate Selection

Take a piece of paper and draw a picture of two funnels side by side. At the top of one funnel write the word *Male.* At the top of the other funnel write the word *Female.* Under the male funnel write the word *Contact.* Under the female funnel write the word *Commitment.* Use the pictures of the funnels to explain the way many people decide to get married.

Young people do not go together very long before they discover that the young man wants contact and the young woman wants commitment. (Point to the appropriate funnel as you speak.) Seeing his girlfriend's emotional needs, the young man begins to treat her special and, in return, expects her to give him some physical contact. So, she lets him hold her hand.

Before long, the young man wants more contact, but before the young woman will permit this she wants more commitment. Then he makes more commitment, and she allows him more contact. He wants more contact, but she requires more commitment. By now you get the picture. The farther down the funnels the couple go, the more slippery it gets, and they find themselves backing into a marriage that they both know is not in their best interest. Remind your teen of the accelerating effect alcohol and drugs will have on that trip down this funnel.

Couples who choose this path to marriage do not marry because each person in the relationship possessed the qualities the other wanted in a spouse. They allowed themselves to be driven by passion and found they were sliding down the slippery slopes of these duel funnels, backing their way into a marriage that, in retrospect, they realized wasn't the best choice for them. That's sad, but that's the way many people enter marriage.

There Is a Better Way

Remind your children that choosing the person they will marry is the second most important choice in their life. Next to the choice of their faith, nothing will affect their future more. A choice that important should not be backed into because passions got out of control.

Make sure your child realizes that his or her spouse will change your family dynamic significantly. For one thing, that person will bring an entirely different gene pool into your family history. I'm not sure where young people place this irrevocable fact in the priorities of their mate choice, but my guess is that very few give it much consideration at all. Nevertheless, this should be one of the most important considerations in mate selection.

Girls Are at Greater Risk in Serious Courtships

Your teenage daughters need to know that among the many unfair things about life are these two facts:

1. Teenage males are driven by testosterone.
2. Teenage girls get pregnant.

It is important for your daughter to set the physical limits to be respected in a young man's relationship with her.

A father who raised two daughters once said to me, "I taught my daughters to avoid two kinds of guys. First of all, I told them to avoid the guy who didn't respect the limits they put on their relationship, because he's not a gentleman. Second of all, I taught them to avoid the guy who didn't test their limits, because he might not be normal."

Because the woman's body bears the child, she is at a much greater sexual risk in any teenage encounter than the male. It's not fair, but that's life, and your daughter needs to know that.

Be sure your son knows that if he gets a girl pregnant, he is just as responsible for impregnating her as she is for allowing it. There is no double standard of morality with God. He holds young men just as responsible as young women for being virgins when they marry.

There Is No Safe Sex Outside of Marriage!

God has designed sex so that you cannot steal its pleasures outside of marriage without putting yourself at great risk. Even when intercourse results from a commercial transaction with a prostitute, Paul says, "Do you not know that he who is joined to a harlot is one body with her? For 'the two,' He says, 'shall become one flesh'" (1 Corinthians 6:16). Once body fluids mingle, you share sexual risks with all the people with whom you have had sex and with all the people with whom each one of them has had sex. This is what Paul is talking about.

According to Scripture, this unifying nature of sexual intercourse is unalterable. You cannot change it. There is no way to stop it. You cannot put it into neutral.

So when people who are not married to each other have sex, they inevitably complicate each other's lives. Either they are exposing each other to a history of sexually transmitted diseases, or they are eroding each other's ability to form a permanent sexual bond with a future marriage partner.

That's what makes sexual sins unique. They are sins against the body. In 1 Corinthians 6:18, Paul states: "He who commits sexual immorality sins against his own body." Notice, he didn't say that sexual pleasure is sin. He says that when you find it in some place other than the fantasy of marriage before marriage and in marriage after you are married, it will inevitably complicate your life.

The public health system can provide teenagers with accurate information about the physiology of sex, pregnancy, and sexually transmitted diseases. But what about the theology and morality of sex? These are the most important issues of sex education.

The sexual information youngsters acquire through the public schools and health offices may make them careful and cautious, but it will not make them sexually responsible. Regardless of how sexually well informed your teenagers may be, they are at the mercy of their sexual urges unless they have a morally healthy conscience in sexual matters.

How do young people acquire this kind of conscience? They must understand that God designed sex for marriage. They need to know that any time two people start to have sex, they are exposing each other to a sexual history that only each of them knows.

The more people each of them have had sex with, the greater risk each of them poses for the other. Having sex with a variety of partners makes it less likely you will be true to the person you marry. God designed sex to bond two people to each other for life. There is no way to ignore this divine principle and escape the consequences. *Outside of marriage there is no safe sex!*

Remind your teens that they will take their sexual history into marriage. You will want to warn your teens about becoming engaged to someone without knowing that person's sexual history. Even people who have never had any symptoms of sexually transmitted diseases may be silent carriers of an STD virus or bacteria.

You are only as sexually safe in marriage as your spouse is sexually faithful to your marriage. Once a spouse goes outside of marriage and has sex with someone else, that person's body fluids have been mingled with that of the spouse. That person has committed adultery and brings that mixture of body fluids back into his or her marriage. This is one of the reasons adultery is such a grievous sin.

Sexual Intercourse Forms a Pleasure Bond

The pleasure of sexual orgasm is divinely intended to form a bond between two people to make them one for life. God has designed sex and marriage so that there is no way people can be sexually active outside of marriage without being affected permanently by that activity.

Caution your daughter never to believe that she is "as good as married" until she is married. Remind your son that a couple is never "as good as married" until they are married.

Warn your son about the consequences of thinking that you can be married in God's sight without assuming legal responsibility for your wife. Using this rationale to gain sexual privileges before the legal marriage will often generate guilt in the wife that clouds their sexual relations after their marriage.

The Body's Bonding Ability

The body's bonding ability can be compromised. The idea of *safe sex* suggests that you can have intercourse with a number of people without your life being permanently affected. Such an idea ignores the power of sexual pleasure to bond one human being to another.

God designed your body to become bonded to the person with whom you share the intense pleasure of sexual orgasm. What happens to that bonding ability when you experience such intense pleasure with a number of different people?

Explain to your teens that the bonding ability of their bodies is analogous to the nature of any other bonding material. For example, a piece of adhesive tape forms its strongest bond with the first surface to which it is applied. If you remove it and apply it to another surface, it will still stick, but it does not adhere as tightly as at first. Each time you remove it and reapply it, you will notice that the adhesive quality is compromised more and more. Eventually all the adhesiveness is gone, and it will no longer adhere to any surface.

In many ways our bodies are like that. The more sex partners your teens have had, the more difficult it will be for them to be true to the person they eventually marry. You can't fool the body. *Sexual sins compromise the bonding capacity of the body.* They weaken the strength of the pleasure bond a person will eventually be able to form with his or her spouse. Your child needs to know this.

Promiscuous sexual behavior before marriage becomes a habit that marriage is not likely to break. When a person gets hooked on using a variety of bodies for selfish sexual pleasure, it will be difficult for that person to limit his or her desires to a spouse. This is why it is important that a young couple inquire about each other's sexual history before they ever become engaged.

Review this information dealing with the theology and morality of sex frequently with your children. Once they understand why the Scriptures confine intercourse to marriage, they are more likely to respect these limits. However, expecting them to uphold a standard of morality they do not clearly understand is very unfair.

Saving Sexual Intercourse for Marriage Simplifies Life

I believe God wants a man and woman to enter marriage sexually pure because He knows it will greatly simplify that couple's life together. Some people may not be able to attain this ideal, but every young man and every young woman needs to know that it is possible. Your teens need to be encouraged and given an opportunity to attain this ideal.

Let your children know that one out of three high school seniors, both males and females, have never had intercourse.[2] They are still virgins. Express your confidence in your children's moral strength to put themselves in that number.

As you can see, the information contained in this chapter makes it clear that sexual purity has to do with much more than virginity. Maintaining sexual purity before marriage keeps your body chemistry from being contaminated with the history of the body chemistry from previous sexual partners.

Assure your teens that you know sexual purity is not the norm for our culture. Their peers will try to convince them that they are missing a lot. And it's true; they will miss a lot.

What Your Sexually Pure Teens Will Miss	
•	Your teens will never have to worry that a rash on their body is evidence of some sexually transmitted disease. They will miss that!
•	Your teens will never have to take an AIDS test. They will miss that!
•	Your son will never have to worry that some young woman is going to inform him that he has gotten her pregnant. He will miss that!
•	Your daughter will never have to panic when she misses a menstrual period for fear that she is pregnant. She will miss that!

So, it is true; by keeping themselves sexually pure your children will miss all of these things in life.

In addition, sexual purity before marriage will spare them from comparing the sexual performance of their spouse with that of previous partners. There have been no other lovers! Their history of sexual lovemaking began together. When you are not comparing your married sex life with previous experiences, you believe that the sex life you discover and develop in your marriage is the best sex life in the world.

Teach Your Son to Be Sexually Protective of Women

Being sexually active before marriage is just as damaging for your sons as it is for your daughters. For example, when a young man gets married, he often finds his wife has been emotionally and sexually damaged by other young men who said and did all the things necessary to open her to their sexual advances. Then, once they sexually tire of her, they abandoned her.

As a husband, he now has to live with the history of sexual abuses imposed on his wife by other men before she married him. The early years of their marriage may be largely consumed by helping her work her way through these issues to find healing from the emotional pains and bruises of her past. And, in many cases, these same young men who abused his wife are living with a wife who was bruised by other men's broken sexual relationships with her.

So, what goes around comes around. The young man who sexually abuses young women for his own pleasure before he is married often finds himself married to a woman who has suffered the same abuse at the hands of other men before marrying him. Often, such a woman is convinced that, "Men are only interested in one thing!" She will have such mixed feelings about her own sexuality that it may take her months, or even years, to receive the healing that frees her to celebrate sexuality in marriage.

Encourage your son to be sexually protective of women. Help him to see the wisdom of choosing a woman for his wife who has not allowed herself to be sexually used by other men. Then their marriage will be free from the clouds of a regrettable sexual history.

As you can see, restricting sex to marriage is primarily for our protection, not for our confinement. God knows that when sex is taken outside of marriage, sooner or later everybody suffers. This is why the Scriptures require healthy sexual behavior to be confined to marriage for both men and women.

> Flee sexual immorality. Every sin that a man does is outside the body, but he who commits sexual immorality sins against his own body.
>
> —1 Corinthians 6:18

> But I say to you that whoever looks at a woman to lust for her has already committed adultery with her in his heart.
>
> —Matthew 5:28

These are just two of the practical reasons the Bible gives for fleeing sexual misbehavior. Be sure you explain them often to your children. Help them to see how poor sexual judgments made in moments of passion can cast a long shadow over their future.

Sexual sins can burden your teens with unwanted pregnancies or even shorten their lives from sexually transmitted diseases. This is what makes sexual sins unique. They are sins against our own body. They are not the most wicked sins we commit, but they are the most life complicating. God will forgive us of sexual sins, but we are left to live with the consequences of our choices.

God has given you the responsibility for being the primary sex educators of your children. The guidelines offered here are to help you assume this role. Edit and improve them to fit the needs of your family. As you discharge your responsibility wisely, you will have the joy of sharing with your children what few families can...open and healthy communication about sex.

In chapters eighteen and nineteen I will talk to you about healthy conversations a mother can have with her daughter and a father can have with his son once their children are engaged.

Chapter 17

Before Your Children Say "I Do"

Training your child for mate selection and marriage is one of your greatest parental responsibilities. Helping your son or daughter choose a spouse wisely is one of your contributions to your child's future happiness.

When you consider how little help we give our young people in knowing how to select a mate, it is a wonder that our national divorce rate, which is about 50 percent of first marriages, is no higher than it is.[1] Think about it... the government actually requires young people to have more training to take an automobile on the public highways than is required for them to obtain a license, get married, and raise a family. So any help your teens are going to get in selecting a spouse has to come from you.

If you have a healthy marriage, in all likelihood your children would like to find someone like their parent of the opposite sex. A son may want to find a wife who has many of the qualities of his mother. A daughter may want to find a husband who has many of her father's qualities.

Many people who have suffered the pain of divorce can look back on their broken marriages and see that the flaws they discovered in their spouse after the marriage were clearly visible before the marriage. They were simply blind to them at the time. Had they known how to become aware of these things before they married, in all likelihood they would have made a different choice.

Your Children Need Your Help

As you can see, whether you are in a healthy marriage or have suffered the pain of divorce, your children need your help in choosing a mate. No, they do not want you to tell them whom to marry. Nor do they want you telling them whom they cannot marry. So, you have to begin to train them in this process of selection long before they need to put it into practice. In fact, this dialogue needs to begin while your children are still in high school. And, if you choose your opportunities wisely, your teens are likely to welcome discussing with you, from time to time, the qualities and character of the person they would like to marry someday.

As you talk with them, remind them good-naturedly that you also have a special interest in this person because that person will become the parent of your grandchildren—not just your son-in-law or daughter-in-law. So, while you are warning them about the dangers of the *double-funnel theory of mate selection* I talked about in the last chapter, begin to discuss with them more practical ways of choosing the person they want to marry.

Warn them that if they allow romantic attraction to be the driving force in their selections, they will be playing Russian roulette with the rest of their lives. More often than not, the resulting marriages will be painfully disappointing. If at all possible, you want to protect them from that.

Of course, all of us want to marry a person who physically excites us. However, wise people will use their heads to carefully screen their matrimonial prospects before they allow their hearts to fall in love with those prospects.

When your youngsters are in senior high school, begin taking advantage of the informal opportunities you will have to start them thinking about the personality and character they want in the person they will marry. You and I both know they already have the physical qualities well in mind.

Explain to them that during the years a young person is growing up, each person gradually defines his or her character by the choices he or she makes. Once a person is old enough to graduate from college, that person's character is fixed and can be easily seen in attitudes and behavior. It is very important to know what to look for and to realize you are not going to change another person's character.

The Public Transportation Model of Mate Selection

Choosing a mate is somewhat like deciding which train or bus to board. People who depend on public transportation will readily see the comparison. Through the painful experience of getting on the *wrong* train or bus and winding up at the *wrong* destination, they have learned how important it is to pay careful attention to the signs on the front of the vehicle before they decide to get on board. They know where they want to go. So, they want to be sure that the train or bus they board will get them there.

They are not willing to risk arriving at the wrong destination because they carelessly forgot to notice the signs on the front of the bus or train before they boarded it. They know that once they are on board, they are not going to get the driver or conductor to go off the planned route to take them someplace else. The vehicle they board will arrive at the destination indicated by the sign on the front of it.

So, experienced travelers board a vehicle with confidence. They know where they want to go. They have looked carefully at the sign on the front of the bus or train. They know the vehicle is headed for the destination they want to reach, and they are not about to get on board unless the bus or train is going where they want to go.

Teach your children how to read the signs.

In some respects, the people your children will meet in senior high school and college are a lot like buses and trains. If your children learn how to read the signs clearly displayed by the attitudes and behavior of young people around them, they can tell the kind of future toward which these people are headed. If that's not where your children want to go, then they will need your help in developing the wisdom and determination not to travel with people like this.

Character and ambition are more important than looks.

Today, the *drop-dead gorgeous girl* and the *handsome hunk* are the cultural stereotypes that often dominate a young person's mate choice. However, you and I know it takes more than an attractive body to make a desirable spouse.

When your children are in their junior year of high school, look for opportunities to talk to them about ways of identifying a person's character and ambition. Remind them that people can be very deceptive.

Later, if your child finds himself or herself in a relationship with someone who proves to be disappointing, strongly encourage your child to end the relationship. Assure him or her that it is better to suffer the pain of a broken friendship and grieve the loss than to suffer later the pain of a broken marriage.

During their senior high school years, your children may think it is a little too early to think about someone they would like to marry someday, and so may you. However, it takes time and practice for your child to learn how to skillfully assess the character of his or her friends. These observations are not meant to be critical or judgmental. It's a matter of protecting your child from the kind of people who can bring pain and disappointment into his or her life.

One of the practical functions of dating is the opportunities it provides your teens to learn how to discern the characteristics they want or do not want in the person they finally marry. This is why it is wise for your children to socialize with a number of people at the same time. It makes it easier to keep the physical relationships from overheating and gives them more practice in judging a person's character before they are ready to get serious with anyone.

How Do You Begin This Kind of Training?

Your might begin by asking your teen something like this: "Of course, you're not old enough to even think about getting serious with anyone now, but do you ever think about the kind of person you would like to marry? I know you want to marry someone who is physically attractive—at least I did, but what are some of the other important qualities you hope to find in the person you will marry someday?"

As your children share with you, commend them for good character qualities they identify as important in a spouse. Make sure they understand that if these qualities are not visible in the person's attitude and behavior while they are dating, the person will not change after they are married.

What you see is not always what you get!

Talk to them about the importance of using their *ears* more than their *eyes* in choosing a spouse. They may wonder what you mean by this, so explain that a person's appearance is largely the result of his or her genes and good personal grooming. This is what captivates your eyes.

However, the person's conversation comes out of the attitudes and values he or she has chosen to accumulate and store up in the heart from the events and circumstances of life. Is that person more critical than complimentary of others? Does his conversation indicate that he is at peace with himself and with his life? Is her attention always focused on herself, or is she thoughtful of others? Does he always seem to feel cheated, rejected, or abandoned? Is she dependable and responsible? Does he dwell on the negative things that have happened to him in life? Has she learned to turn her tragedies into triumphs? Does that person see himself or herself as a *victor* or a *victim* in life?

Marriage will not change any of these character traits! Make sure that your teens knows that if they don't want to travel through life with a person who sounds like this, they shouldn't get on board thinking they can change the way that person is headed. They should trust the kinds of things their ears hear as they train themselves to listen discerningly to the people around them.

Our eyes are usually focused on what is physically desirable to us. That's why it is important to remember that no one stays young forever. Time alters the physical appearance of everyone. Gravity takes its toll on all of us. Appearance declines over time, but a person's character is enhanced over time. The way a person looks is important. Being neat and attractive enhances anyone's appearance. However, what a person chooses to talk about and how a person acts are even more important. You don't live with *how a person looks.* You live with *how a person lives.*

Jesus said that what a person talks about comes from experiences that person has chosen to store up in his or her heart over time.[2] By listening carefully to a person's conversation you can tell a lot about that person's history and how that person has chosen to deal with it. In conversation you can get an emotional preview of what it would be like to live with that person if you chose to marry him or her. These habits of the heart have been formed over many years, and marriage will not change them.

By helping your children learn some simple listening skills that reveal how a person is choosing to deal with the things that happen to them in life, your children will be able to choose their friends—and, eventually, their mates—more wisely.

Encourage your children to pick up on things like this when they are around their peers. Initially, your children may not see the connection between choosing their friends and choosing their mate. However, as you continue to talk about the need to carefully select the people they will marry, it will become obvious to them that at the appropriate time one of their friendships will turn into a love relationship. Inevitably, they will marry one of their friends.

Choosing Friends

The following information will provide you with some advice your teens should find valuable in choosing their friends.

1. Choose friends who share their faith and values.

I'm not suggesting that your children exclude people who are different from their circle of friends. Including some of these people among their friends will broaden your children's world and deepen their appreciation for different views of life. However, people who share their faith and values will bring out the best in them and provide them with the support they need when things in life are not going well. This is why it is wise to form our closest friendships with people of like values and faith.

When your children begin to think about marriage, remind them that marriage not only joins two people, but it also joins two families. During courtship, a couple may not see this as a very important factor. However, when families share similar faith and values, the family members are able to provide greater support for the marriage of their children.

Religious feelings run deep. Being married to someone of a different faith often results in each person in that marriage neglecting his or her own faith. This denies the couple the joy of a "shared commitment to spiritual discovery."[3] Christians, as well as those from other faiths, are urged by their leaders not to be *unequally yoked together.*[4] There is strong evidence that interfaith marriages are at higher risk for divorce.[5] The earlier in life you can communicate this to your children, the better it will be for them and their marriage.

2. Choose friends who have learned to be happy.

Happiness is a choice people begin making for themselves very early in life. Sooner or later we all discover that we cannot choose happiness for anyone but ourselves. The earlier in life your teens make this discovery, the wiser they will be in the choice of their friends.

If they have a friend who is unhappy, help them to see that their friend's unhappiness is the result of choices that person has made throughout life. That person's unhappiness is not rooted in what has actually happened to him or her, but rather in the way that person has chosen to interpret the things that have happened.

We live with stories about life... not facts!

Remind your children that each of us is confronted with painful challenges in life. This is one of the ways life treats us all very much alike. However, none of us live with just the facts of our lives. We live with a story we tell ourselves about the facts of our lives. Some people are naïve enough to believe that facts are facts and that there is only one *right way* to interpret them.

However, a brief visit to any courtroom will reveal how many different ways the same set of facts can be seen. Skilled lawyers can build many stories around the same set of facts—and so can we!

Each of us chooses our own unique way of interpreting the facts of our life. Of course, we believe the version we have chosen to be the only *true* version. The stories some people tell themselves about the facts of their lives overwhelm them with anger, guilt, anxiety, sadness, and depression. Others choose a version that helps them rise above whatever has happened to them and be happy in spite of it all. These are the kinds of people your children should want for their friends.

Until unhappy people are ready to see that the facts of their history can be viewed in more creative ways, not even God can help them discover a version of their lives that results in their happiness. I had not worked with people very long as a therapist before I discovered this fact: "Until the pain of remaining the same hurts more than the pain of changing, people prefer to remain the same."[6]

This was certainly proved to be true in my own life. My birth was the cause of my mother's death. I could never change that fact, but I did have a choice about how I would live with it. For nineteen years I chose to see myself as my mother's murderer. This left me feeling angry, depressed, and guilty for being alive much of the time.

However, one day as a teenager I stood at my mother's grave and realized she was only nineteen years old when she died. What a tremendous price she had paid to give me life. From that day until now I have chosen to see my mother's death as adding to the value of my life—not as making a murderer out of me.

Some people choose to see the painful things that have happened to them in negative and destructive ways rather than in positive and creative ways. This is a basic difference between happy and unhappy people.

Help your children to see that happiness is a choice. Two people who choose to be happy can make each other happier, but regardless of how happy one of them may be, that one person cannot make the other person happy. That must be his or her personal choice.

This characteristic is particularly important in choosing a spouse. In the idealism of our youth, we believe we are the missing piece to someone else's puzzle of happiness. We see making unhappy people happy as our mission in life. Nothing could be further from the truth. If a person cannot be happy without us, they will never be happy with us. When a happy person devotes himself or herself to making an unhappy person happy, the happy person usually sacrifices his or her own happiness.

Marriage never makes anyone happy. Marriage simply intensifies the state in which marriage finds you. If two people are happy before they marry, they can find greater happiness in marriage. However, if either of them is unhappy, that person will be even unhappier after marriage. The hope that marriage will "make me happy" has been proven to be a false hope for those naïve enough to believe it.

Unfortunately, people make the mistake of believing they are unhappy because they are unmarried. They are sure that if they marry the right person they will be happy. They have never assumed responsibility for their own happiness. Once they are married they are still unhappy, but marriage gives them someone else to blame for their unhappiness.

3. Choose friends with compatible goals in life.

As mentioned earlier, our friends tend to bring out the best or the worst in us. When friends share similar goals, they tend to encourage and support each other in reaching those goals. When friends of the opposite sex have clearly defined vocational goals, their focus tends to be more on their vocational goals and less on the physical dimension of the relationship. This makes it easier for them to control their passions.

However, be sure your children understand that work-related issues will have a major bearing on their marital happiness. For example, there is a big difference between a dual-worker marriage, a single-career marriage, and a dual-career marriage.

The *dual-worker marriage* is the most common form of marriage in the United States. It is comprised of a husband and wife who both have jobs that do not require a college education. Over the years, couples have adjusted to this form of marriage, but it does deny their children a full-time parent in the home.

In *single-career marriages*, one spouse helps to put the other through college and any graduate training necessary to achieve career goals. When this is a shared dream, it can strengthen a couple's commitment to each other.

However, in *dual-career marriages* both spouses want to achieve career goals that require at least a college education. Since few couples can afford to go to college at the same time, a couple has to determine whose educational goals will be met first. This can present them with uncomfortable levels of stress early in the marriage.

Advancements in their careers can also bring tremendous stress on their marriage. If both are offered promotions that would require each of them to live in a different part of the country, their marriage would be challenged.

They will also have to decide how the responsibilities of their marriage will be equitably divided. The issue of when to have children and how the responsibility of parenthood is to be shared can also be the source of uncomfortable debate.

These are just some of the factors that make dual-career marriages a higher risk for divorce.[7] All these vocational patterns should be given important consideration when children evaluate whether a friendship should move toward marriage.

4. Choose friends you can trust.

Some people are fun to be with, but they are very shallow. They lack the capacity to share the deeper parts of themselves with anyone else.

They are awkward and uncomfortable with others who try to share more deeply with them.

These people can brighten up life in lighter moments. However, in marriage they can leave you feeling lonely and sometimes even guilty for overwhelming them with your need to share the deeper parts of yourself with them.

Other people are glad to hear you talk about the intimate personal details of your life, but they cannot be trusted with them. They will betray your confidence and leave you feeling deeply wounded. In the next section of this chapter I will give you information to teach your children how to develop the kind of intimate friendship each of them needs and still be protected from those who cannot be trusted.

The Wheel Theory of Love

The *Wheel Theory of Love* is a good tool for helping your children explore the potential for friendship each person presents while protecting themselves from the pain of rejection and betrayal. It defines four stages through which friendships grow.[8]

1. Establishing rapport

You can take a lot of social pressure off your teens by helping them understand how friendships are formed. They will be relieved to know that no one person can be a close friend to everyone. There is a certain chemistry that attracts people to each other. When it's there, you know it. When it's not, you know that, too. And this doesn't mean that there is anything wrong with anybody. It simply means that the first stage of building a friendship is finding someone with whom you share a common chemistry.

How do you build a friendship? You develop the skill for talking about common interests, current events, and campus activities. These are not deep subjects. However, by carrying on this kind of light conversation, your teen will discover whether or not he or she would like to spend more time with the other person. Remind your teen that the other person will be making the same decision about him or her at the same time.

2. Mutual self-revelation

The purpose of this stage is discovering whether you can trust someone else. The key word here is *mutual*. You are taking a big risk when you reveal more of yourself to another person than that person is willing to reveal about himself or herself to you.

Tell that person something personal enough not to be shared with everyone, but not so personal it would cause you a lot of pain if it were told. Then wait to see if the other person makes an equal investment by sharing something personal with you.

If your confidence is broken or the person fails to reveal anything personal to you, then you know you do not want to carry the friendship any further. You've reached that discovery with minimal risk to yourself. If the person keeps your confidence and invests in you by revealing something personal, you may be ready to take the next step in building your relationship with that person.

3. Mutual dependency

Now that some level of trust has been established between you and your friend, the two of you will want to be with each other more often. You will begin calling each other more frequently, having lunch together at school, helping each other with homework, going to games together, and enjoying each other's friendship in other ways. So the relationship may be ready to move into the next stage.

4. Mutual need fulfillment

This is a critical stage in the friendship. You risk doing something for your friend. Then you see if that person is willing to do something for you. This gives you an opportunity to discover whether the person is a *giver* or a *taker*.

After you have done a few things for your friend and discovered that person is not thoughtful of you, you have learned something very important about that person—he or she does not know how to give.

People generally come in two categories: givers and takers. Givers tend to make the mistake of believing that if they give enough, they can make a *giver* out of a *taker*. However, you can never give enough to make a giver out of a taker. Just as a *giver* has learned how to give, a *taker* has learned how to take. These people are selfish and inconsiderate. Once your teen has discovered that this is the kind of person they are dealing with, they are wise to end the relationship.

However, if the person gives back in return, the friendship may be ready for another rotation. If so, the rapport between the two people will become closer. They will share sufficient confidence to trust to each other the deeper things about themselves. This will make them want to spend more time together. Consequently, they will be willing to do more for each other. So, the wheel of friendship continues to turn.

At some point, this kind of friendship may turn into a love relationship. Eventually, an engagement to be married may result from this kind of patient, painstaking, persistent building of a love relationship.

Before Your Child Becomes Engaged

When your son or daughter begins to feel he or she might want to become engaged, insist that your child have a serious and honest talk with his girlfriend or her boyfriend about the history each person is bringing into the relationship. The following questions should be answered by each person.

- Have you ever had sex with someone else?
- Have you ever been involved in a pregnancy?
- If so, is there a child as a result?
- Was there an abortion?
- Were you ever sexually abused as a child?
- If so, how was this dealt with, and how has it affected your views of sexuality?
- If you needed therapy because of childhood sexual abuse, would you be willing to go for treatment before the engagement?
- Have you ever had a sexually transmitted disease?

- If so, what was it?
- How was it treated?
- Was the disease cured, or is it simply in remission?
- Are you willing to be tested for a sexually transmitted disease *before* the engagement?

As sensitive as these questions may be, your son or daughter deserves to know these things about a person before committing to marriage. In some cases, what they discover may end their relationship. However, this should come as a relief to everyone concerned. Even though grief over the loss is inevitable, it does not begin to compare to the bitterness and disappointment of discovering this information after an engagement or marriage.

During this time of discovery, they should also be honest with each other about their family history. Is there a history of mental illness in either family? Any areas that might prove to be troubling after the engagement and marriage should be surfaced and explored.

If either person has been previously married, what was the cause of the divorce? Would the divorced person be willing to allow your child to have a discussion with the previous spouse before the engagement?

Some people are offended at the thought of raising such intrusive questions, but we are talking about your child's future. We are talking about what should be a lifetime commitment. I feel you are only demonstrating a healthy parent's love for your child when you insist that these issues be raised *before* there is any engagement to marry.

Once Your Child Is Engaged

When both families have agreed to the marriage, it is time to face a more important question. What should get the most attention, the wedding or the marriage? Unfortunately, in our culture the wedding tends to get more attention than the marriage.

As parents, we take great care in seeing to every detail of the wedding: the rehearsal, the rehearsal dinner, and the reception have all been planned for months. We want to be sure that the wedding comes off without a hitch.

However, the wedding is simply a traditional ceremony. It is important. I don't mean to trivialize it, but all the weeks and months of planning that go into your children's weddings are just for one day. *Marriage is for life!* Preparing our children for marriage is much more important than planning their wedding. Parents need to keep these priorities in sharp focus.

Taking advantage of the engagement period to talk to your children about marriage is by far a greater gift for them than the most extravagant wedding. Drawing on your own experience, you can tell things you have learned about married living that you believe will be helpful to them.

What Is It Like to Be Married and in Love?

Years ago, the Lord gave me this definition of married love, and I have used it to help thousands of couples define the practicality of marriage:

> Married love is a persistent effort on the part of two people to create for each other the circumstances in which each can become the person God intended him or her to be, a better person than he or she could become alone.[9]

Notice, married love is an effort. People who stay married work at it. If the marriage is to be fulfilling for both partners, the effort has to be mutual and persistent. No one person can love enough to make a marriage work. The husband's task is to create the circumstances in which his wife can flourish. She will need to do the same for him. In that kind of environment, each person will grow into the person God intended him or her to be—a better person than either of them could have become without the other.

Before the Wedding

Most of us would have welcomed help in managing the awkwardness of our wedding night and the first few weeks of marriage. This phase of marriage has been so fantasized that it often falls short of what a couple expects. You can make these early weeks of marriage much easier for your children by having a talk with them a couple of weeks before they are married.

The next two chapters contain some practical guidelines for conversations both parents can have with their son or daughter, with specific information for a father/son talk before a son's wedding and a mother/daughter talk before a daughter's wedding. I hope these suggestions will help you to create memorable moments with your children that will deepen your relationships.

Make expectations of the wedding night realistic!

Often couples have so idealized the wedding night that it is impossible for their experience to fulfill their fantasies. Help them to adjust their expectations by walking them through the realities of their wedding day. The pace of the last several days before the wedding ceremony will be frantic. So many details have to be remembered. There is the stress of the rehearsal. After that, comes the enjoyable but emotionally draining rehearsal dinner. The level of excitement on the wedding day is impossible to anticipate. After the ceremony the photographer will have to have his day. Finally, attention has to be given to the details of the reception, the need to be loving and hospitable to all family members and guests, the opening of the gifts, the garter ritual, the throwing of the bride's bouquet, and on it will go.

You might want to say to your son or daughter, "By the time you get where you are going for the night you will be exhausted. So, be considerate and sensitive to each other. Remember, you have a honeymoon in front of you. You may want to make love on your wedding night, but both of you may be so worn out that you agree what you need most is a good night's rest. Don't let that disappoint you. You have your honeymoon and the rest of your life to make love. So, lower your expectations about your wedding night. Don't worry about disappointing each other. Just be comfortable. This will make your wedding day much more enjoyable for you."

Now it's time to set aside some special time with your son or daughter. Use the material in the following two chapters to plan these preparation times.

Chapter 18

A Father's Premarital Talk With His Son

Some time before the wedding, have a night out with your son. Do something both of you enjoy doing together. However, be sure the activity is consistent with having a serious talk about marriage.

Then, tell your son that just as he wants his wife to be sensitive to his needs and meet them for him, he will want to be sensitive to his wife's needs and meet them for her. He should be able to distinguish between his needs and her needs.

Honestly acknowledge: "I'm your dad. I have the same hormones rushing in my body that you have rushing in yours, and I know how much you anticipate a sexual feast on your wedding night. However, it's very important for you to be sensitive to your wife's romantic needs on that night as well. If you want her to continue to be sexually exciting for you in the future, then stay romantically exciting for her."

When I talk with couples, I try to teach what I practice. This changes considerably what I teach. For example, at the conclusion of one trip when Priscilla and I had been away from each other for the longest time since we had been married, I wanted her to know how much I had missed her. When she arrived at the airport, I gave her a card. The card showed a cute little kitten lying sideways with a sad look on his face, and on the inside it said: "I've been sad without you and missing you."

When we got to the car, there was a pink rose and another card waiting in the seat where I knew she would be seated. When we arrived home, on the pillow where I knew she would be sleeping with me that night was a dozen red roses and another card. We had been married ten years at that time.

Tell your son that if he and his wife want to keep the sparkle in their marriage, he has to stay romantic, and she has to stay erotic. If he doesn't stay romantic, and she doesn't stay erotic, their marriage is going to be Boredom City after the first two or three years. Their lovemaking will become routine, mechanical, predictable, and boring. The bubbles and the excitement will be gone. The newness will have worn off. The resulting dullness and boredom will set both your son and his wife up for some outside person's seductive traps.

So before your son's wedding, let him know that if he wants to be a happily married man for life he has to be romantic for life—not just during the time he is winning his wife's love.

Priscilla and I have some friends who envy our relationship so much they tell us they can hardly wait until we are "old married people." Well, if we can help it, we are never going to be "just old married people." We are going to stay newlyweds. We are going to keep the excitement in our relationship.

A Wife's Fantasies Are Different From Her Husband's

Your son should know that his wife's fantasies are just as real to her as his are to him, but they are different from his. For example, he can hardly wait to feast his eyes on her nakedness. This is something women need to understand about men. Regardless of what a wife thinks about her body when she looks in the mirror, her body is gorgeous to her husband. The wise wife will resist saying to her husband, "You are just saying that because I know what you want." Instead she will say something like, "Honey I really appreciate that; it means a lot to me to know that I'm still attractive to you."

Every wife needs to know that she continues to be attractive to her husband. Tell your son to realize that just as he fantasizes about her nakedness, she fantasizes about being in his arms and hearing him tell her how wonderful she is to him.

As you begin to realize how different a couple's fantasies are, it becomes obvious that God has designed marriage so that you cannot be selfish and succeed in it.

Erotic versus Romantic Needs

A wife has less need to be erotic because she has fewer erotic needs than her husband. A husband is going to find it less important to be romantic because he has fewer romantic needs than his wife. So each person has to learn to give a kind of love they do not have as great a need for if both of them are going to find their needs met in each other. As I said above, God has designed marriage so that you cannot be selfish and succeed in it.

In your talk with your son, remind him that one of the biggest challenges in marriage is for each spouse to imagine what life would have been like had they been born a member of the opposite sex. So say something to him like, "Son, you will need to learn to think like a woman and to feel like a woman if you are going to fulfill your wife's romantic needs. She has different hormones than you. She has grown up with different cultural expectations than you. You need to become a specialist in anticipating your wife's romantic needs and meeting them for her. You are to take the initiative in meeting her needs. You are to love her as Christ loves the church. He anticipates our needs, and He is there for us."

Advise your son to let his wife teach him how to make her body feel good. Many married men are unaware of female anatomy. It's as if we are willing to do whatever preparation work is necessary for us to get what we want, but it never dawns on us to ask our wife to show us what feels good to her. Suggest to your son that he ask his wife to guide his hands and tell him what feels good to her.

A wife may be thinking, *Well if my husband really loved me, wouldn't he know what makes me feel good?* No. The most loving husband in the world is not a fortuneteller. He cannot read his wife's mind. She knows her body better than her husband. She knows what turns her off. She knows what turns her on. It is unfair for her to keep him in the dark about what sexually excites her. So, advise your son to let his wife teach him what feels good to her.

The Mystery of Orgasm

One of the big mysteries of the honeymoon is why orgasm occurs so easily for the husband and sometimes seems so difficult for the wife. This is due partly to the different levels of orgasmic skills the husband and wife bring into the marriage.

Sexual orgasm is something you learn how to do. Like any other learned behavior, it improves with practice. Since men are more likely to masturbate than women, and masturbate more frequently than women, they often enter marriage with more highly developed orgasmic skills. However, with more practice the wife develops orgasmic skills that are just as advanced as her husband's. Couples would be more comfortable with these differences if someone would explain the circumstances responsible for them.

One other question that arises early in some marriages is, "Why does orgasm happen so quickly for the husband and more slowly for the wife?" Well, this is just another evidence God has designed marriage so you cannot be selfish and succeed in it.

Let your son know that if his wife is going to achieve orgasm, it will take twenty minutes to an hour from the beginning of foreplay until she has an orgasm. This is the normal response time for a healthy woman.

Often early in the marriage the husband is thinking, *Come on, honey. Come on!*

And the wife is thinking to herself, *Slow down and enjoy the trip, sweetheart.*

In most cases, giving your son this kind of information before his wedding night will be invaluable to him. Let him know that every time he needs an orgasm, his wife may not need one. He should never leave her with the feeling that her orgasm is an essential proof of his manhood. When she wants an orgasm, then he has the privilege of providing one for her, but it should fulfill her needs, not his.

There are times when she may say something to him like, "Honey, I just want to make you happy this time." As long as he is meeting her romantic needs, he should not feel selfish in allowing her to meet his erotic needs. So his wife is never pressured to have an orgasm for him. When she has an orgasm, she has it for herself.

Within the first twenty minutes of foreplay, her body will tell her what she needs from her husband to bring her to orgasm. Then, verbally or nonverbally, she should guide her husband's activity in raising the level of her sexual excitement to give her the pleasure she deserves and he delights to bring her.

Practical Sexual Advice From the Bible

When the wife wants orgasm, her husband should provide that for her before he climaxes. Would you believe that this kind of practical advice is in the Bible?

Here is the way the Scriptures read from the King James Version, "Let the husband render unto the wife due benevolence" (1 Corinthians 7:3, KJV). Didn't those King James translators have a nice way of putting it? "Due benevolence"...what does that mean? When the wife needs an orgasm, her orgasm comes first. Why? Because God designed the wife's body so that she can continue to enjoy lovemaking after she has experienced orgasm. The husband finds this difficult or impossible. So, once he has provided her the pleasure she needs, then she provides him with the pleasure he has been anxiously anticipating.

"Due benevolence" implies that early in the marriage a couple should discover the frequency of each other's need for orgasm. This is the pleasure each of them is to duly provide for the other. So, when a four-times-a-week man is married to a four-times-a-month woman, you have some negotiating to do. Over time, you come up with a frequency that leaves him feeling loved and doesn't leave her feeling used.

This is all part of the father/son talk before the marriage. Help your son to understand that his wife will enjoy meeting his needs even if she doesn't have an orgasm. Every newly married man needs to know that. Just as he is excited to see how she's going to react to some romantic surprise he has planned for her, she's excited to see what her body does to excite him and fulfill his needs.

Chapter 19

A Mother's Premarital Talk With Her Daughter

Tell your daughter how important it is for her to be sensitive to her husband's erotic needs. It will help her if you will tell her frankly how you got and kept her father's attention before you were married. You might say something like, "Honey, you and I both know that there is a certain amount of flirtation and seduction involved in getting a man's attention, and as a wise woman, you shouldn't stop that after he marries you."

Remind her that her flirtatious seduction of him is part of what made her attractive to him. It will be an important part of *keeping* her attractive to him. A wise woman continues to flirt with and be seductive with her husband.

Reassure your daughter that it is normal for her husband's fantasies to be more visual and auditory than hers. In talking with your daughter, say something to her like, "Share your nudity freely with your husband, honey. He needs that. You may tend to be shy with him at first, but get over this as soon as possible."

Let your daughter know how much it means to a man for his wife to be sexually free enough to initiate sex with him, especially when she feels a need for orgasm, but also at other times. Let her know that it is inconsiderate for a woman to put the burden of initiating sex on her husband all the time.

If your daughter questions this advice, explain to her, "Well, honey, how would you feel if your husband came home some night and found that the candles you had lit in the bedroom were emitting an obviously sexy fragrance? Then he notices that you have romantic music playing softly in the background. Then although you thought the negligee you were wearing would light any normal man's fire, your husband simply sits down in the family room and begins to read the paper or watch the news on television. How would you feel?"

You might want to tell her, "If your father were to respond to me that way, I would feel devastated. It would be obvious to me that he no longer found me sexually desirable."

Help your daughter to understand that her husband needs to know that she finds him sexually desirable. Remind her to never forget that.

Some wives make the mistake of assuming that simply accommodating their husband's sex needs leaves their husbands feeling sexually fulfilled. This may leave him feeling *serviced*, but it does not leave him feeling *loved*. Every husband needs to know his wife finds him physically desirable.

I've talked to many men who have committed adultery. I always ask them, "What was there about this woman that made her so attractive to you?"

Many, many times, with sadness in their voices, they have said to me, "I guess it was that she left me with the feeling that she physically desired me."

In such moments I have often found myself thinking, *Why should a man have to go outside of his marriage to find a woman who makes him feel that she physically desires him?*

Help your daughter to understand that just as she needs to know that her husband sexually desires her, he also needs to know that she finds him physically desirable. By initiating sexual contact and sexual activity with him, she is drawing him closer and closer to herself. She needs to feel as free to touch him erotically as he is to touch her.

Of course, committing adultery is never justified. It is not only a very destructive sin against the marriage, but it also makes it even less likely that the fire a spouse had wished to be kindled in his or her marriage will ever be lit. A couple takes a big step toward protecting their marriage from this agony when they keep alive their passion for each other.

As her mother, give your daughter permission to play "Show and Tell" with her husband on their honeymoon. You can't imagine how liberating this will be for her. After all, each of them has discovered what sexually feels good to them. One fun part of the honeymoon is to share their discoveries with each other. This will probably end up in a discussion about what couples of faith should be able to enjoy in their lovemaking.

Let her know that God wants His married children to enjoy creative freedom in their lovemaking. He doesn't really say much about regulating a married couple's sex life. He simply gives us three guidelines:

1. Since our bodies are temples of the Holy Spirit, whatever is done in our lovemaking should not bring physical or emotional harm to either partner.[1]

2. Since we are "heirs together of the grace of life," whatever is done should be done by mutual inclination and consent.[2] There should be no coercion. You talk about what you want to try. You try it. If you like it, you keep it in your sexual repertoire. If you don't like it, you try something else. Over the years, stay creatively experimental so that you build a growing repertoire of sexual activities with which both of you feel comfortable.

   You may want to go to the personal section of a major bookstore and choose a sex manual that you would feel to be appropriate for your daughter and give it to her before she leaves on her honeymoon. This could be a fun gift for your children on their honeymoon—especially since it came from the bride's mother. What a unique step toward a wonderful start in your relationship with your new son-in-law! And scanning the contents before you wrap it up for your daughter may bring some delightful surprises to your husband.

3. Third, as people of faith we are not to have unnatural sex. A careful reading of Romans 1:21–27 makes it clear that women of faith do not have sex with other women, and men of faith do not have sex with other men. However, this pas-

> sage has nothing restrictive to say about the sexual freedom God wants His children to enjoy in marriage.

In your conversation with your daughter, be sure you make her comfortable enough to raise any remaining questions she may have. Trust me; she will never forget this conversation. Regardless of how close the two of you have been, this time together will more strongly bond you to each other. Urge her to pass the tradition on to her daughter once she becomes engaged.

The challenge of being the primary source of information about sex for your children does not end with their wedding. In the next chapter, I will be talking to you about ways you can enrich your children's marriage after they say "I do."

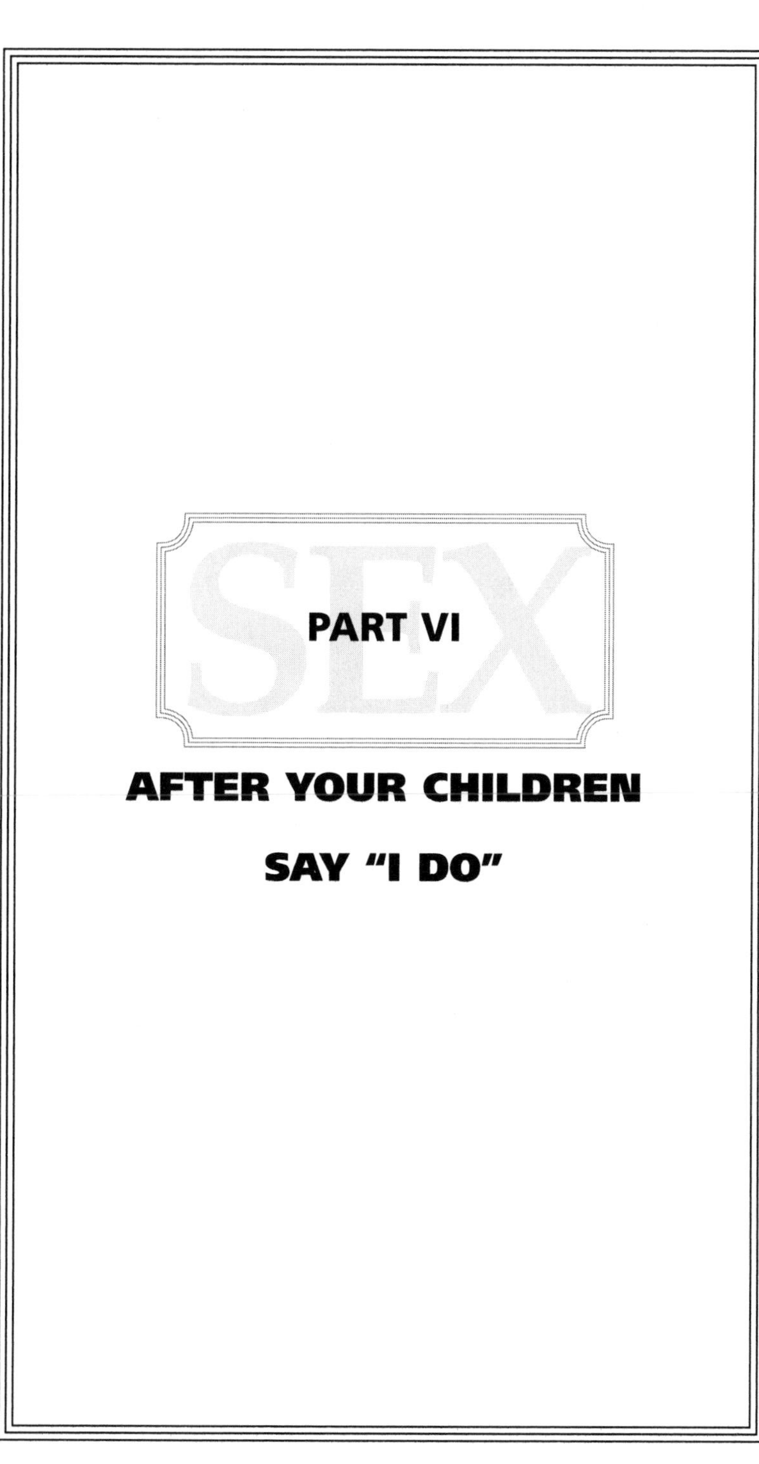

PART VI

AFTER YOUR CHILDREN SAY "I DO"

Chapter 20

Monitoring Your Children's Marriages

Pregnancy, parenting, midlife, and aging all bring special challenges to a couple's sexual relationship. Parents who have already dealt with these issues in healthy ways can provide their children with rich resources in dealing with these issues.

We usually associate words like *aftercare* and *perpetual care* with surgery and cemeteries. Few of us ever think of them as having anything to do with marriage... especially our child's marriage.

However, by lovingly monitoring your child's marriage through the transitional stages you know are ahead for them, you can provide the kind of *aftercare* and *perpetual care* that make these transitions safer and more comfortable for them. In this chapter I will be making some practical suggestions for parents who want to provide this kind of healthy monitoring for their child's marriage.

Monitoring Is Different Than Mentoring

Today, a growing number of couples want to be mentored through the early part of their marriage. You need to understand the difference between *mentoring* and *monitoring.* A *mentor* is someone who performs a very different service than a monitor. A mentor is a trusted guide, tutor, or coach.

The marriage mentoring movement is a rather new attempt to help couples build marriages that last for life. Many religious organizations are developing marriage mentoring programs to help couples during the first year or two of their marriages.

Couples who grew up in homes where their parents modeled a healthy marriage for them will see mentoring simply as a resource for marital enrichment and growth. However, other couples who grew up in divorced families, stepfamilies, or single-parent families have never had the opportunity of learning how to be married from people who have succeeded in the challenge. Many of these couples can benefit greatly from a relationship with an older couple trained to mentor couples through the adjustment period of marriage.

The newly married can seek help from their mentors in dealing with nonsexual issues they might be reluctant to share with their parents. The older couple can offer them more objective help than you, because their view of the marriage is not prejudiced by a parent-child relationship with either spouse.

Trying to be marital mentors for your own children is fraught with all kinds of risks and dangers. Many times when you know how deeply your child has been hurt by his or her spouse, you are tempted to remember the pain long after your child has forgiven his or her spouse and forgotten those issues they shared with you. However, your ambivalent feelings toward your child's spouse may continue to smolder.

If your child and his or her spouse want to be mentored by another couple, commend them for caring that much about the longevity and success of their marriage. Skilled and well-trained mentors can provide secure and neutral space for a newly married couple to negotiate their differences and resolve their conflicts.

Mentoring Is *Not* Counseling

Although marriage mentors should have special training for mentoring couples, they are *not* marriage counselors. Healthy mentors will make this point very clear to the couple they are mentoring. Mentoring takes place in a much more informal environment than counseling. Often mentoring occurs while the two couples are enjoying some mutually desirable social activity together.

Mentors usually meet with a couple three to six times during the first year of marriage. Their primary function is to model a healthy marital relationship and to share some practical ways the couple can keep their commitment to God and to each other healthy through the years.

As a caring parent, be sure to inquire about the training of those who may have accepted the responsibility of mentoring your child's marriage. Responsible mentors will not get involved in sexual counseling. Unless a mentoring couple has had professional training in managing sexual marital issues, opening these intimate boundaries in a mentoring relationship could put both couples at sexual risk.

Parents Can Be Healthy Monitors

However, if over the years you have built an open relationship with your child in defining the role sex plays in a healthy life before they are married, this provides the basis for your understandable concern that your child and his or her spouse enjoy a healthy sex life after they are married. So you are in an excellent position to perform an invaluable service to your child by *monitoring* their sexual relationship from time to time during their marriage.

Your success in this effort is dependent upon both you and your child clearly understanding the role of a monitor. A *monitor* is "one who watches, keeps track of, or checks usually for a special purpose." Your purpose in monitoring the sexual relationship your child has with his or her spouse is just to be sure this part of their marriage is growing and maturing in a healthy way. It also allows your child an opportunity to benefit from the information and experience you have gleaned through the years.

In the best of all possible worlds, a mother and daughter or father and son are comfortable in openly discussing sexual issues with each other. When this is the case, it is usually safer and more comfortable for a daughter to seek counsel from her mother and a son from his father. However, in some cases, for a number of reasons, the child may have access to only one parent. In that event, the one parent needs to be comfortable enough with the sexual issues of life to discuss them in a healthy way with either a son or daughter.

Monitors Are Overseers

Without intruding into this intimate and sensitive area of your child's marriage, you can wisely monitor their relationship. In doing so, you must clearly understand the difference between a *monitor* and a *mentor*. Mentors are teachers and mediators. Monitors are overseers. Monitors want to be sure that whatever they are monitoring is going well.

Wise parents can monitor their child's marital sexual relationship without arousing resentment or making their child feel that his or her privacy is being intruded upon. If things are not going well, as a loving monitor you can help your child and his or her spouse to identify areas that need attention and point them to appropriate sources of help.

Monitoring Your Child's Early Married Love Life

When you remember how sexually awkward you probably felt during those first few weeks and months of marriage, you will quickly see how helpful it would have been if you had found someone you could trust with this intimate area of your life. If a son has a father he can talk to or a daughter has a mother she can talk to about how to deal with those moments of sexual awkwardness of early marriage, it helps them become more relaxed and patient in achieving a comfortable and enjoyable sexual adjustment.

Sexual Insensitivity Can Cause Lasting Pain

Sometimes in those sensitive moments of sexual intimacy, a husband or wife can do clumsy things or make mistakes in judgment out of ignorance, embarrassment, or impatience. Even though the one partner did not intend to deeply offend or hurt their spouse, the emotional pain can last for several years. In some cases the marriage never does overcome it.

I have known many couples who have suffered through years of marriage because of such mistakes. Careless remarks or impatient gestures made in such uneasy moments carry with them the excruciating memories of sexual rejection, which can take a lasting, painful toll on a couple's sexual pleasure.

If your children have someone they respect who can assure them that sexual awkwardness is normal during the first few weeks and months of marriage, it will relieve the anxiety of thinking that their sexual relationship should have been going better, sooner. As their parents—and marriage monitors—that is an important role you can fill. Help your child to see that being loving, kind, and patient with each other will prevent most of these impatient remarks or sudden impatient gestures that leave one or both of them feeling painfully rejected and misunderstood. This is one of the functions of healthy parental aftercare you can provide for your child's marriage.

If you have the kind of open relationship with your children that we've been talking about in previous chapters, then you are in a perfect position to help your child and his or her spouse to create the kind of emotional climate necessary for learning the art of lovemaking. Assure your child that as the two of them tune into each other spiritually and emotionally, their bodies will inevitably follow their hearts.

Making Love versus Having Sex

There is a big difference between *making love* and *having sex*. Sexual skills can be learned by any couple who loves each other. However, love can only be experienced and expressed. If your child *loves* his or her spouse, then the skills for enjoying an exciting sex life can be learned through good information from healthy sources, the willingness to experiment, and plenty of patience, practice, and time.

Some people have learned to be *sexual pros* by being promiscuous, but they are very lonely. They know how to *have sex,* but they don't know how to *make love.* Other people love each dearly and are deeply committed to their marriages, but they are starving for wild passionate love because they never learned healthy sexual skills. As a healthy parent you do not want your child to suffer from either of these dilemmas.

So reassure your children that as their love deepens for each other, they will become more relaxed and able to learn more and more about the erotic art of making love. After all, sexual lovemaking is not something you do *to* each other or *for* each other. It is something you enjoy doing *with* each other.

If you have kept your marriage sexually alive and growing, you will always be at least two decades ahead of your children in this wonderful adventure. Depriving them of the benefit of that experience if and when they need it would be sad.

In the beginning of marriage we are all sexual amateurs. However, the longer we live together, the more relaxed and skilled we can become in exploring and discovering the pleasures God wants us to enjoy in the sanctity of marriage. As long as we are healthy, we never get too old to enjoy sex. Tell your child that!

Is Your Child's Married Love Life Any of Your Business?

Absolutely! After all, your marriage and family will be deeply affected by any sexual problems that develop in your children's marriages. For example, suppose your daughter marries a man who shows little or no sexual interest in her. This would be devastating for her. In most cases, the wife takes the blame for her husband's lack of sexual interest in her. I don't know that a man is able to realize how devastating it feels to a woman when she is not able to sexually excite her husband.

On the other hand, I have known women who stayed in emotionally abusive marriages for years because they were too ashamed or embarrassed to talk to anyone about it. They even feared to raise the subjects with their spouses because they were convinced they would only confirm what the women already suspected—that they were the cause of it. Loving parents can help their daughter realize how abnormal this is and urge her to confront her husband with their need of professional help.

On the other hand, suppose your son marries a woman who is too sexually anxious or afraid of his body to tolerate touching his genitals or allowing any of his seminal secretions to touch her. If you have raised him to be comfortable talking to you about the sexual issues of his life, and you, as his father, inquire about how he and his wife are doing sexually, he has an opportunity to tell you his concerns. Then you can explain to him how abnormal his wife's reactions are and urge him to confront his wife with their need to seek professional help to remedy their problem.

The Initial Approach

After the first two or three months of the marriage, find a private moment when you can inquire frankly about how your child and his or her spouse are getting along sexually. Before asking any questions, say something like this to your child: "You know how open and frank our family has always been in discussing the sexual side of life. So, I feel I would be failing you as a father (mother) if I didn't have a talk with you about how your sexual relations are going in marriage. I know some of the questions I'm going to ask you may appear to be intrusive, but I love you so much I just can't be at peace until I know that the two of you are building an open and loving sex life."

Before you have this postmarital discussion with your child, mentally rehearse the way you want to pose your questions. This will help you to be as discreet as possible. Then you can begin to question your child about the sexual issues of the marriage relationship. A mother may want to ask her daughter some of the following questions:

- Are you comfortable with your husband's body?
- Is he comfortable with your body?
- Have you been able to show him what feels good to you?
- Has he been able to show you what feels good to him?
- Are there ways in which you would like for him to give you pleasure that make him uncomfortable?
- Are there ways in which he would like for you to give him pleasure that make you uncomfortable?
- Has intercourse been painful for you?
- Has orgasm been difficult for you?
- Does he provide orgasm for you when you need it?
- Are you satisfied with the frequency of your love sessions?
- Is your husband satisfied with this frequency?

When a father is talking with his son, in addition to the questions above, he may want to ask these questions:

- Can you talk comfortably with your wife about the sex life you want?
- Can you make her comfortable enough to tell you the kind of sex life she wants?
- Is your wife patient at times when maintaining an erection is difficult for you?
- How have the two of you managed times when you have prematurely ejaculated? (Assure your son that performance anxiety can be the source of erectile difficulties and premature ejaculation. Assure him that if this is the source of his problem, with time and experience it will diminish. If it doesn't, with professional help, these problems can be easily treated.)

If the information you get from intimate conversations with your child indicate things are going well sexually in the marriage, you will be relieved. However, if your conversation reveals that there are some serious sexual problems in your child's marriage, your child and his or her spouse will be very grateful to you for caring enough to inquire and direct them toward appropriate sources for help.

You know that *you are not qualified to provide this kind of help*. However, you are in a position to recognize their need for sexual counseling. You will want to urge your child and his or her spouse to see a competent professional person who shares their faith and has been trained to do sexual counseling.

Then, at the risk of being thought to be a little too nosy, keep inquiring about the issues that concern you until you know they are being satisfactorily addressed. When the issues have been resolved, your child will thank you for this—and so will his or her spouse.

Indications of Sexual Problems

As a parent you should be sure your children know that it takes from six months to two years for some healthy marital partners to achieve a comfortable level of sexual satisfaction. Often, frequency of lovemaking is a sensitive issue during this adjustment period. The husband may want sexual relations more frequently than his wife. Or the wife may want to make love more often than her husband.

In the early months of the marriage, sexual intercourse may occur as frequently as once a day to two or three times a week. For young married couples to be making love less than one time a week or more than once a day on a regular basis is very unusual. This usually means that the needs of one partner are being disregarded and those of the other are being neglected.

As I mentioned earlier, in the beginning of the marriage, reaching orgasm may be somewhat difficult for the wife, and refraining from premature ejaculation may be a similar problem for the husband. A few months into the marriage it may be reassuring for you to remind them of this.

There are some issues that should raise your concerns, including: an obvious lack of sexual desire on the part of either spouse; the husband's inability to erect or to maintain an erection; the wife's lack of lubrication, pain upon penetration, or inability to achieve orgasm. If your information indicates any of these problems, clearly explain to your child that these are treatable problems, but they are not self-correcting. That is, time is not going to heal them. Get a commitment from your child to address these issues with his or her spouse as soon as possible.

Self-help Is Less Threatening

In the beginning of their marriage relationship, couples are more open to self-help approaches to any sexual problems they may be having. Suggest that the two of them engage in an open, loving, and honest definition of their difficulty. Once they are agreed on the nature of their problems, suggest that they go to the self-help section of a major bookstore or library and together scan books that address the areas that concern them. After examining the credentials of the authors to be sure of their professional qualifications, they should agree to purchase one or two books. Then, they will need to commit themselves to reading and discussing together the suggestions the authors make about dealing with their sexual issues. Finally, in good faith they need to agree that two or three times a week they will follow the instructions of the authors until they have resolved their issues.

If the self-help approach has not resolved their issues or significantly reduced them in six months, the two of them should seek the help of a competent sex therapist. Usually the earlier a couple gets into therapy, the sooner they resolve their problem.

Care should be taken to be sure that the therapist shares or, at least, will respect their faith in his or her treatment approach with them. The couple can express these concerns to their physician. He can help them find a sex therapist who meets these needs.

What If One Person Refuses Any Kind of Help?

What often happens in a marriage where one spouse is unwilling to deal with sexual problems is that sooner or later the frustration of normal needs for affection and sexual pleasure make a husband or wife vulnerable to an adulterous affair. When this happens, the spouse who has had the affair often gets blamed totally for all the sexual problems in the marriage. Sexual frustration in marriage is never an excuse for adultery! What other options are available when your child finds himself or herself in such a position?

Seek professional help

Encourage your child to make a personal appointment with his or her physician and bring the concerns to the doctor's attention. Ask him for a referral to a sex therapist who will respect their faith. Urge your child to go alone for a consultation. In most cases, the information he or she receives will be helpful, and therapists can be skilled in getting the reluctant spouse into counseling.

Should this effort fail, as a last resort your child may have to consider creating a preventive crisis.

The role of a preventive crisis

A *preventive crisis* is a crisis that is deliberately created to avoid adultery or divorce. Here is how you go about it.

If your child's spouse is refusing to get sexual counseling for a problem, encourage your child to confront his or her spouse with this proposition: "Both of us know we have sexual problems. I am willing to accept responsibility for whatever contribution I am making to these problems. I am willing to go to a competently trained sex therapist that shares or, at least, will respect our faith. The only thing I am unwilling to do is to remain in this kind of relationship, which is destroying both of us and our marriage."

Nearly always, creating this kind of preventive crisis results in the couple getting the kind of professional help needed to correct the sexual problems that are threatening the marriage. By giving your child this kind of advice you are demonstrating that you care enough for them and their marriage to support their determination to get the relief they need. In the process, you prevent the whole family from suffering the pain and conflict that would be provoked by a marital affair or divorce.

Monitoring Your Child's Child-Bearing Years of Marriage

Most couples need from two to five years to master the skills required for marriage. Remind your children that one of the most loving things they can do for their future children is to be sure both of them know how to be married *before* they try to learn how to be parents. These are two different sets of skills. Rarely can a couple learn them simultaneously.

Preparing the marriage for children is one of the most important parts of parenting. Remind your children that newborns add stress to the marriage; they do not relieve it. If a couple has taken the time and made the investment necessary to strengthen their love bond to God and each other, then celebrating the creation of a new life will add tremendously to the joy of their marriage.

The conception and birthing experience should be shared events. Encourage your children to participate together in the birthing classes recommended by their obstetrician. Talk with them about the sexual adjustment that may be necessary during the last trimester of pregnancy and the first few months of the baby's life. Be sure they know that the physical depletion of childbirth will take its toll on the sex drive of the mother for a few weeks. Remind them of the many different ways they have discovered for meeting each other's sexual needs that do not involve vaginal intercourse. However, as a mother, you can share with your daughter, and, as a father, you can share with your son the practical role these lovemaking techniques can play in seeing that their love life continues through the pregnancy and during the early months of the baby's life with as little interruption as possible. Hugging, kissing, body massage, caressing, genitally petting each other to climax, and oral activity couples find enjoyable are among the expressions of love available to couples during these months.

As much as your child and his or her spouse will love the baby they have made together, always urge them to keep their love for each other stronger than their love for their child. After all, their love for each other produced the child. And their love for each other will provide their child the secure family environment he or she will need to grow up to be a healthy adult.

Monitoring Your Child's Midlife Marriage

Crises are so common in midlife that when one occurs, we often refer to it as a *midlife crisis*. A number of factors converging during midlife can be responsible for triggering such a crisis. Here are just a few that you can help your children to be prepared for.

Your children's children begin to graduate from high school and leave home.

Once this starts to happen, one parent or the other begins to anticipate the emptiness of the home when all the children are gone. Sometimes this is referred to as the *empty-nest syndrome*. You can relieve some of the grief and depression accompanying this syndrome by reminding your children that their home never has been a *nest* and that it won't be *empty* very long. You can also share some of the practical ways you dealt with them leaving your home to begin their own families.

Shortly after the last child leaves home, some of your children's older children will begin to bring the grandchildren home. (And you will become a great-grandparent!) The wise couple prepares to enjoy the brief respite they will get between these times. Remind your children to think ahead to set some goals for enjoying themselves in this season.

Your children will be confronted by their own mortality once they enter midlife.

When your children can no longer double their ages and expect to be alive at that time, that knowledge will be troubling to them—as it probably was to you and is to most people. It is during our forties and fifties when we usually begin to notice this. Aging starts to take its toll on us—and on our children—at about this time.

Most people notice that not only are they getting older—but also their bodies are showing it! There is nothing wrong with wanting to look as young as possible, but aging has its advantages as well. Remind your children of this. When you have lived long enough to discover that every time the wind blows the boat is not going to sink, a certain comfort and confidence enter your life.

Midlife couples cannot depend on spontaneity to motivate their sex lives. They need to schedule their lives more often, including scheduling time for sex. I remember a friend of ours who used to remind us of this. When we would ask her and her husband to go out with us on Friday night, she would look at us with a little twinkle in her eye and say, "Can't we go some other time? Friday night is Arnie's (her husband) night." Then we would all laugh.

Arnie was in his eighties—and he still had *his* night! He was an inspiration to all of us younger men.

As your children approach midlife, urge them to talk about their love life more with each other and to take the time to creatively plan it.

Midlife affairs are almost always an attempt to deny aging by getting involved with someone much younger. A strong marriage usually survives this kind of an affair, but the wounds are deep, long lasting, and unnecessary. Advise your children of this.

As your children age, model for them how older couples stay in love. Continue appropriate expression of affection in front of them. When they see you walk holding hands or arm in arm with your spouse, they know that although there may be a little snow on the rooftop, there is still fire in the furnace.

Tell them the truth about sex in the later years, just as you talked with them about sex when they were children. Making wild passionate love may take a little longer, and the frequency of your sex needs may have decreased considerably, but everything that used to work still works just fine. As you age sexually together, the intensity of your passion may lessen, but the intimacy of your passion intensifies—and that's not a bad trade off.

Looking back on a lifetime of lovemaking together helps you to see that the love bond between you has been strengthened by the storms you've weathered together. And the celebration of that bond has been intensified by the growing number of times you remember refreshing yourselves together at the love springs you have found in each other's body.

Epilogue

Well, we have reached the end of our journey together. However, you and your children will continue your trip together through life. My hope is that this book will make your family's excursion through life more intimate, exciting, and satisfying by helping you be more open with each other about the sexual side of life.

As you have discovered, a healthy family is never finished helping each other avoid the explosive damage sexual misbehavior can bring to them. Nor is there ever an end to the exciting sexual discoveries we can discreetly share with each other along the way.

I have tried to make this book like an old friend you want to stay in touch with over the years. It is written so that you can begin benefiting from its contents wherever you happen to be in life. And, if you are just beginning to have your children, I hope you will find yourself often going to the shelf where you have stored this book. That way we can continue our conversation over the years while you are helping your children discover the wonderful gift of their sexuality and teaching them to be good caretakers of it.

May they see the wisdom of saving sexual intercourse for marriage and still celebrate the joy of this special gift while they wait for that special person God will bring into their lives! In your older years, may you still be discovering sexual secrets that you can encourage your children to anticipate! After all, God has not called us and our children to deny our sexuality, but to discipline our sexuality and dedicate its celebration to the creation of strong marriages and healthy families.

Appendix A

Commonly Asked Questions About Sex: Dealing With Delicate Issues

The questions explored in this appendix are among those most frequently asked in marriage and family seminars I've conducted across the country over the years. They have not been organized in a particular fashion. With the exception of some editing for the sake of brevity, the questions and the answers are presented in the same manner they were presented in the seminars.

Q. ***When we find out our teenager is having oral sex with someone, should we forbid her to see him any more, or should we strictly chaperone the relationship?***

A. First, make it clear to your daughter that you do not approve of single young people indulging in oral sex. Then clearly explain to her the reasons for your objection.

1. Remind your daughter that God created sex for marriage. When she has sex with anyone outside of marriage (before or after she is married), she complicates her life and the other person's life.

2. Review with your daughter the risks of contracting sexually transmitted diseases through oral intercourse. Most young people make

no attempt to protect themselves when engaging in oral intercourse. Be sure she understands that when she has oral sex with someone, she is having oral sex not only with that person, but also with every person with whom that person has had any kind of sex.

3. Oral sex is just as much a violation of one's virginity as genital intercourse. There is no such thing as *technical virginity.* Any time an orifice of the body is penetrated sexually, whether it's your mouth, your anus, or your vagina, you have had intercourse.

The moral ignorance in this country is demonstrated by the prevailing opinion on many college campuses and high school campuses that until a man's penis goes into a woman's vagina, that couple has not had sex; therefore, mutual petting to orgasm, oral sex, or even anal sex is not having sex.

While we are defining intercourse morally, let's also define adultery morally. Many times a married man or woman will say, "We didn't go all the way." However, any time you give to another person what belongs exclusively to your spouse—even a French kiss—you have violated the bond of your relationship. The word *adultery* means "to another." It comes from two Latin words: *ad*, meaning "to," and *alter*, meaning "another." Whenever you give to another what belongs exclusively to your husband or your wife, you have violated that relationship. From a strict biblical point of view, that violation ends the relationship that began with your wedding.[1]

When I am helping couples to heal from adultery, I tell the spouse who has been offended by the affair, "Your marriage has ended. Even though the license is still on record in the courthouse, in God's sight your husband's (or your wife's) adultery broke your marriage. Now you have a choice; you can recommit to a new marriage, or you can walk out of this man's (or this woman's) life." Most of the time, couples choose to recommit to their marriage.

Then, I suggest that the couple renew their vows, set a new wedding date, and exchange new rings. I advise them to treat the recommitment to each other as though it was a brand-new marriage covenant between them.

Q. ***What do you think would be an appropriate age for our teenager to start dating one on one?***

A. Going with groups of boys and girls should not begin before the sophomore year of high school. Going out with another couple, or two other couples, should not begin before the junior year of high school. Going out with someone alone should be reserved for the senior year of high school. I would still stick to this schedule, even though your teenagers are going to protest wildly.

The last thing we need to do is to rush young people into serious relationships. Even though they protest loudly, if they conform to the rules you have set down for them, ten years from now they will look back and say, "Mom and Dad, we didn't like it at the time, but we are sure glad you put the guidelines there for us."

Q. ***If a person engages in self-pleasure without fantasy or pornography, with whom does that person bond?***

A. Himself or herself. I have referred to this as *narcissistic masturbation*. Such a person usually carries into marriage the need for a secret life of masturbation that is highly likely to become disturbing for his or her spouse when it is discovered. So, why do that?

It's unnecessary in the first place. Why not just fantasize about being married? Be a good steward of your sexuality before you're married. It will help you be a loyal spouse.

Q. ***How do you reinforce abstinence before marriage to your children when you yourself did not practice abstinence, and your children know that?***

A. Mature parents want to protect their children from the mistakes they made. Be honest and up-front, and say to them, "I do not want you to have to deal with the complications of life that I had to deal with because I didn't wait until I was married to have sex with someone. So, this is why I can tell you that sex before marriage does not simplify your life—it complicates your life. I would like to protect you from those complications if I can. I hope you'll see the wisdom of my advice. It is not going to make me love you any less if you do not heed my advice, but it is going to complicate your future. It will also add tension and anxiety to my life as your parent if you choose to be active sexually with others before you are married."

Tell them honestly, "When you get married and have children, you will want to protect your children from the mistakes you have made. Right now I'm the parent, and you're the child, and I'm trying to protect you from the mistakes I've made."

Q. ***How can I help my adult son who is still suffering emotionally because of a childhood sexual abuse by an uncle? How can I help my adult daughter, who was sexually abused by her brother?***

A. Both of these people need to get into counseling or therapy. God can help them deal with the sexual abuse they experienced—and caused—under the guidance of a biblical counselor, a professional person who knows God and knows Scripture. Your children have already lived too many years in the shadows of the past. They can have futures free from the shadows of the past. But obviously, the past is not self-correcting. Time alone is not going to make it go away. So the earlier you can encourage them to get the help they need, the brighter their futures will be.

Q. ***If I caught my three-year-old pleasuring himself, would that be an open door for a sexual spirit to enter his life?***

A. No. Such a belief is superstitious and has no basis in Scripture. Don't be bound by that kind of superstition. If every three-year-old child who pleasured himself or herself were demon possessed, we'd have a nation full of demon-possessed people. Don't think that God is going to discriminate against your child. Deal with that behavior as a normal part of life, and your child will grow out of it in a few years.

Q. ***How do we talk to our children about homosexuality, which has become so accepted and normalized? Almost every teenager is exposed to others their age who have engaged in homosexual activities. Many of them feel a need to recruit others into their circle of activities. How do we explain this behavior to our kids?***

A. I believe homosexuality is unnatural. Why is it unnatural? Homosexuality is unnatural because two members of the same sex cannot naturally reproduce. One of the obligations that we have as human beings is to produce children in whose bodies God can live and be expressed. How can a woman who is sexually linked to another woman, or a man who is sexually linked to another man, reproduce?

Your children will understand this explanation. Explain to them that some people may be born with a genetic predisposition to homosexuality, but people become homosexuals largely because they experience repeated orgasm with members of the same sex. The orgasm reinforces the person's bondage to the stimulus that produced it. That's why children need to be protected from an overexposure of sexual experiences with children or others of the same sex. Sexual orgasm will eventually build an attachment between the child and the source that stimulates him or her to orgasm. This needs to be explained to your child.

Q. We're really struggling with the awareness that our teenage daughter's friends are having oral sex and masturbating with partners. One of them even says she is a lesbian. Should we limit our daughter's involvement with these friends?

A. If you don't exercise control over the friendships of your children as much as is possible, God will hold you accountable. You need to establish clear guidelines for your children, protecting them from sexual environments that could endanger or hinder the Christian perspective of sexuality that you have tried so hard to teach to them. Once you set down the guidelines, if your children choose to disobey you, God will not hold you responsible for what happens to them as a consequence of their misbehavior.[2]

Your children may despise you for your stand on their relationships for a while. They may oppose you with derogatory name-calling or bad attitudes in order to make you feel so bad that you'll let them do what they want to do. But if your experience has taught you that this behavior is going to complicate their lives, out of love for them, you must deny yourselves the reward of their smiles, hugs, and friendship for as long as it takes. Let them know that you are going to be fair in what you expect of them and firm in your response to them. But in spite of the fact that you're going to be firm, you are still going to be friendly.

Q. ***How does a child keep thoughts on marriage if that person does not know his or her future spouse yet?***

A. Why do male children put on adult male hats and neckties, and why do female children put on adult dresses and shoes, if not to fantasize about being grown up and married? We all imagine ourselves in the future. Anticipating that you are going to grow up and get married is a normal, natural anticipation for a child. That's what you want to tell your child.

Q. ***If you are a single parent, how do you explain the sexual questions to your children of the opposite sex?***

A. You give them the answers they are seeking, frankly, honestly, and without embarrassment. If you are a single mom raising boys, you do the same thing that their father would do if he were in the home. One of the things you can do as a mom is let your sons know how special sex is to a woman, but also let them know how physically driven they are. Give them the same guidelines for taking good care of their fantasies that we suggested fathers give their sons. Single fathers should do the same thing for the daughters. Have the same talk with your daughters that we suggested mothers have with their daughters.

Q. ***If someone has not been trained to associate sex with marriage but with shame, can they be healed from this?***

A. Absolutely. God wants to set a person free from this kind of bondage. Good information and godly counsel can assist in the process.

Q. My sixteen-year-old son refuses to allow his male pediatrician to examine his genitals. He becomes very agitated and will not pull down his underwear or let the doctor examine him even though I am present. Is this normal, or should I fear he's had a negative past experience?

A. I'm not sure. He may just be shy and easily embarrassed, or he may have had an unpleasant experience. That's something you need to talk to him about and then proceed accordingly. If you have good rapport with your son and ask him about it in an appropriate setting, he'll probably tell you. Then you can cry with him, have compassion on him, and see that he gets the help to put this behind him. If he reassures you that nothing has happened, and you believe him, then encourage him to grow out of this shyness as he grows up.

Q. How should parents deal with the situation when they find two same-sex children around six years old who are showing each other their genitals? I know I handled it badly; how can it be corrected now?

A. At a time when it's convenient, tell your children, "I made a mistake when I discovered you showing your genitals to your friend." Children are great forgivers. Only adults try to act like they never make mistakes. So, when you tell your child, "When I found you and your friend looking at each other, I didn't handle my response to you very wisely, and I want you to forgive me." For your child it will all be over. Then you can emphasize that it is normal to be curious about how the genitals of other boys and girls look, but it will be healthier for your child to remember to keep his or her genitals personal and private.

Q. ***Are there scriptures relating to courting and dating?***

A. Not that I know of. However, Christians in many countries simply follow the traditional cultural mate selection process. No cultural mate selection system is perfect. Perfectly harmonious marriages are not typical of any culture.

Q. ***How should I respond when I discover my child pleasuring herself?***

A. Sooner or later observing parents are likely to discover their children pleasuring themselves. Prepare for this moment so that it does not embarrass you, shock you, or overwhelm you. A wise way to manage this is to back out of the situation and pretend that you didn't see what you saw. Show your child the same respect that you would want if your child barged into your bedroom while you were having intercourse. Later, remind the child of the importance of thinking about marriage when he or she is having pleasant feelings in his or her genitals.

Respect the child's privacy, but take advantage of the situation later by using it as another opportunity to remind your children to keep their fantasies about growing up and getting married. If the child is pleasuring himself or herself in front of other people, then you will need to calmly stop the activity. Later address the inappropriateness of the social context in which the activity was taking place.

Q. ***What do I do if I discover my child and a group of his or her friends engaging in some kind of sexual play?***

A. Sexual curiosity is normal for children. This is usually pursued in games of mutual exploration. A certain amount of this activity is a normal part of growing up. Here are some suggestions for managing this kind of situation.

1. Don't panic. Remember this is something every parent faces. Your children are not sexual profligates. You probably engaged in this kind of activity when you were a child. So remind yourself that you got through it without it ruining your life, and so will these children.

2. Calmly break up the activity. If only your children are involved, separate them and direct them into other separate activities. If other children are involved, send them home. Then later call their parents and tell them what you found, just as you would want them to call you if they found your child involved in this kind of activity in their home.

3. When you are calm, have a talk with your children. Remind them that their genitals are the personal private parts of their body. Go through your whole speech with them again, reminding them that their genitals are not to be shared with their playmates. Their genitals are personal and private.

As long as the activities are limited to innocent games of discovery, don't punish the children the first time you catch them. Just stop the activity. Later, reinforce your teaching about genital privacy and body privacy.

If other episodes follow later, then noncorporal punishment is appropriate. You may want to ground your children or give them other forms of discipline. Do not use a form of corporal punishment for their behavior because you don't want your children to associate physical pain with sexual pleasure in the disciplinary process.

When your children are old enough, they will want to spend the night with friends and have their friends spend the night with them. Be sure you know personally the parents who will be supervising your children during their night away from home. Make sure their beliefs and values are similar to yours.

If you can't provide a separate bed for your children's overnight friends, then limit the number of times you permit him or her to have a friend over for a night. Why? Because when you put two bodies together in a double bed, let alone in a single bed, there's likely to be body contact. Although a certain amount of exploration is normal, you don't want to create the circumstances where this is frequent, where more life-complicating patterns of behavior may be reinforced.

Monitor the times when your children are having friends overnight at your house very carefully. Make sure that parents of your children's friends do the same when your children are spending the night with their children. Children who are spending the night with each other need to be well supervised.

Q. Why should parents be so careful in these situations?

A. Remember, I said earlier that sexual orgasm tends to form a link, a bond, a tie, between the experience and the source of excitation. So, if you have two boys often sleeping together for long periods of time, and they mutually bring each other to orgasm, what's going to happen? The source of the stimulus will be more and more attractive because of the pleasure provided by that stimulus. If two girls sleep together, and they get involved frequently in mutual sexual pleasuring, what's the normal thing to expect?

Many times homosexual activity early in life, especially if it's between an older male and a younger male, or an older female and a younger female, creates an attraction to members of the same sex because they have become a frequent source of sexual pleasure. A bond has formed between the pleasurable memory and the stimulus that produced it. That bond is not genetically formed. Its formation is not mystical. It is just a consequence of sexual history.

Q. Suppose you surprise your teenage daughter and her boyfriend, or your teenage son and his girlfriend, while they are engaging in sexual activity. What should you do?

A. This is certainly reason for concern...but it isn't a cause for panic. Panic never helps anyone, young people or their parents.

If this should happen to you, withdraw from the scene as discreetly as possible. Later, after everyone has had a chance to be properly clothed and to regain their composure, engage in a healthy dialogue with the teens about the risks involved in such sexual experimentation and the wisdom of reserving deeper sexual intimacies for marriage.

When you discover them you may want to say something like, "I'm very disappointed to find the two of you like this and to see what's going on. Get presentable, and when you're presentable we need to talk."

Talk with them about the risks they take when they engage in sex outside of marriage. Don't moralize to them, and don't dangle them over hell by a thread. Ask them such things as, "Do you understand how what you are doing can seriously complicate both of your lives?"

Show as much concern for your teenager's friend as you do for your own teenager, and hope that the teenager's parents will do the same if they find the same thing going on in their home. Address the inappropriateness of the activity, the far-ranging complications of that activity, and how, in retrospect, they will wish it never took place.

In your talk, remind them of the risk of pregnancy. Although they have received careful instructions in junior high about how to use condoms, there are many people who follow that routine and still become parents. Abstinence is the only sure way to avoid pregnancy. There is no foolproof way for avoiding pregnancy outside of abstinence. I have talked to parents who conceived a child even though the wife was on birth control pills. I have talked to couples who used a diaphragm with spermicidal jelly, but they still got pregnant. I have talked to parents who were using condoms, yet conceived children.

Teenagers should know that that there is no "safe sex" outside of marriage. So you may want to continue, "What are you going to do, son, if you get my daughter pregnant? How are you going to deal with that? Have you given that serious thought?"

Then you can say something to your daughter like, "Honey, what are we, as your parents, going to do if you get pregnant? This has nothing to do with our love for you. This has to do with complicating your life. We would live through it. We would love you through it, and as a family we would get through it. But this is a permanent part of your history that your mom and dad wish you would protect yourself from."

It is important that you talk to them about the risk of pregnancy, the risk of sexually transmitted diseases, and about the hurt they would inflict upon each other when the relationship ends because of an unwanted pregnancy. This is especially important information to discuss with fifteen-year-old, sixteen-year-old, and even seventeen-year-old kids who are living in the home. The likelihood that they will marry the person they are dating at that age is very remote. Tell them, "I know you probably are talking about how much you love each other, (and if they are both Christians) and I know you both love the Lord, but have you stopped to consider that the likelihood the two of you will spend your future together is very remote? What you are doing right now is going to leave both of you damaged and hurt when you break up. It's going to leave my daughter feeling that men are only interested in one thing. She's going to carry that into her marriage with some other man. And, as a young man, it is going to grow calluses on your conscience. If you have been able to use my daughter as a source of your pleasure, you'll use somebody else's daughter in the same way."

Have the courage to talk to them eye-to-eye about the reality they are creating for each other and the complications they are bringing to each other's life. Will that totally cure them? Well, we'll leave that with the Lord, but your task is responsibly managing situations like this. The information I have given you here is an appropriate way to manage the situation.

You would hope that both the young man and the young woman would benefit from such a talk, but whether they choose to benefit from it or not is their responsibility. You were responsible as a parent, and God will hold them accountable for how they choose to respond to your loving and frank conversation.

Q. Can the Lord cleanse your sexual fantasies?

A. Yes, He can. If you have been promiscuous, ask God to help you impose on yourself a six-month discipline of celibacy. Ask Him to help you have no sexual contact with anyone and not to masturbate for six months.

What practical purpose will such a discipline serve? If you have been sexually promiscuous and have eroded your conscience in this area, then the commitment to sexual abstinence must be long enough to reestablish these important sexual boundaries in your conscience. Then be sure to limit your sexual fantasies to having sex with your future spouse so you will be able to form a sexual bond with a person God will send into your life.

Q. Who sets the limits of physical contact in a dating relationship?

A. In seminar discussions I am often asked why so much of the responsibility for setting limits on a couple's physical contact rests with the girl. Although the Scriptures define the same moral standards for both sexes, two biological facts determine my answer.

1. Teenage young men experience much higher levels of testosterone and hormonally induced sexual excitement than teenage young women. This makes the guys less aware of the needs for limits at the very time when they are required.

2. Teenage young women get pregnant.

Morally, young men are just as responsible for the stewardship of their bodies as are young women. However, young women are hormonally better prepared to be the limit setters—and their risks are much higher if the relationship gets out of bounds.

As unfair as it may seem for nature to thrust

such a responsibility onto young women, this is a fact that is not likely to change. Therefore, parents who are raising daughters need to face this reality squarely so they can help their daughters come to terms with it. Explain to your daughter that the more she keeps the physical activity of a relationship above the shoulders, the easier it will be for her to control it.

Your son's conscience will also give him a strong desire to control his behavior. He will feel better about himself when he respects the boundaries Scripture sets for his behavior. He knows intercourse belongs in marriage, and he wants to respect that fact.

Teach him to be sensitive to the sexual risks a young woman assumes in going with him. Help him understand the wisdom of keeping his relationship free from the moral concerns that inevitably result from being sexually active before marriage.

Be sure your son understands that only when he is financially capable of supporting a wife and has provided her with the emotional security of marriage does he have the right to expect her to go all the way with him.

Appendix B

Helping Your Child to Understand Pregnancy

In this appendix you will find many diagrams that thoroughly describe the process of ovulation, fertilization, and implantation during pregnancy. You can use these diagrams to discuss pregnancy with your children. Take the time for them to get a full understanding of each diagram, and refer back to them each time your child and you discuss the issues of pregnancy.

Diagram 1

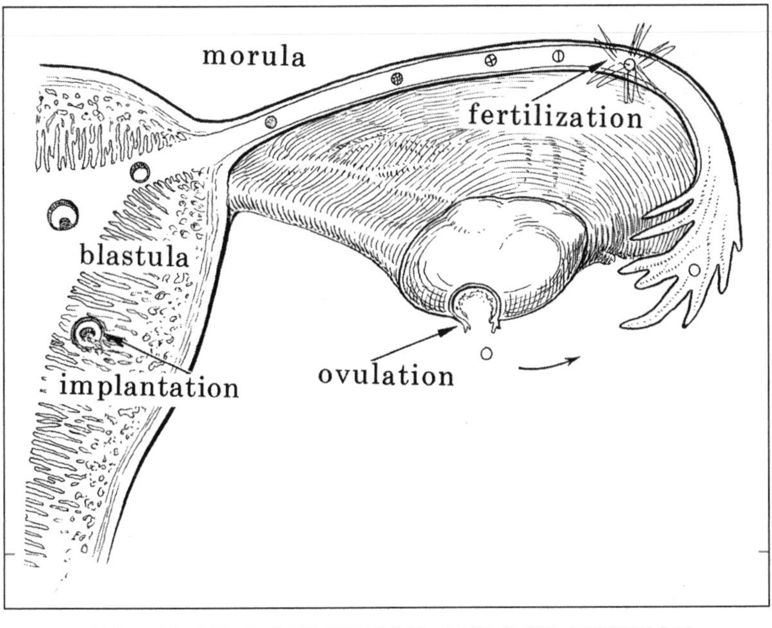

OVULATION, FERTILIZATION, AND IMPLANTATION

Diagram 2

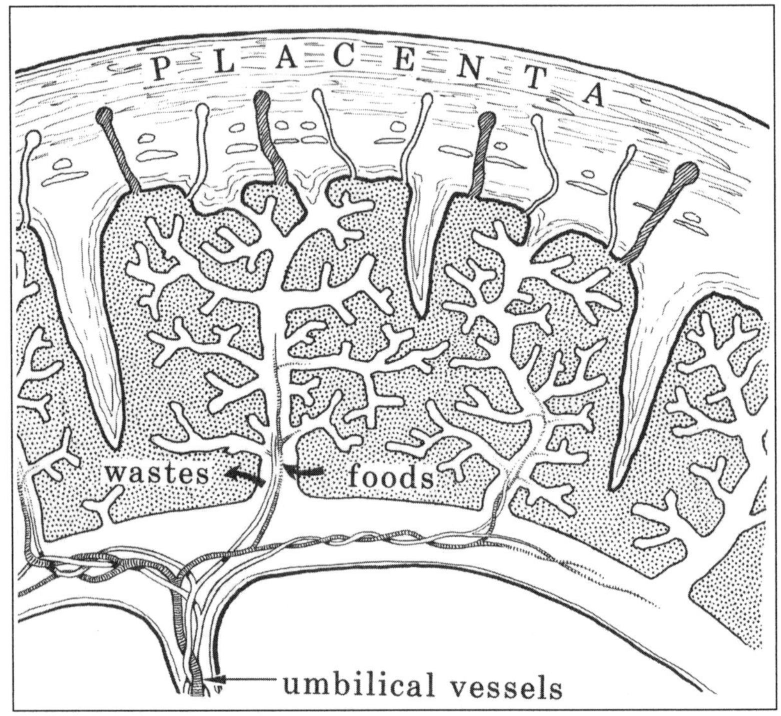

THE UMBILICAL CORD

Diagram 3

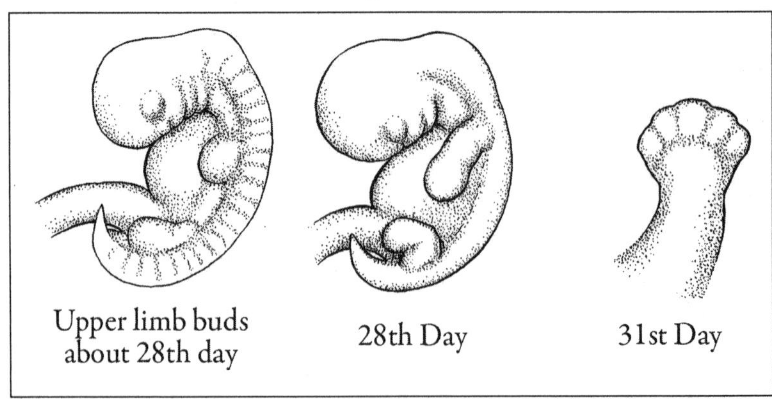

EMBRYONIC DEVELOPMENT OF HAND AND ARM

Diagram 4

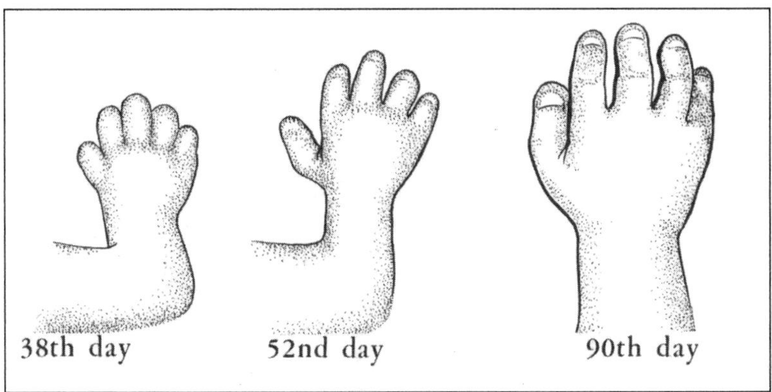

Hand Development Detail

Diagram 5

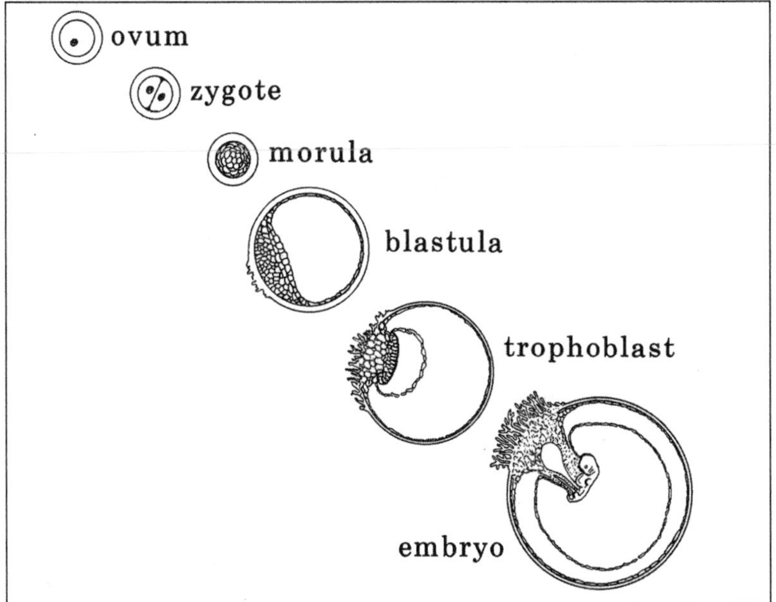

EMBRYONIC DEVELOPMENT

Diagram 6

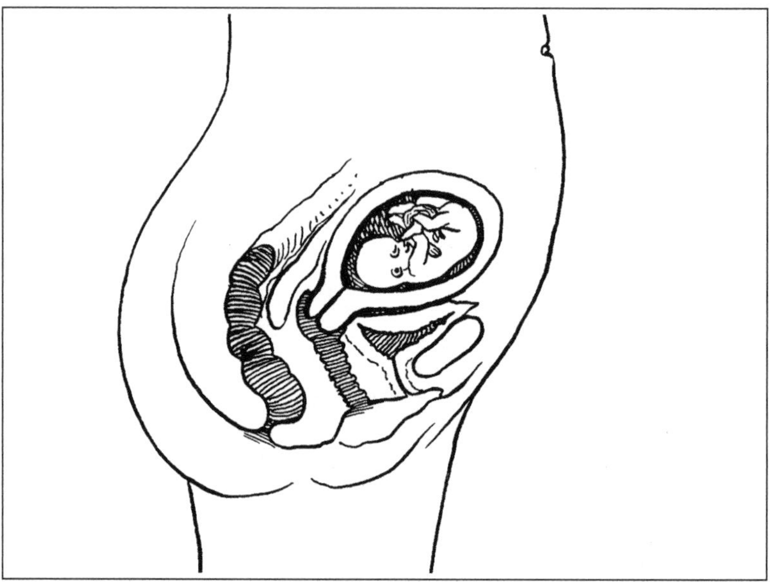

THIRD MONTH

Diagram 7

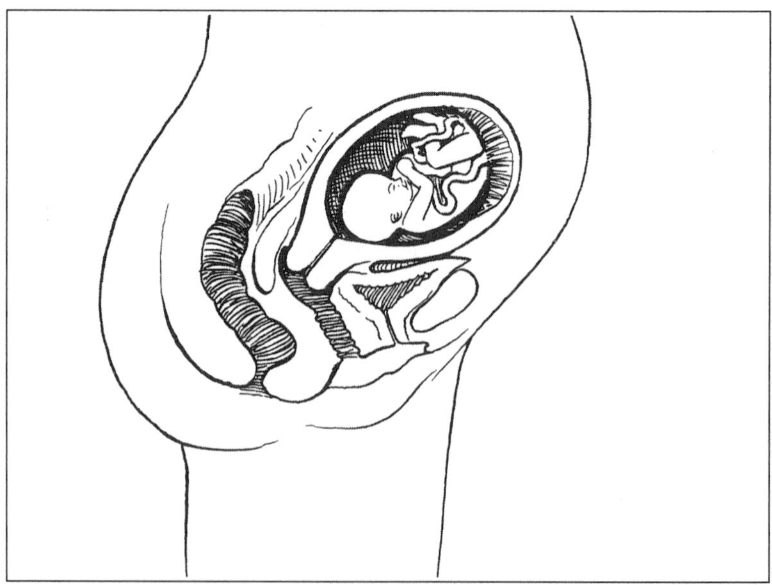

FOURTH MONTH

Diagram 8

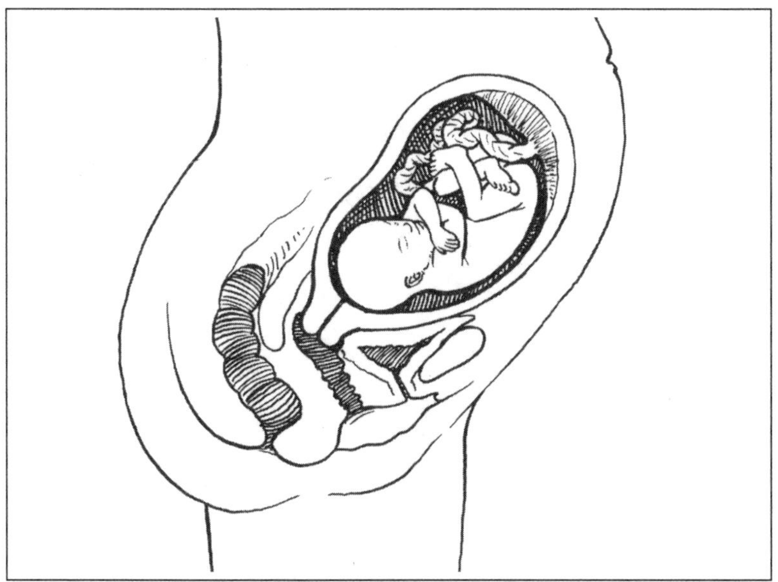

FIFTH MONTH

Diagram 9

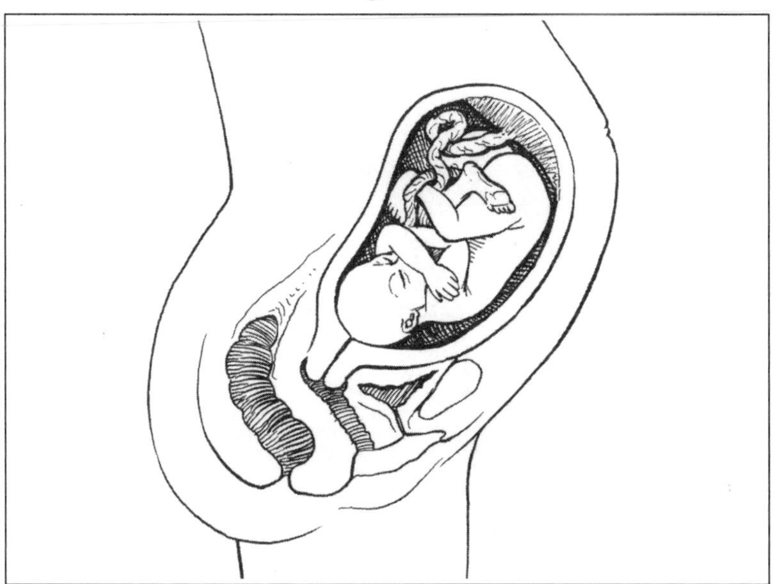

SIXTH MONTH

Diagram 10

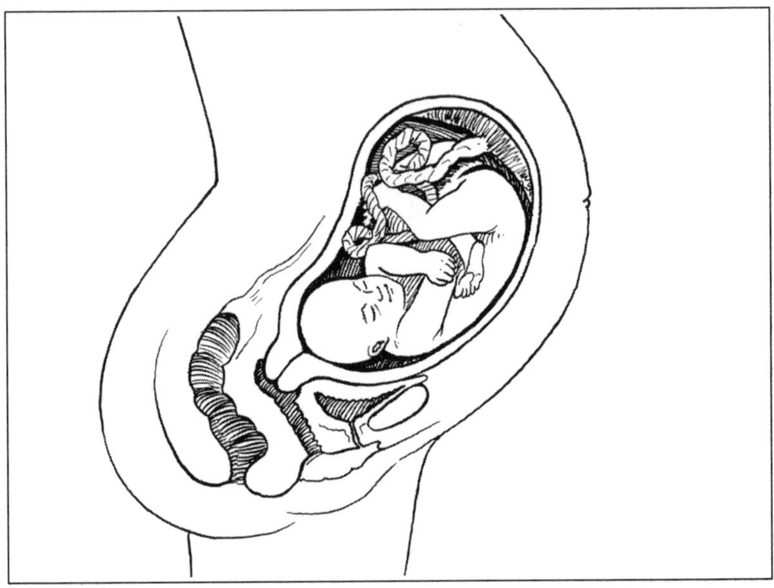

SEVENTH MONTH

Diagram 11

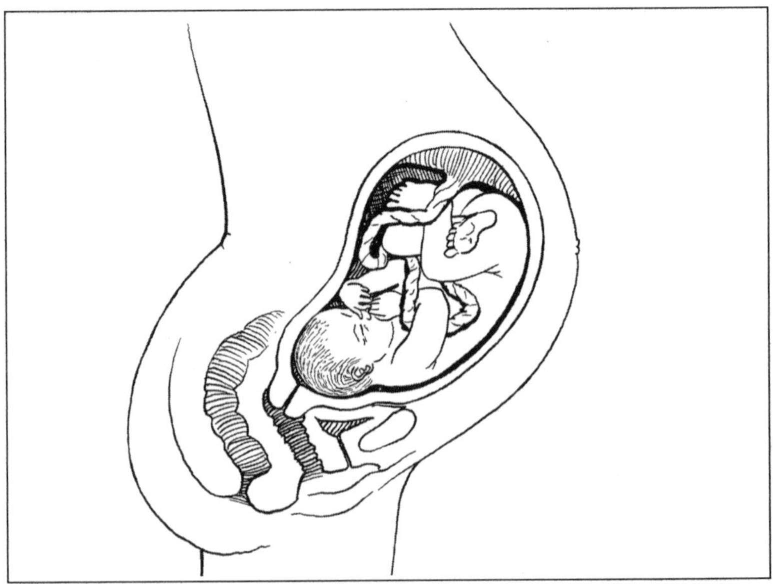

EIGHTH MONTH

Diagram 12

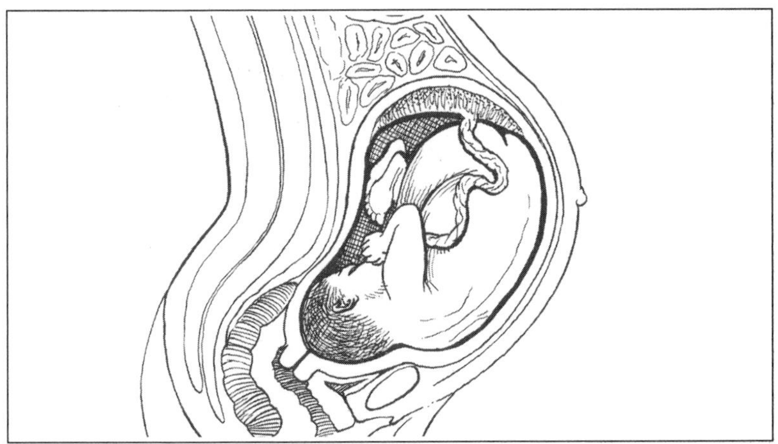

NINTH MONTH

Diagram 13

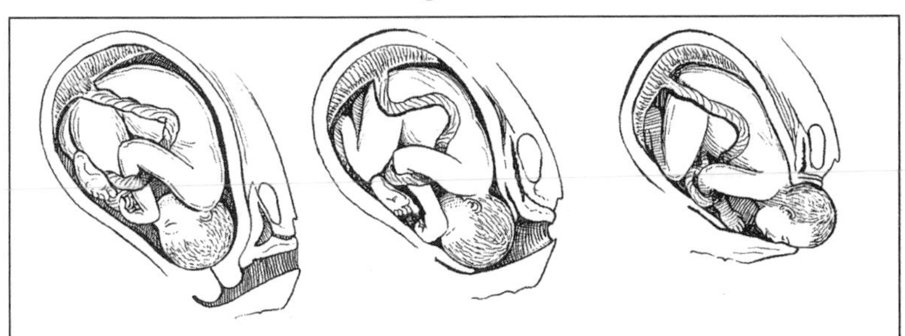

STAGES OF BIRTH

Diagram 14

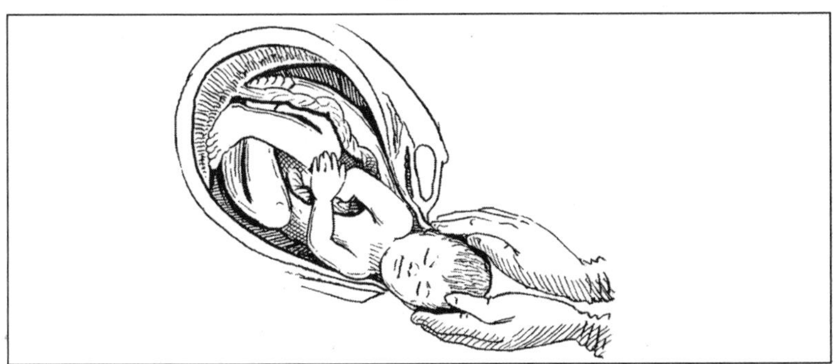

BIRTH, FINAL STAGE

Notes

Chapter 1: Sex...Sacred or Secular?

1. Richard Dobbins, "Breaking the Silence of Your Bedroom" (unpublished manuscript).

2. Genesis 1:26–28.

3. Psalm 8:5.

4. Psalm 9:8; Daniel 12:1–3; Romans 14:12; Hebrews 9:27.

5. First Corinthians 6:19–20.

6. Genesis 2:16–17.

7. Genesis 1:26–27.

8. Matthew 6:26.

9. Romans 14:10–12.

10. B. Miller, "Families Matter: A Research Synthesis of Family Influences on Adolescent Pregnancy" (Washington DC: National Campaign to Prevent Teen Pregnancy, 1998).

Chapter 2: What Does the Bible Say About Sex?

1. Genesis 1:26–28.

2. Genesis 1:31; 2:21–25.

3. Leviticus 18:22–30.

4. Genesis 38:4–10.

5. First John 3:15.

6. Luke 1:35.

7. First Timothy 3:16.

8. First Corinthians 7:1–6.

9. Matthew 19:10–11.

10. Matthew 19:12.

11. Second Kings 9:32.

12. First Corinthians 7:1–2.

13. John 2:3–11.

14. First Corinthians 6:13–20.

15. First Corinthians 6:17.

16. First Corinthians 6:16–17

17. First Corinthians 7:2–4.

18. First Corinthians 7:4–6.

19. James 3:2–10.

20. First John 1:9.

21. Genesis 2:18.

22. First Corinthians 7:2–4.

23. Psalm 127:3.

Chapter 5: Protecting Your Children From Sexual Abuse

1. "Child Sexual Abuse," American Academy of Child & Adolescent Psychiatry, No. 9, updated July 2004, http://www.aacap.org/publications/factsfam/sexabuse.htm (accessed July 20, 2005).

2. "Confronting Child Sexual Abuse With Courage," From Darkness to Light, http://www.darkness2light.org/faq/faqs.asp (accessed July 20, 2005).

3. National Adoption Information Clearinghouse (HHS), "2. What Is Child Sexual Abuse," *Parenting the Sexually Abused Child*, http://naic.acf.hhs.gov/pubs/f_abused/f_abuseda.cfm (accessed August 29, 2005).

4. From the American Academy of Child & Adolescent Psychiatry, as viewed at http://www.aacap.org/publications/factsfam/sexabuse.htm, July 20, 2005.

5. "Sexual Abuse of Children—the Greatest Global Hidden Epidemic," Press Release, October 3, 2003, eMediaWire.com, http://www.emediawire.com/releases/2003/10/prweb82627.htm (accessed August 31, 2005).

6. "A-Z Guide: Sexual Abuse," drgreene.com, http://www.drgreene.com/21_1185.html (accessed September 1, 2005).

7. "Child Sexual Abuse," http://segnbora.com/abuse.html (accessed September 1, 2005).

8. "Why do people sexually abuse children?", Sexual Abuse/Trauma, allaboutcounseling.com, http://www.allaboutcounseling.com/sexual_abuse.htm (accessed July 20, 2005).

9. "Childhood Sexual Abuse," from Safe Place Ministries, http://www.safeplaceministries.com/childhood_sexual_abuse%20article.htm (accessed July 20, 2005).

10. Ibid.

11. "Crimes Against Children by Babysitters," Juvenile Justice Bulletin, September 2001, http://ncjrs.org/html/ojjdp/jjbul2001_9_4/page3.html (accessed July 20, 2005).

Chapter 6: Helping Your Child When Abuse Has Happened

1. "Child Sexual Abuse: What Parents Need to Know," Planned Parenthood of Nassau County, Inc., http://www.plannedparenthood.org/pp2/ppnc/files/ppnc/media/factsreports/childsexabuse.pdf (accessed September 1, 2005).

2. "Abuse Facts," Good Touch/Bad Touch, http://www.goodtouchbadtouch.com/abousefacts.php (accessed July 21, 2005).

3. Statistics About Kids and Abuse, "Special on Criminal Background Checks," North America Youth Sport Institute, http://www.naysi.com/FYI/fyi_32.htm (accessed July 21, 2005).

Chapter 7: Your Child's World...Invaded From Space

1. London School of Economics, January 2002, quoted in Randall Caselman, "Compliments From the Master," sermon dated May 15, 2005, http://www.churchofchristusa.com/Main/detail.asp?id=915 (accessed August 29, 2005).

2. Valdemar W. Setzer and George E. Duckett, "The Risks To Children Using Electronic Games," http://www.ime.usp.br/~vwsetzer/video-g-risks.html (accessed August 29, 2005).

3. See Proverbs 4:23; 22:6; Matthew 12:34–35.

4. "The Effects of Electronic Media on Children Ages Zero to Six: A History of Research," prepared for the Kaiser Family Foundation by the Center on Media and Child Health, Children's Hospital Boston, http://www.kff.org/entmedia/upload/The-Effects-of-Electronic-Media-on-Children-Ages-Zero-to-Six-A-History-of-Research-Issue-Brief.pdf (accessed September 1, 2005).

5. Deborah Johnson, "Raise Parent's Awareness of Risks, Benefits of Cyberspace," *AAP News*, February 2003, http://www.aap.org/advocacy/JohnsonCyberspaceAware.htm (accessed July 21, 2005).

6. Miriam E. Bar-on, "The Effects of Television on Child Health: Implications and Recommendations," *Arch Dis Child* 83 (October 2000): 289–292, http://adc.bmjjournals.com/cgi/content/full/83/4/289 (accessed September 1, 2005).

Chapter 8: Pornography...How Big a Threat for Children?

1. "Recent Statistics on Internet Dangers," ProtectKids.com, http://www.protectkids.com/dangers/stats.htm (accessed July 21, 2005).

2. Larry Eldridge Jr., "Damage of Porn," ABC7chicago.com, http://abclocal.go.com/wls/news/connectwithkids/print_081104_cwk_porn.html (accessed July 21, 2005).

3. "General Statistics on Pornography and the Internet," Keeping Kids Safe, Clear Traffic Safe Net, http://www.cleartraffic.com/keeping-kids-safe.htm (accessed August 29, 2005).

4. "Helping Kids Use the Internet Safely," Child Development Institute, http://www.childdevelopmentinfo.com/health_safety/web_safety_for_kids_teens.shtml (accessed July 21, 2005).

5. Margo Whitmire, "50 Cent's 'Candy Shop' Sweetens Hot 100," Daily Music News, http://www.billboard.com/bb/daily/article_display.jsp?vnu_content_id=1000816645 (accessed August 29, 2005).

6. You can read these lurid lyrics at http://www.azlyrics.com/lyrics/50cent/candyshop.html (accessed September 1, 2005).

7. Ephesians 5:19.

8. Genesis 1:27; 2:20–25.

9. First Corinthians 6:13–7:4.

10. The Testimony of Dr. Mary Anne Layden, "The Science Behind Pornography Addiction Hearing," November 18, 2004, before the U. S. Senate Committee on Commerce, Science and Technology, http://commerce.senate.gov/hearings/testimony.cfm?id=1343&wit_id=3912 (accessed August 29, 2005).

11. Ibid.

12. Ibid.

13. Marjorie Hogan, MD, FAAP, "Media Education Offers Help on Children's Body Image Problems," *AAP News*, May 1999, http://www.aap.org/advocacy/hogan599.htm (accessed August 29, 2005). Also, "Growing Up With Television," Kids' Wings The Little Red Schoolhouse, http://suzyred.com/takstv.pdf (accessed September 1, 2005).

14. Johnson, "Raise Parent's Awareness of Risks, Benefits of Cyberspace."

15. "Keeping Kids Safe on the Internet—They Will Meet a Predator in a Chat Room," Clear Traffic safeNet, http://www.cleartraffic.com/keeping-kids-safe.htm (accessed July 21, 2005).

16. Tracking Where Kids Have Been Online, Media Awareness Network, http://www.media-awareness.ca/english/resources/special_initiatives/wa_resources/wa_shared/backgrounders/tracking_kids_online.cfm (accessed August 29, 2005).

Chapter 9: When the Body Begins to Change

1. W. Kyman, "Sexuality Education for Parents," *Journal of Sex Education and Therapy* 21: 151–157.

2. *Merriam-Webster Dictionary Collegiate Dictionary*, 11th edition (Springfield, MA: Merriam-Webster, Inc., 2003), s.v. "puberty."

3. "Wellness & Safety: Tips for the Adolescent Boy," Children's Healthcare of Atlanta, http://www.choa.org/default.aspx?id=515 (accessed July 22, 2005).

4. B. M. King and J. Lorusso, "Discussions in the Home About Sex: Different Recollection by Parents and Children," *Journal of Sex and Marital Therapy* 23 (1997): 52–60.

Chapter 11: Avoiding Traps With the Opposite Sex

1. Meg Meeker, MD, *Epidemic: How Sex Is Killing Our Teens* (Washington DC: Lifeline Press, 2002), 21.

2. Ibid., 194.

3. *With One Voice: America's Adults and Teens Sound Off About Teen Pregnancy, A National Survey* (Washington DC: National Campaign to Prevent Teen Pregnancy, April 2001).

4. Meeker, *Epidemic: How Sex Is Killing Our Teens*, 11.

5. Donna Johnson Edwards, "Talking Tech: My Kid's New Best Friend—a Punk or a Predator?", richmond.com, January 4, 2005, http://www.richmond.com/printer.cfm?article=3409635 (accessed July 22, 2005).

6. Ibid.

7. Ibid.

8. Quoted in "Child Molesters: What You Need to Know to Help Safeguard Your Child," http://www.ktk.ru/~cm/molester.htm (accessed September 1, 2005).

9. Stuart Wolpert, "Teenagers Find Information About Sex on the Internet When They Look for It—and When They Don't, UCLA's Children's Digital Media Center Reports," UCLA Health & Medicine News, http://www.medctr.ucla.edu/santa-monica/news/detail?rad_id=5876 (accessed August 30, 2005).

10. "Chat Safety Summary," Chat Room Safety, UKChatterbox, http://www.ukchatterbox.co.uk/article/17 (accessed September 1, 2005).

11. Wolpert, "Teenagers Find Information About Sex on the Internet When They Look for It—and When They Don't, UCLA's Children's Digital Media Center Reports."

12. "Pornography Addiction: Did You Know…," Fires of Darkness Ministries, http://firesofdarkness.com/pornography_addiction.htm (accessed July 25, 2005).

13. Eldridge, "Damage of Porn."

Chapter 12: Discussing Masturbation and Fantasy

1. "Teens Who Watch a Lot of TV With Sexual Content Have Sex Sooner," Parenting of Adolescents, About.Com, http://parentingteens.about.com/odthe/teensexuality/a/teen_sex8.htm (accessed July 25, 2005).

2. Ibid.

3. "Sexual and Reproductive Health: Masturbation," Aetna InteliHealth: Teen Topics, http://www.intelihealth.com/IH/ihtIH/WSTHW000/23414/23451/266765.html?d=dmtContent (accessed September 1, 2005).

4. Matthew 5:28.

5. First Corinthians 7:4.

6. First John 1:7–9.

Chapter 13: Alcohol, Drugs, and Sexually Transmitted Diseases

1. Mary Huser, et al., "Whose Kids? Our Kids! Teens, Sex and Alcohol," Cooperative Extensions Publications, http://cecommerce.uwex.edu/pdfs/B3706_10.PDF (accessed July 25, 2005).

2. "Substance Abuse and Risky Sexual Behavior: Attitudes and Practices Among Adolescents and Young Adults," February 2002, Kaiser Family Foundation, http://www.outproud.org/pdf/CASASurveySnapshot.pdf (accessed September 1, 2005).

3. Ibid.

4. "Survey Says Teens Mix Risky Sex With Alcohol, Drugs," excerpt by Zach Howard, Reuters Health, at PreventDisease.com, http://www.preventdisease.com/news/articles/teens_sex_alcohol.shtml (accessed August 30, 2005).

5. "Adolescents and the Media," *Adolescent Medicine,* edited by Victor C. Strasburger, MD, and George A. Comstock, PhD (Philadelphia, PA: Hanley & Belfus, Inc., October 1993).

6. Substance Abuse and Mental Health Services Administration, *National Household Survey on Drug Abuse: Main Findings 1997* (Rockville, MD: Substance Abuse and Mental Health Services Administration, 1999), quoted in "Alcohol Use and Abuse: A Pediatric Concern," *Pediatrics* 108(1) (July 2001): 185–189, http://pediatrics.aappublications.org/cgi/content/full/108/1/185 (accessed September 1, 2005).

7. Meeker, *Epidemic: How Sex Is Killing Our Teens*, 14.

8. "Facts About Sexually Transmitted Diseases (STDs)," http://www.teenshelter.org/std.htm (accessed July 25, 2005).

9. Ibid.

10. "Teen Sex and Pregnancy," Facts in Brief, the Alan Guttmacher Institute, www.agi-usa.org/pubs/fb_teen_sex.html (accessed July 25, 2005).

11. Meeker, *Epidemic: How Sex Is Killing Our Teens,* 154.

12. J. S. Santelli, et al., "Multiple Sexual Partners Among U.S. Adolescents and Young Adults," *Family Planning Perspectives* 30(6) (November/December 1998): 271–275.

13. Meeker, *Epidemic: How Sex Is Killing Our Teens*, 154.

Chapter 15: Protecting Your Teens From Tragedy

1. "Teen Sex and Pregnancy," Facts in Brief, the Alan Guttmacher Institute.

2. Matthew 6:21.

Chapter 16: Choosing a Life Partner

1. Second Corinthians 6:14.
2. "Teen Sex and Pregnancy," Facts in Brief, the Alan Guttmacher Institute.

Chapter 17: Before Your Children Say "I Do"

1. "U.S. Divorce Rates," Ontario Consultants on Religious Tolerance, Religioustolerance.org, http://www.religioustolerance.org/chr_dira.htm (accessed July 25, 2005).
2. Matthew 12:34.
3. Howard and Charlotte Clinebell, *The Intimate Marriage,* available from religion-online at http://www.religion-online.org/showbook.asp?title=1900&C=1714 (accessed July 26, 2005).
4. Second Corinthians 6:14–18.
5. "Divorce Rates Among Inter-faith Marriages," Religioustolerance.org, http://www.religioustolerance.org/ifm_divo.htm (accessed July 26, 2005).
6. Available in art form from www.prichardprints.com.
7. Beverly Baskin, "Dual Career Couples—Facing the Stress of Success: How Families Cope, Part 1," SelfHelpMagazine, http://www.selfhelpmagazine.com/articles/wf/dualcar.html (accessed September 1, 2005).
8. Ira L. Reiss, "Toward a Sociology of the Heterosexual Love Relationship," *Marriage and Family Living* XXII (May 1960): 139–145.
9. Available in art form from www.prichardprints.com.

Chapter 19: A Mother's Premarital Talk With Her Daughter

1. First Corinthians 6:19–20.
2. First Peter 3:7–8.

Appendix A: Commonly Asked Questions About Sex

1. Matthew 5:27–28.
2. Ezekiel 18:20.

You are more than you realize!

We know that you have found fresh new insight and information in *Teaching Your Children the Truth about Sex*. For more practical teachings, please visit Dr. Dobbins at **www.drdobbins.com**!

Dr. Dobbins helps you understand, define, talk about, and modify your feelings. This is a great independent or group study.

ISBN: 0971239115

Every person has a presence. How do you affect other people? How does good and evil impact your presence? Discover the power of presence in this life-changing teaching.

ISBN: 0971231109

Find out more about yourself!

Visit your local bookstore
or
www.drdobbins.com

Strang Communications,
publisher of both **Charisma House** and ***Charisma*** magazine, wants to give you

3 FREE ISSUES

of our **award-winning** magazine.

WWW.CHARISMAMAG.COM

Since its inception in 1975 *Charisma* magazine has helped thousands of Christians stay connected with what God is doing worldwide.

Within its pages you will discover in-depth reports and the latest news from a Christian perspective, biblical health tips, global events in the body of Christ, personality profiles, and so much more. Join the family of *Charisma* readers who enjoy feeding their spirits each month with miracle-filled testimonies and inspiring articles that bring clarity, provoke prayer, and demand answers.

To claim your **3 free issues** of *Charisma,* send your name and address to: Charisma 3 Free Issues Offer, 600 Rinehart Road, Lake Mary, FL 32746. Or you may call **1-800-829-3346** and ask for Offer # **96FREE.** This offer is only valid in the USA.

Charisma
+CHRISTIAN LIFE
www.charismamag.com

5567